WORDS
THAT HAVE
MOVED
THE
WORLD

"People, be good."

Complete Sermon
preached by John Ruskin
at the age of four

WORDS THAT HAVE MOVED THE WORLD

George Target

BISHOPSGATE PRESS LTD.

British Library Cataloguing in Publication Data

Words that have moved the world.
1. Sermons, English
I. Target George
252   BV4241

ISBN 1 85219 015 9
ISBN 1 85219 025 6 Pbk

All enquiries and requests relevant to this title should be sent to the publisher, Bishopsgate Press Ltd., 37 Union Street, London SE1 1SE

Printed by Whitstable Litho, Millstrood Road, Whitstable, Kent.

Contents

A Little Clearing of the Throat before Starting

A fine Sunday morning on the High Street, any High Street: Ashford or Bath, Darlington or Gloucester, Kingston or Peterborough, perhaps Winchester or Canterbury . . . anywhere at all in the four corners of our air-conditioned wilderness.

Let it be Norwich, a Fine City, on the other end of the line from London's Liverpool Street Station. Except that not even the *Official Guide* claims a proper High Street.

"Largest corn and cattle market in the whole kingdom," it almost says here, "focus for agricultural commerce, the manufacture of mustard, boots and shoes, keg and bottled beer, and confectionery. Home of thriving insurance and banking companies whose business is world-wide, important engineering products, and a variety of prosperous light industries. Superb shopping and personal service amenities, modern entertainment in the shape of local radio and television, contemporary cinemas, dance-halls, theatres, bingo clubs and other amusements, many public houses licensed for music, facilities for sport and recreations such as football and boating, restaurants catering for all tastes from fish-and-chips to Chinese take-away, splendid museums, noted art collections, and a wide range of churches and chapels representing most shades of theological opinion . . ."

And, because it's Sunday morning, you can say *that* again!

"Most shades of theological opinion . . ."

Down there, on the water-meadows along by the River Wensum, in pride of place, naturally, is the Anglican cathedral: mellowed stone, the shadows soft, almost purple, the arches strong, the windows gleaming, the tower four-square, tiered, ribbed and banded and embossed, the spire an ascension . . . and this touch of golden fire at the height of all, the Cross triumphant.

Or is it the wind-driven Cockerel of Betrayal crowing thrice?

Anyway, elsewhere and nearly everywhere, there's a different church for each Sunday of the Liturgical Year: All Saints from Andrew to Swithin, Benedict to Peter Hungate or Peter Mancroft or Peter Parmentergate, Clement to Michael-at-Coslany or Michael-at-Plea, Eltheldreda to my Lady Julian herself . . . Saxon Towers and Norman Arches, Fan-Vaulted Porches and Sanctuary Knockers, Early or Late Perpendicular Naves and Fine Timbered Roofs,

1

Decorated Chancels and Transepts with Painted Bosses, Stone Monuments and Memorial Brasses, Old or New Stained-Glass, Fifteenth-Century Knapped Flintwork, Sixteenth-Century Lecterns, Seventeenth-Century Pulpits, Eighteenth-Century Fonts, Nineteenth-Century Altar Furnishings, and *URGENT* Twentieth-Century Appeals for Repairs, Restoration, and Maintenance.

Not to forget the Chapels and Gospel Halls and Upper Rooms: Assemblies of God, Baptists, Christadelphians, Christian Scientists, Greek Orthodox, Jehovah's Witnesses, Latter-Day Saints (better known as Mormons), Methodists (Primitive or otherwise), Mount Zion Pentecostals, Presbyterians, Roman Catholics, Seventh-Day Adventists, Spiritualists, and United Reformed.

And what about the Faithful Remnant of Southcottians and Flying-Roll Jezreelites?

All manner of other Assemblies and Meetings and Gatherings, assorted Rites and Ceremonies, Proper Lessons and Psalms and various Revised Orders of Service, Masses and Family Communions, Creeds and Litanies and Prayers and Thanksgivings upon Several Occasions, Collects, Epistles and Gospels, Hymns and Anthems and Voluntaries, pipe or electric organs, harmoniums, pianos, unaccompanied voices, twangling guitars, and (loudest and most cheerful) the great silver sin-no-more blare of the Salvation Army Band playing in their Citadel.

Yes! Praise ye the Lord! Halleluiah! Amen!

But, most of all, *listen* to the Word of that Lord!

* * *

Which is what those congregations will sooner or later be doing: listening to the Ministry of the Word, the words of preaching, the "Message for this morning hour" . . . the Sermon.

First and always a Text, some sort of general introduction, smiling references to programmes seen on television, anecdotes, cuttings from the papers, contemporary parables, instant gimmicks . . . here a formal address read from a complete script, there a lecture from notes, elsewhere an exposition or straight exegesis, down the road a high proclamation, round the corner a meditation . . . apologetics, interpretations, moralisings, judgements, devotionals, slow-motion discussions, harangues disguised as exhortations . . . some penny-plain or tenpence-Technicolored, some delivered with blessed assurance or intellectual arrogance, some in humility or diffidence, some dragged to the limits of endurance, some brief to this side of the perfunctory, some passionate, some casual, most of them trying to stand six feet above contradiction, all of them falling short of the Glory.

For who dares boast of any Glory these days?
How clear are the words? How sure are the voices? How certain the sound of the trumpet?
And how many souls *are* there in the pews under the conviction of these present unhappy confusions?

"A mere numerical assessment," states the Professor of Religion at your nearest University, using the appropriate synodical language, "would undoubtedly disclose an apparently weaker Church, whereas a qualitative evaluation in terms of allegiance and commitment would probably reveal a stronger one in that there are likely to be fewer nominal members."

Agreed, the Truth is not to be measured out in pews filled . . . but the brutal fact is that, this Sunday and every Sunday, most people are at home, many still in bed, or eating their bacon-and-eggs and fried tomatoes, enjoying that second cup of tea or coffee, starting to read the papers, or already watching the telly . . . or cleaning the car, digging the garden, painting the backdoor, playing with the kids, having a bath, doing the weekly wash, getting dressed to go out, waiting for the pubs to open, cooking that nice bit of beef or lamb or pork for lunch . . .

"Go to *church*?" say the voices. "You've *got* to be joking!"

*   *   *

Yet there *was* a time . . .

Indeed, if you have ears to hear, there still *is* a time . . . still those who are not Ordained Ministers of any church or sect, neither the son nor daughter of such a Minister, who come stalking in from that air-conditioned wilderness with words of fire and roses on their parched lips.

Except who wants to know? Who cares enough to listen?

Open your mouth to say anything unpopular or controversial or too close to home *these* days, and you'll be told to go peddle your troubles as far away as possible.

Prophetic utterance?

Go read the Astrology columns!

*   *   *

Here, then, as a reminder, are the words of one such Preacher.
Who stood under the lamp on the corner, and said:
"The other evening I was walking through the streets of the city . . .
"*Which* City?"

3

"There is only one city, though its name may be spelt in many ways: Alexandria or Athens, Babylon or Berlin or Birmingham, Calcutta or Cape Town or Carthage, Florence, London, Los Angeles, Madras, Madrid, Melbourne, Moscow, New York or Norwich, Paris, Peking, Rome, Rio de Janeiro, Singapore, Turin, Washington, Vienna . . . even Jerusalem.

"For it was built by Cain, and those streets are paved with shining promises and broken hearts.

"And, walking through this city, in an alley between the supermarket and the Bingo Social Club, I saw a cardboard box of peaches, rich and succulent, golden in the gleam of flickering neon . . . delicious, tempting, irrestistible . . .

"Peaches? Summer fruit left in an alley?

"In *this* city?

"So I picked one out . . .

"And it squelched to a sticky pulp in my fingers.

"Rotten, they were all rotten . . . been left for rubbish, garbage, trash.

"And, like it or not, so are we, as a people, as a nation: rotten, ripe for destruction, the ultimate rubbish dump.

"So listen, all you comfortable ladies and gentlemen who can't be bothered with the millions of your brothers and sisters who had no place to sleep last night, no place to lay their aching heads, those who've had no breakfast this morning, those who won't be having any lunch, any dinner, any supper, any sustaining snacks between meals, any crisps, any bars of chocolate with fruit and nuts, any cups of tea or coffee to keep going on, and who will probably be dead by the end of the week . . .

"Listen, all of you who live on the income from investments, staying fat on the sweat of those who work for your idleness, who toil in poverty so that you can cultivate the Finer Things of Life . . . you who trade the innocent for thirty pieces of cupro-nickel-silver, and the poor for a portfolio of shares . . . yes, and sell the sweepings of the floor, the rubbish of the wheat as good bread . . . you who sip vintage wine when your brothers thirst for clean water, you who spend more on a seat at the opera than your sisters spend on food for a month or even a year, you who drive around in flash cars when children rot for simple lack of love . . .

"All of you who waste our days buying on the cheapest market and selling on the dearest, making profits at whatever social cost, cheating and lying in the name of Good Business Practice – all within the small print of the various Rules and

Regulations . . .

"You who pack fewer items into larger packets, and charge the same old prices, who give short weight and short change . . . you who've already traded in your soul . . .

"Watch it! Your day is coming!

"The bills are soon due for payment!

"Because you have sold the starving on your money markets, and you generate mass-unemployment for your own economic advantage.

"You exploit the poor, trick the needy of their rights, and tempt the inadequate to violence and crime.

"And fathers and sons lust after the same whores on television, read the same porno-magazines, and your wives and daughters and sisters prance naked in your strip clubs.

"And listen, you women who anoint yourselves with the finest oils and lotions, who lie on soft mattresses, and sprawl on your interior-sprung divans, eating choice meats and crystalised fruits . . . who glister in your latest fashions, who paint and preen and perfume your flesh, who wear silk, and ignore the whimpering of babies in the slums of Liverpool and Glasgow and Manchester and Camberwell Green . . .

"You are feasting over an open grave, flaunting your own shrouds!

"Your time is coming!

"Listen, you who despise the truth, and hate those who won't be bought by your inducements and bribes and honours, you who refuse to hear the cry for justice . . . and all you self-important politicians who chatter about a Higher Standard of Living, who lie about Peace and prepare for war . . . who smile and smile and rehearse your sincerity . . .

"Your time is coming!

"You, whose every altar is decked with gold and silver while men and women starve, whose priests are clothed in embroidered vestments while children shiver in the winds of winter.

"What have your performances of Choral Evensong to do with God? What have those Revised Orders of Service to do with works of mercy?

"You may light all the candles and burn all the incense you like, furnish your churches and cathedrals in all manner of finery, and you will not please God.

"Let there be no more of your bellowed hymns, for you only deafen yourselves with the booming of your mighty organs.

"For you prefer gold to God, doctrines to truth . . . when all

God wants is justice to be done, integrity to flourish . . ."
But, by then, the Prime Minister had heard enough of all this nonsense, and demanded that Politics be kept out of the Pulpit, and the Chairperson of the Party insisted that such blatant bias be removed from the media of mass-communications.

And, of course, the Archbishop agreed about this uneducated layman from the working-class . . . though he was naturally more concerned about that bitter denigration of the Revised Orders of Service.

"Your rustic rabble-rousing may be all very well for militant revolutionaries and impractical idealists," he said, "but we live in the pragmatic world, where balance and sensible compromise are, at the ending of the day, the only way forward. So go back from whence you came," he said, now smiling at the little play on words he had prepared, "and keep your woolly rhetoric for your sheep."

Then answered Amos, and said: "I was no prophet, neither was I a prophet's son, but I was an herdman in the howling wilderness of Tekoa, and a gatherer of sycomore fruit: And the Lord took me as I followed the flock, and the Lord said unto me, *Go, prophesy* . . ."

*　　*　　*

For, yes, it was Amos who spoke the first version of those words seven-hundred-and-fifty years or so before Christ.

Any old Bible Commentary will give you all the unnecessary facts . . . though don't pay more than tenpence for it. Bound to be one accumulating dust on the lowest shelf in your nearest *Save the Children* or *Oxfam* shop.

"Tekoa," it'll likely say, "an inconsiderable village in a narrow ravine surrounded by hills overlooking the Dead Sea . . ."

When it's the living truth that matters.

Mind you, he spoke in Hebrew to the people of ancient Israel . . . but, like us, they had recently never had it so good, lived at a time of unprecedented material prosperity, worshipped money in the bank, knew success as the ownership of consumer-goods, and relished pleasure by the plate and glass and mouthful.

As nearly always, the rich were getting richer and the poor were getting desperate . . . though government statistics were massaged to produce the usual telly-coloured haze between election promises and the actual numbers of those not gainfully employed. Morality was replaced by Instant Moralism, common honesty was manipulated by fast talkers with an eye to the Main Chance, and principles were corroded by expediency.

And so, under the burden of Prophecy, in stalked Amos from his

6

wilderness with those words of fire on his indignant lips . . . as if Francis of Assisi should preach about Holy Poverty at the Lord Mayor's Banquet, or a Jehovah's Witness conduct a Bible Study in Saint Paul's Cathedral on the End-of-the-World implications of the latest Stock Exchange scandal.

Can you even *begin* to imagine it?

Anyway, Amos said what he had to say . . . especially to the Archbishop.

* * *

"Your wife shall be an harlot in the city, ravished on the public street, your sons and daughters shall be butchered, and you shall die in a corrupted land.

"Trouble? You hardly know the meaning of the word!

"Pollution will get worse than it already is: smoke, smog, fumes, chemical waste – all these will darken the sun at high noon, poison the lakes and rivers and the seas, and turn the earth to sterile ash. Quite apart from all the synthetic plagues and murderous gases you've got stockpiled. And your bombs and rockets and nuclear-warheads . . . where will you hide when, inevitably, something goes wrong?

"What will be Top of the Pops on *that* day? There'll be more panic and terror in the streets than singing, louder howling than that of your transistor radios.

"Man and women and children will die all over the city, drop and rot where they fall. There'll be so many putrefying corpses piled up that it'll be quite impossible to bury them. Dead silence . . .

"And even the beautiful girls in their summer dresses, and the young men in their bright clothes, will die with the rest of us, for their golden youth will not help them!

"Yes, the Top of the Pops will be a funeral dirge.

"There'll be a lot of useless tears shed on *that* day, and the evening of it will be an hour of bitter despair!"

* * *

And when he had finished, and not before, he stalked back to his flocks and fruit.

"Good riddance!" said the Prime Minister. "Who does he think *he* is? How many voted for *him*?"

"There ought to be a law!" said the Party Chairperson. "Which we'll be introducing during the next Parliamentary Session!"

7

"A sad case in need of treatment," said the Archbishop, doing his best to be charitable.

By the end of the week the outrage had dropped out of the headlines . . .

But, by the middle of next week, next month, next year, the next decade, it had all come to pass even as it had been foretold.

What does the actual date matter? What's time in the Light of the Mystery they call Eternity?

*   *   *

This book is about such preaching, about words which moved the world: or *would* have done had enough people taken enough notice.

And that's usually the trouble: the preaching is heard, often by many – but few listen, and fewer still take enough notice to do anything very much about it.

"He that hath ears to hear," said Christ, "let him hear."

Meaning that good preaching is more than aural wallpaper with an ecclesiastical pattern . . . because if the understanding isn't reached, the Message hasn't been preached.

The word itself will tell us what it ought to be.

"Preaching" is used to translate the Greek New Testament word *kerygma,* a "proclamation" by a herald. The preacher is thus seen as a special messenger sent by the King of kings to proclaim the Gospel or Good News of Salvation . . . with all the overtones of high silver trumpets.

An obvious fact to remember about heralds is that it was the *content* of their messages which mattered, not the mere *form* in which they were delivered: sometimes it was a sealed letter from king to king, sometimes a speech read aloud from a manuscript, sometimes the display of a flag of truce or surrender . . . and, according to Shakespeare, the French Dauphin sent his herald with a barrel of tennis-balls to Henry the Fifth as a mark of contempt.

Heralds, then, do not always have to use spoken words . . . all they have to do is *deliver* their message.

True, the English word "preaching" derives from the Latin *praedicare,* "to proclaim," with its roots in *dicere,* "to make known," and *dictus,* a "saying" or "word." All of which has come to mean the "pronouncing of a public discourse or address by a clergyman on Sacred subjects in connection with an Ecclesiastical Function."

(Thank *you,* Samuel Johnson.)

In short, a Sermon: from the Old German *swer,* "to swear an oath," akin to the Latin *sermo,* "conversation," with *sermo* an extension of *ser,* "series" . . . all of which may properly define it as a "serious conversation" or "series of words about a serious subject."

Usually, of course, delivered in a pulpit, from the Late Latin *pulpitum,* a word of obscure origin, meaning "trestle or scaffold" . . . a platform on which a Reader in the Early Church would stand to read the Scriptures.

This practical custom started when the Jews returned to Jerusalem from the Captivity in Babylon: "And Ezra the Scribe stood above all the people upon a high place, or platform of wood, which they had made for the purpose in the street that was before the Water Gate, and opened the Book of the Law of Moses, and read therein distinctly, and afterwards gave the sense, so that all could hear the reading with understanding."

Any of the standard encyclopaedias and histories of Christianity will chart the Rise and Decline of the Pulpit Sermon, from the passionate simplicities of the Apostles to the theological complexities of Paul, through the demented sterility of the Middle Ages to the Golden Age of the Protestant Reformation and the Silver Days of George Fox and John Wesley and Jonathan Edwards . . . and then Moody, Spurgeon, Billy Sunday, Billy Graham . . . John Wimber . . .

But what it has come to *be* is another matter entirely!

*　　*　　*

Even without such an encyclopaedia it's self-evidently true that the Protestant Reformation replaced the Mass with the Sermon.

The Mass was a visual Sacrament, an act which spoke through ritual gesture and mystical symbolism, and could be understood even at its deepest levels by an illiterate worshipper . . . whereas the Sermon was a discourse which, like a book, could only present its religious information in words.

So, in attempting to bring the Word of God to Luther's "unlettered plough-boy," the Protestant Church paradoxically lost touch with the illiterate, and ceased to be able to preach without formal words. Scholarship took over from the more flexible forms of traditional culture: the Sermon ousted folk song and dance and drama and non-verbal art. The Pulpit was built higher than the Altar . . . and the people, instead of participating with all their senses in a Sacrifice, merely listened to a man telling them what they should believe.

And the combination of this verbal Protestantism with the invention of printing gave the Bible into the hands of these listeners – who then became readers . . . which created the cultural pattern that is now destroying the structure of the Church.

For the Gospel became Literature, the Word became words, and almost ceased to be Good News.

Biblical Christianity turned into a mere literary sub-culture.

And, because of television and the entire electronics communications industry, and the consequent turning back to an aural and visual and tactile culture, contemporary Western society is becoming more and more *non*-literary, fragmented and immediate rather than coherent and sequential. Yet the Church persists in presenting its Message in a literary way . . . and wonders why so few are listening.

*   *   *

Because of all these and many other factors, it is now admitted by everybody (except those with an almost desperately vested interest) that contemporary preaching is having what's known as a "bad Press."

Once upon a time the famous preachers were Princes of the Pulpit, spell-binders, personalities, the Terry Wogans and Robin Days and the Beatles of their age.

Apart from such Stars, the more typical Sermon was described by Somerset Maugham at the beginning of this century: "The Vicar expounded twice on Sunday the obvious passages of the Scriptures, in twenty minutes or so, making for the benefit of the vulgar a number of trite reflections in a slovenly language compounded from the Authorised Version and the daily papers."

With much evidence from Literature that the sadly typical hasn't improved since then.

For one example among many, there's *Elmer Gantry,* a character melded by Sinclair Lewis from several notorious American Ministers:

"He never said anything important," but "always said it sonorously" in a "cello of a voice, welcoming as a brass-band, and uplifting as a cathedral organ." And his Sermons "related imaginary anecdotes for edifying purposes as though they were sober truths of his own experience," which "grew more glutinous and improbable" with every retelling. The novel ends as Elmer prays at the "beginning of a Crusade for complete morality" . . . with his eyes on the "charming ankles" of a "new girl" in the choir. "Dear Lord," he thunders, "we shall yet make these United States a moral nation!"

It would be a comfortable way out to deny that this prevailing image of the preaching clergyman has little basis in fact . . . except that fiction can tell the sort of truth which our laws of libel prevent being told about living preachers you can hear any Sunday.

No, the decline is now reaching the bottom of the ancient barrel.

Only three hundred years ago it was possible for Richard Baxter, the Puritan preacher, to have a high and urgent vision of his task: to preach as a "dying man to dying men."

Today it's equally possible to regard many preachers as the intellectually confused speculating aloud in front of the hungry sheep . . . who "look up, and are not fed."

True, even as recently as the nineteen-sixties, William Barclay could still claim that there was "preaching today which will stretch a man's mind to the limit, and which is an education to listen to."

So that decline must have recently been both steep and rapid, because the only way you can be hit by the headlines as a preacher these latter days is to clamber on the Billy Graham band-waggon . . . or doubt the existence of God, deny the Virgin Birth of Jesus, or question the fact or necessity of the Resurrection. Either way you'll also make Prime Time on television.

Dribble the more usual lukewarm milk-and-water from the bottom of the barrel, and you'll be doing very well indeed to catch the attention of anybody . . . except the front three rows of the Faithful in the creaking pews.

*   *   *

The reasons are depressingly obvious, and have been proclaimed with the tongues of men and of Angels.

"Because thou sayest, I am rich and increased with consumer-goods, and have need of no new knowledge . . . and knowest not that thou art wretched, and miserable, and poor, and blind, and naked . . ."

Or, to use another brand of High Rhetoric, the Parson has gone the way of the world, hunted with the Squire many times too often, dined at the Rich Man's table while those "poor men at his gate" have gone on looking up, and still "are not fed" . . . with neither the crumbs from beneath that table, nor the living Bread he was paid to preach.

And for too long have the material demands of kings and governments been preached as the very Commandments of God, the dogmas and traditions of the Church been taught as the words of Jesus Christ.

"Preachers become flatterers," said Austin Farrer, "we charm your ears . . ." The result, as he well knew, was that they "run the risk of disgusting the best part" of their congregations.

Yet another factor is that most clergymen feel obliged to preach well to the theological right of what they actually believe. They blame this on the "innate conservatism" of those in the pews – but the result is that they propound doctrines from the pulpit which they'd never defend at street-level . . . and some they can't even believe over a mug of steaming cocoa in the kitchen.

And the preacher who refuses to speak as a Prophet to a sick society becomes irrelevant, a curious relic from times past rather than a sure foundation for new building.

So the brutal fact is that most people are now voting with their buttocks: the pews are emptying because we can no longer accept (not even by faith) that the preacher is any closer to God than we are, that he "knows" any better than we do. And who (except their compilers) can work up much enthusiasm over theological crossword-puzzles?

Even in the recent past, such preachers could ascend into the pulpit as though to the top of Mount Zion, look down on us from a greater height than can be measured in feet or metres, and distribute the loaves and fishes of the Higher Learning. Indeed, they were often the only educated men for miles around . . . but, today, twelve-year-old boys and girls probably know more about Science and Mathematics and Biology and Computer Techniques. And the rest of us prefer group discussions, the give and take of arguments between equals, talking among friends . . . conversation rather than homiletics.

The pulpit, then, has lost most of its status as a witness-box, and is now a dock in which more than the preacher is on trial.

Yes, the pulpits are as full as ever – but the pews are not . . . and that easy-chair in front of the telly confronts a greater challenge. The Weather Forecast may be just as often wrong as the theologians . . . but at least it's about the real world we live in. And we choose to make our own interior journey rather than trudge that old route-march along the well-trodden highways, wander on our own lonely pilgrimage with crusty wholemeal bread and hunks of good cheese rather than accept the tattered maps and packets of dry biscuits and processed gunge issued from the Vestry at such appointed times as shall be thought meet and expedient.

* * *

Standard preaching is based on what most of us believe to be dubious assumptions: that the preacher is better informed than we are, that a twenty-minute lecture is a more efficient method of communication than ten minutes of genuine conversation, that monologues are superior to dialogues, that a prepared statement avoids the need for verifiable answers to real questions, that it's more blessed to listen than to take part . . . that verbal epiphanies always show forth more than any other showing forth . . .

We are drowning in such one-way words, and could do with some

12

of those actions which speak louder.

No, we have suffered from too many manipulators, too many religious demagogues able to play on the emotions of a crowd, too many grubby ecclesiastical politicians sounding the "patriotic" trumpets, too many slick apologists using the high skills of language to sell what should be the free gift of Salvation.

Who needs the smooth words of the powers that be? the greasy tricks of the evangelistic trade? the windly rhetoric of the hollow men?

*   *   *

Don't believe *me* about the futility of such preaching.

Mingle with a congregation after any Sunday morning or evening Service, and ask around on the subject of *last* week's Sermon.

"*Last* week? Well, er, you know, wasn't it, er . . ."

And then there'll be a wry smile and self-deprecating shrug.

Mind you, few will remember all *that* much of the one they've just heard – probably the text, perhaps an illustrative anecdote . . . but *last* week's thousands of words have swirled away down the Orwellian Memory Hole . . . leaving *what* behind?

True, there *will* be exceptions, Christians keen enough to have taken notes, or the preacher might have been on a high . . .

But mostly, unless you're a realist, it'll be a depressing few minutes – though I commend such consumer testing to every clergyman who isn't already persuaded by his own experience of preaching to those emptying pews.

*   *   *

The Sermon, then, is now a sacred relic, a dubious thing of withered skin and dried bones enclosed in a reliquary of fond remembrance, still encrusted with the jewels of past glory, wrapped in a soft cloth of sentimental piety . . . and exposed to the few remaining Faithful on Sundays and other High Days.

Yes, it was *once* the major form of Christian teaching: congregations could neither read nor write, and so the Clerks (or Clerics) would *speak* the Word of God to them, and then explain what it meant. There were also signs of the Faith all over the churches and cathedrals in which they worshipped, symbols of the Holy Mysteries, sermons in wood and stone and stained-glass and precious metals, lessons taught with the voices of silence . . . but, generally, the Good News of Salvation was delivered in words from the pulpit.

However, times have changed, and are rapidly changing . . . yet

13

the churches are extremely reluctant to change with them.

Candles have been superseded by electric-lamps . . . and still they use candles on their altars – or even electric-lamps that *look* like candles, complete with flickering flames and imitation guttering wax and all.

"It's a long and venerable tradition, you know, a memorial linking us to our brethren of the Early Church in the catacombs . . ."

The human voice can now be amplified, and television cameras can bring the remotest figure into immediate close-up . . . and still our preachers prefer to ascend into the pulpit to be better seen and heard by those a few feet away in the back row.

* * *

But, whether we like it or not, we now live and have our being with television: that universal coloured blur in the corner of the room . . . a world of visual images, things seen rather than heard, experienced rather than merely spoken about.

Yes, words remain essential: we have a verbal faculty which offers the best current means for communicating certain abstract information – especially that based on words. We are word-using creatures, which is one way of defining our rational nature, and those special ideas and concepts capable of definition in words at all are obviously central to our experience of being human.

Even then we find it necessary to use facial expressions, hand gestures, and perhaps unconscious body-language when trying to reach the frontiers of words. We often feel emotions we can't express in any other way than by hugging or kissing or loving . . . and who could possibly define the perfume of a rose? or the taste of treacle-toffee? or what it's like to nurse a sleeping baby in your cradling arms?

And these days the cartoon is understood quicker than the catechism, the advertising slogan is mightier than the Sermon . . . the medium more interesting than the message.

There are few sights more frustratingly sad for those who care than that of a Church whose time has at last come again, but whose thoughts linger on remembrance of things past.

* * *

The root mistake of these committed sermonisers, from which sprouts most of the others, is the assumption that because people are reasonably *literate* they are therefore *literary*.

But, for example, newspapers are literate without being literary in

14

the old-fashioned sense, and usually devote as much (or more) space to dramatic pictures as words. Stories and news-items are told quickly in bold headlines and crisp paragraphs, sentences are short, words are simple, and everything is varied with all manner of typefaces and graphics. Each page makes a total impact, information is presented immediately, nothing is much more important than anything else, wars and football and politics and robbery with violence, famine in Africa and Princess Di wearing new clothes, the breasts and bottom of the girl on page three and an old woman mugged in her own home by teenage thugs, *now* all at once, shock, horror, rape and chips . . . Wow!

Again, the advertisements (on the backs of which all this is printed) rely even less on words: for one visual image sells a million bars of soap or chocolate, the logo of one brand-name can corner the market.

While television, the leader of the competitive pack, involves the viewer *in* the experience of reality, and often dispenses with words altogether. A well-directed programme is alive with colour and movement and sequences of dramatic intensity, several acknowledged experts will deal with various aspects of the subject, there's give and take, perhaps conflict of evidence or opinion, clash of personalities . . . music at key moments . . . and we are thus drawn into the disturbing actuality of direct involvement.

With this complex richness as a daily norm of expectation we go to church on Sunday . . . and have to listen to one man talking at us in a loud voice for as long as he dares to go on.

*　　*　　*

There is an added factor to be considered in any examination of the effects of television on the Sermon: most talking heads on the screen are in close-up, inches away from us . . . and the technique of presentation is to underplay, understate, talk quietly and naturally. Newscasters and interviewers are trained to remember that they are in the same room as their audience, not to shout, not to make big expressive gestures, not to be too forceful or dynamic. In other words, not to ham it up, but play it down: that's not a Public Meeting "out there," but two or three gathered together.

So we are now conditioned to being spoken to conversationally in a person-to-person way . . . and even Presidents and Prime Ministers no longer address us on television as though we were an unruly school assembly, but are coached in smiling sincerely and putting on special confidential or reassuring voices.

But the typical clergyman in the pulpit still blunders on in the old way, trying to present what should be an intimately personal content by standing fifty yards away from most of his congregation, and speaking with that loud voice of strain in what he hopes is a sacred silence . . . though some of them can't even manage that, but mumble into their notes, and are largely unheard.

*   *   *

Yes, some preachers *are* trying to drag the Church backwards into the contemporary world . . . and they run Courses in the Techniques of Radio and Television and Communications Theory.

And there's a jokey message sellotaped to the wall in every training studio: *Television isn't just a brightly-lit pulpit.*

So they at least know the name of the game.

But most of our clergy persist in confining their best endeavours to the Sermon.

However, like the lace and embroidered costumes and distinctive clothes many of them wear while doing it, the whole performance is archaic, and they are merely going through the motions which *used* to work once upon a more authoritarian time.

*   *   *

An even better comparison for the Sermon is with the hand-written illuminated manuscript, once the best way the Church had to preserve and pass on its teachings. And such manuscripts are nearly always beautiful, just as some Sermons have been . . . but now we have printing-presses and photo-copiers, data-processing and retrieval systems, and the proper place for antiquities is a museum.

Again, gargoyles and episcopal gaiters were once the forms by which the Church expressed its sense of the grotesque and the dignity of its prelates: the custom of the country today is to watch *Spitting Image* and wear unisex jeans and trainers.

No, the Sermon is only a carefully preserved survival, an anachronism, probably the major barrier between Jesus Christ and the world . . . and the Church is clinging to its legendary past because its present is drearily uncomfortable . . . while the future doesn't bear thinking about.

The quicker we can get rid of it, the quicker we can release Christ from the rock-tomb of words we have erected over Him with such theological care and exactitude.

*   *   *

Understandably enough, many preachers are often passionate (even desperate) in their defence of the Sermon as a means of communicating the old old story to those who have already voted with their buttocks by no longer sitting in the pews to "come under the sound of the Gospel."

"The preacher's throne is the pulpit," wrote Matthew Simpson when secular doubts were first beginning to undermine their religious confidence. "He stands in Christ's stead; his Message is the Word of God; around him are immortal souls; the Saviour, unseen, is beside him; the Holy Spirit broods over the congregation; Angels gaze upon the scene; Heaven and Hell await the issue."

The preaching of Sermons is the "highest, holiest activity to which a man can give himself," wrote William Sangster, a popular Methodist preacher at Westminster Central Hall just after the Second World War. "It is a task which Angels might envy and for which Archangels might forsake the Court of Heaven."

"There is nothing like it," wrote Martyn Lloyd-Jones, another popular preacher of the time. "It is the greatest work in the world, the most thrilling, the most exciting, the most rewarding, and the most wonderful."

Apart from that descent of the earlier high-flown rhetoric into this modern banality, the idea is always the same: the Preacher remains a Prince of the Church, and the Sermon is his Chosen Instrument of Power.

Indeed, Donald Coggan, when he was Archbishop of York, was indignant at being expected to preach from a "poor, paltry little stand," the "sort of temporary contraption from which any man might have scorned to give out the Notices of the Week." True, he afterwards denied that an "elaborate setting" was ever "called for" . . . but obviously hankered after the "magnificence" of some pulpits he'd recently seen elsewhere: "Thrones indeed!" he said . . . and I must agree that costly embroidered vestments *would* look even more incongruous behind a "contraption" instead of high in carved wooden glory. The only questions being why a Living Faith in Jesus Christ needs either Archbishops *or* vestments? pulpits *or* Sermons?

True, not all of them are quite so solemn about it . . . and William Wand, former Bishop of London, is not above a little High Table facetiousness: "A mundane, but none the less serious, danger for the Harvest preacher," he wrote in his *Letters on Preaching*, "is that of physical contact with the decorations. If he is wearing his best stole, the row of tomatoes on the pulpit ledge can be quite devastating. And his best point can be ruined if he knocks a small pot-plant from the same point of vantage into the lap of the Colonel's Lady underneath."

Though *that* sort of Anglican cosiness, with the Colonel and his

Lady setting a Good Example to the tenants by sitting in the front row of the pews, is an element in what has driven most of the rest of us out of the back rows.

* * *

One of the latest in this rear-guard of defenders is John Stott, "an impenitent believer in the indispensable necessity of preaching." He's currently a respected Evangelical theoretician of the Sermon, considered by most conservatives to be a preacher in the mainstream of their tradition . . . and his book, *I Believe in Preaching,* published in 1982, is already a minor classic among those who accept the "absolute primacy of the Bible" as "God's Word written . . ."

With typical Evangelical enthusiasm he starts by attacking those who question the continued usefulness of the Sermon, calling them the "prophets of doom," and he agrees with Donald Coggan that it's a "specious lie" to point out just how ineffectual it is in the Britain of today. Indeed, they unite in alleging that to be critical of the Sermon as a means of communication is to do the work of "Our Father Below" – a donnish pleasantry for the Devil, borrowed from *The Screwtape Letters.*

Which is the standard response of those with a weak case in these over-heated acres of the Christian vineyard: "We are doing the work of Christ, and, if you disagree, *you* are doing the work of the Devil." Even to doubt at all is to be damned as a "bitter controversialist."

However, once uncovered from its undergrowth of Biblical texts, which are amassed to establish a "Theology of Preaching," their case is simple: the "unbroken tradition in the Church of nearly twenty centuries."

Christ preached, the Apostles and Disciples preached, the Greek and Latin Fathers preached, the Friars and Reformers preached, the Puritans and the Evangelicals preached, Spurgeon and Moody and Billy Graham have preached . . . therefore *we* have to go on preaching.

Well, yes, of course, Christians *must* tell other people about the Good News of Jesus Christ: the only question is whether or not the Sermon remains the best way of doing that telling?

Yes, those who have heard what they believe is the Word of God are indeed called upon to speak it to others: but why do we have to ascend a pulpit to do the speaking?

So, by thus confusing the generic act of preaching, or proclaiming, with what is merely one of the forms used by preachers in the past, an Evangelical case is thus made out for the Sermon.

But there is a clear distinction between *preaching*, which is the

generalised telling of the Good News, and *sermonising,* which is what
goes on inside a church. Christians are commanded to "preach the
Gospel to everybody" . . . but that *doesn't* mean delivering prepared
Sermons to congregations of more or less convinced believers.

The Apostles spoke as they got the chance to everybody who'd
listen, sometimes to sympathetic crowds, often to actively hostile
mobs – but very rarely to a docile or captive audience. Whereas
within existing groups of believers they devoted themselves to
praying and *teaching,* the communion of bread and wine, and
fellowship.

These days, as with so much else, the Church does almost the exact
opposite: *preaching* to its own, and trying to *teach* those who don't
want to know and are not even listening.

*   *   *

However, it's not only the Evangelicals who see the Sermon as the
answer to most questions, because many Church Leaders are
disturbed and depressed by the "moral chaos" of this country, the
present apathy of their churches, the accelerating decline in
membership, and the obvious lack of Christian witness in our
contemporary society. Archbishops and Bishops, Moderators and
Presidents and Elders . . . all have lamented, and all have hankered
after the Good Old Days.

Yet, of *all* people, these Leaders are probably the most responsible
for the conditions they complain about. "If the blind lead the short-
sighted, shall they not together end in the nearest ditch?"

But let us grant them sincerity in wanting to do something about it.

Then the question becomes *what*?

Donald Coggan, one among many such, wants the Gospel
"proclaimed" . . . but perpetuates what seems to be the typical
confusion between generic proclamation and the Sermon as merely
one of the *means* of proclaiming. For his "vision" is of "giving our
people" the "opportunity of listening, Sunday by Sunday, to a
steady, intelligent, interesting exposition of the things most surely
believed among us."

In fewer words, more of the same: more and longer Sermons.

*   *   *

Another even more implausible argument is that the Sermon is
unique as a form of discourse.

"Here are God's people," claims John Scott, "assembled in God's
presence to hear God's Word from God's Minister."

Yes, but why does that Minister have to preach that Word of God as it has always been preached? Merely *because* that's the way it has *always* been preached?

He could just as well sing or dance, or mime or act or manipulate puppets, or draw, or put on a slide or light show, or make a dramatic mixed-media presentation, or arrange a "happening" . . . or even invent an entirely new method of proclaiming the Good News.

Why does it *need* to be a Sermon?

"God's people" can still be "assembled in God's presence to hear God's Word from God's Minister," and "hear" it without a word being said . . . for ancient truths do not *have* to be proclaimed in ancient ways, and does God need a tongue to speak?

* * *

Prebendary Cleverly Ford, Honorary Director of The College of Preachers, has also tried to re-establish this supposed quality of the Sermon: it's uniqueness as a traditional part of a sacramental Service.

"Preaching," he claims, though less elegantly than John Stott, "in the context of a congregation of people of faith worshipping God as known in Christ as Lord in the presence of the Divine Spirit stands in a class by itself."

Though he goes on to elaborate the notion that the Sermon has this unique value because of its *context*. True, he doesn't describe *all* of the possible factors involved, but it's easy to admit their cumulative effect. First, there's the special building in which the Sermon is preached, decorated with Christian images and symbols, and traditionally sited with its longitudinal axis pointing towards the East – thus being on stream to absorb the mysterious tides of solar energy. Then there's the choral and congregational singing, the ritual gestures and liturgical words of the Service, the emotional character of the readings and responses, even the archaic vestments worn by the preacher . . . all eyes directed towards him, silence, no distractions allowed . . . everything contributing to the inducement of that sense of awe and strangeness in which his words can work with power, and perhaps assume a significance they don't possess.

But, again, the undoubted fact that a method is unique doesn't necessarily mean that it remains effective.

The British Public School is a unique method of education . . . though who would claim that therefore it's the best? Yes, it once did the job it emerged to do – but now, under pressure from changed circumstances, it's changing.

And the University Lecture is a unique method of communicating information . . . though who would claim that it's the only or the most effective way? It's been described as "facts and opinions passing from the notebook of the lecturer to the notebook of the student without passing through the mind of either." And, likewise, the preaching of a Sermon is the equivalent of trying to fill rows of empty bottles in the pews by sloshing buckets of water from the pulpit.

Yes, as the dictation of one precious manuscript to a hundred scribes at a time in the days before the invention of printing, both the lecture and the Sermon once worked well enough – but we have now improved the technology, and can communicate the same content more memorably.

In other words, the mere quality of being unique is not in itself a recommendation . . . especially when the method is so ineffectual in principle, and usually so dreary in preaching practice.

*　*　*

Alan Bennett, thirty years ago in *Beyond the Fringe,* preached what ought to have been the Funeral Oration over the Common or Pulpit Sermon: an hilarious Jumble Sale of flabby jargon, pseudo-scholarship, matey asides, inconsequential anecdotes, condescending slang, totally irrelevant and strained examples of "Spiritual Lessons" drawn from daily life – all utterly pointless . . . and all in that strangulated voice which seems to be issued with theological degrees.

Yet the last time my wife and I attended a Service in York Minster we heard an equally pointless and inconsequential Sermon, though it was even more insufferably condescending . . . and (if it hadn't been so depressing) almost as funny.

*　*　*

And even a former Archbishop of Canterbury, Donald Coggan, has had occasional moments of disquiet: "When a man has been at the job for a good many years, he does well to look back . . . to think of the many hours which he has spent in preparation, reading, studying, thinking, writing . . . and in the actual delivery of what he has prepared. Look at those notes, piles and piles of them. Words, words, more words! What has been the purpose? What has he been trying to do down the years? Has be been trying to prop up an institution, to perpetuate a venerable practice into the late twentieth century?"

And he makes an honest admission: "Some of these practices, good in their day, are best left to history. Let them be buried as relics of the past."

Amen, Brother Coggan, Amen in gentle thunder!

True, as a teacher of preachers, he then understandably enough hastily backs away from the disturbing implications of this refreshing heresy, and goes on to talk about "proclaiming the truth as it has been made known in Jesus" ... thus persisting in the confusion between the *telling* of that truth and preaching Sermons about it.

"But," wrote the Apostle James, "be ye *doers* of the word ..."

And, as the courtiers of King Canute discovered, the running tide will not stay for the speaking of mere words, no matter how lordly ... and neither will the Sermon survive, no matter how dogmatic or desperate its clerical defenders.

*   *   *

The great temples of Babylon and Egypt, Greece and Rome, were once crowded with worshippers ... but now most of them are ruins, visited by archaeologists and tourists.

And most of our cathedrals are now already catering as much for the tourists as for any worshippers, the turnstiles clanking away, the Gift Shops doing a thriving trade in ticky-tat, chink-chink, and the buildings are seen as architectural museums rather than as Holy Places. Unless the Church changes, and returns to its roots in Jesus Christ and love and people and simplicity, the worshippers will continue to leave and the tourists will take over completely.

And fresh thinking about the Sermon, and the differences between preaching and teaching, could well be the pivotal point of that change.

Otherwise the day of the archaeologists is at hand!

So why not start digging away at the foundations of the pulpit before *they* do?

*   *   *

Not long after Amos had stalked back to his wilderness, unheard, another Prophet spoke to our condition.

"It is not for any man to bring a charge against the people," said Hosea, "not for any man to condemn. God's quarrel is with the false priests. *Priests?*" he said. "By day and night they blunder on, and the people are dying for lack of knowledge ... because the priests have rejected knowledge, forgotten the teachings of God, perverted a glorious calling into a shameful trade."

So please don't blame me for the perhaps hurtful truth ... listen to the Prophets.

*   *   *

Why so scathing?

Because Almighty God, Master of Time and Space, Creator of Heaven and your nearest daisy, is being confined to the always-on-Sunday pulpits, silenced by the mewling of self-satisfied clerical voices.

Not, of course, that the Church is failing to communicate – we know only too well what the Church is and does. And its "success" in being seen as a soppy Gas-and-Gaiters Private Establishment Club is in directly reverse ratio to its almost total failure to preach Jesus Christ, and Him Crucified.

True, as many more minor prophets than Gavin Reid have pointed out, "high powered First Division ecclesiastical figures have been saying such things for years." But the depressing fact is that the Church has taken so little notice, insists on mumbling and muttering, pottering in the pulpit, and regards three clergymen mildly disagreeing about Teilhard de Chardin in front of a bowl of plastic flowers on television as the contemporary equivalent of Pentecost.

Briefly, the Church continues to do in the late twentieth century what it wasn't even very much good at in the nineteenth.

So the death of the Church seems to me to be the only hope for Christianity . . . and Jesus can't get out of the Gothic tomb we've built for Him until *we* blow open the door with the fresh air of Faith, Hope, and Charity – and the greatest of these is Love.

And, most certainly, no Church that *still* puts all its dubious eggs into the one pulpit, that still slumbers under the Sermon, *can* survive into the twenty-first century. For on every hand and hoarding, every page and screen, every cartoon and cassette and video, we are confronted and clamoured at by expert communicators . . . and we now know the way it must be done if it's going to be done at all.

Yet, every chance he gets, your actual clergyman put on his fancy dress, climbs as high as possible above the rest of us, and talks down at the few faithful pews for twenty minutes about seventeen words from Deuteronomy – half-an-hour when it's Leviticus.

*　　*　　*

And yet . . . and yet . . . there *have* been times and preachers, Sermons preached in that language of fire and roses, words which have shaken the world.

To have collected them all would have been the work of a lifetime . . . and "of my threescore years and ten" more than sixty "will not come again."

So all I have done is chosen a few which have come my way and moved me for all manner of personal reasons. Such taste is always subjective and one man's meat and drink is another man's indigestion.

Not being a woman, I can't speak for them.

* * *

Merely in passing, even given the wicked and unChristian prejudice against women in the patriarchal Church, it's strange that there haven't been many more women preachers, good or great or otherwise.

Apart from our own Joanna Southcott, the three most curious I've come across are Ellen Gould White, Mary Baker Eddy, and Aimee Semple McPherson – all Americans.

Mrs White was an extraordinary woman, one of the founders of the Seventh-Day Adventist Church in the nineteenth century, but her Revivalistic Camp Meeting Sermons about the special doctrines of that church are obviously of more interest to its members than the rest of us.

The same is true of Mrs Baker Eddy, an even more extraordinary woman, sole founder of the Church of Christ Scientist, whose vast number of expository Sermons on her own book, *Science and Health,* are much too specialised for any but the very Elect.

As for that "gay and lovely evangelical nun," as Sinclar Lewis called Aimee Semple McPherson, we can surely enjoy seeing her "bedecked in American football helmet, pantaloons, and shoulder pads," hurtling across the stage to "grab a tackling dummy while shrieking threats at the Devil . . ."

* * *

Another consideration of choice was length.

Even the better preachers have often been overly fond of their own voices, and have gone on for far longer than the most besotted of us could maintain undivided attention.

The ancient emphasis is on solid extension as the chief of virtues: "Sermonettes," chuckles bright-eyed and bushy-tailed Evangelical wisdom, "makes Christianettes."

Jonathan Edwards and Spurgeon and Campbell Morgan would preach for an hour or longer, the equivalent of twenty-five closely-printed pages . . . and even a contemporary, John Scott, exceeds forty minutes.

Ten such Sermons complete, and you'd have a thick and dreary book.

Block-busters bust little but blocks.

So I have merely given the full flavour rather than every last text and paragraph. This isn't a work of scholarship, but a box of samples, small glasses for tasting rather than crates of two-litre bottles. But at least most of the wine is sweet and miraculous, and hasn't been changed back into ecclesiastically-approved sour milk and water.

* * *

It would have been instructive to have included a few examples of contemporary preaching – if only for comparison with vintages from the Day of Wine and Roses.

But most competent observers agree that there's not much of value to choose from.

Donald Coggan, for one, admits the "sorry plight" of preaching in the Church of which he was so recently Archbishop.

Michael Green, for another. He's an Evangelical intellectual who has stated (with what John Stott praises as "customary forth-rightness") that the "standard of preaching in the modern world is deplorable."

True, he regards John Scott as an exception, " one of the few great preachers in Britain." However, John Stott himself allows that "our worship is poor because our knowledge of God is poor, and our knowledge of God is poor because our preaching is poor." This is no mere pious expression of generalised pseudo-humility, for he goes on to admit that "in the pulpit" he is "often seized" with what he calls "communication frustration," and that he's "unable to convey to others" what he's "thinking – let alone feeling." And he concurs with Michael Green that the "tide of preaching" has ebbed, "and the ebb is low today."

Though there was always Billy Graham, undoubtedly the most highly-publicised mass-evangelist of recent times, and certainly the Big Apple of almost every Evangelical eye. Except that his own words were conclusive: "No one ever called me a great preacher," he said. "There are thousands of better ones." Yes, the statistical handouts of "results" are apparently impressive – but have obviously got more to do with sophisticated methods of crowd manipulation than either the content or the quality of his preaching . . . which even his own colleagues will admit is informal to the point of formlessness.

So, reluctantly, I have accepted these candid self-valuations, and left out our merely famous contemporaries.

* * *

Here, then, are a few of the words which have moved the world: at

once an Anthology, another Funeral Oration, and an Epitaph.
"Come, every one that thirsteth, come ye to the waters . . ."
Better still, try some of this sweet wine!

Che Mountain and the Synagogue

The most famous Sermon of them all was the one preached by Jesus in the morning of the world, when a great multitude of people followed Him, and, seeing them, He went up into a mountain. And when He had sat down, His Disciples came unto Him, and He lifted up His eyes on them, opened His mouth, and taught them in the presence of the multitude, saying . . .

*   *   *

Except that it's extremely unlikely that it was ever preached by Jesus in the form by which we know it in Matthew's Gospel.

"There would hardly be a reputable New Testament scholar today," murmur the comfortable voices in libraries and lecture-rooms, "who would disagree with the view that this is no single continuous discourse, delivered on any one occasion, but is rather an Anthology of Sayings, probably collected by some unknown Disciple who desired to provide his fellow-believers with a Christian Primer for the Conduct of the Sanctified Life. Moreover," murmur the voices, "a close scrutiny of the various texts confirms this hypothesis, in that . . ."

And off they maunder and meander into their gently passionate controversies about the undoubtedly serious difficulties involved in wanting to *quote* the presumed words of Jesus . . . which, apparently, is ever so much more interesting than the *other* sort of difficulties involved in actually *doing* anything about any of those words.

But at the very least we *can* read (if only in totally inadequate translations from a hopelessly corrupt text) what some person or persons unknown (allegedly Matthew or Luke or both, or even somebody using their authenticating names) borrowed from what somebody else (possibly Mark) partly remembered of what somebody else again (thought to be Peter or a Disciple of Peter) probably told him about what *he* partly remembered of what somebody they all merely *imagined* was Jesus might *just* have conceivably said in the middle of a noisy crowd one Thursday morning (or was it the Friday?) thirty or forty years earlier . . .

Though what we can read *still* seems to make more sense to me than the words of these blind mouths grating away on their scrannel pipes of scholarship in recent twittering days.

True, there *is* an obvious problem, which applies to most of the

Sermons ever preached: they were intended to be spoken and so heard by a congregation, not written to be read silently in a book by one reader at a time.

Yet, for all that and much more, it's hardly likely that Jesus would preach in disconnected epigrams, condensed phrase after condensed phrase, or that He would pack quite so many fertile eggs into so small a basket. He left spiritual indigestion to the theological experts.

"We have here, then," murmur the voices, relieved to be back on safer ground, "density of content, aphoristic richness, abundance of maxims and similitudes, abrupt transitions, and the imposition of a symbolic structure more or less poetic in form – all such as to lead the unprejudiced mind to the inevitable conclusion that we are faced by an Ecclesiastically arranged collection of quite possibly Authentic Sayings, almost certainly compiled by some unknown Disciple acting on behalf of the Early Apostolic Church . . ."

*   *   *

And it came to pass, when Jesus had ended these sayings, the people were astonished, for He taught them as one having authority, and not as the Scribes and Theologians.

If only, if *only* we could hear those words as they sounded before they were defused and submerged in the Commentaries.

I say unto you, That ye resist not evil, but whosoever shall smite thee on thy right cheek, turn to him the other also . . .

No, that would never do, would it?

Certainly not for the Ministry of, er, Defence, with its nuclear weapons poised for Instant Second Strike Massive Retaliation.

*   *   *

However, only slightly less famous, there's the Sermon in the Synagogue at Nazareth.

We're told in the various Gospels that when Jesus was about thirty years of age, soon after a fast of forty days and nights in the wilderness, He began to preach in Capernaum, saying: "The time is fulfilled at last, and the Kingdom of God and Heaven is now at hand. Repent ye . . ." And went about all through the whole of Galilee in the power of the Spirit, teaching, and healing all manner of sickness and all manner of disease among the people.

And He came to Nazareth, the little town where He had been brought up, and, as His custom was, He went straight into the Synagogue on the Sabbath day . . .

*   *   *

The domestic setting and form of the Service in the Synagogue, or House of Assembly, probably arose during the Captivity of the Jews in Babylon, when they were exiled from the magnificence of the Temple in Jerusalem, cut off from its system of Ritual Sacrifices.

The building would be both a Place of Prayer and a School of Religious Instruction, a not very large rectangular hall aligned on the consecrated direction of Jerusalem so that everybody present could face the Holy City at the appointed times, and thus be reminded of their Messianic hopes. There'd be seats on one side for the men, and, on the other, behind a lattice-screen, the women would sit on cushions. At the far end was the chest or Ark of painted wood which held the Sacred Scrolls, with a raised seat for the Reader or Teacher next to it. The best or first chairs for the Elders, Scribes, Doctors of the Law, and the Head of the Synagogue were in front of the Ark.

The Service was simple, if lengthy by modern standards:

Chanting of the traditional opening Psalms and Prayers...
"Blessed be Thou, O Lord, King of the world, Who formest the light and createst the darkness, Who makest peace..."

Appointed Reading for the Day from one of the Five Books of Moses in Hebrew, each Verse followed by a translation into the local tongue, the Aramaic of Galilee or Greek or whatever, with the congregation standing to listen, facing Jerusalem.

Commentary on this Reading, usually by an Elder or Scribe as directed by the Head of the Synagogue.

Then the long Prayer of the Eighteen Benedictions of the Great and Ineffable Goodness of God.

Another Appointed Reading from one of the Prophets, with the Verse by Verse translation, and another Commentary.

Finally, the Benediction... "The Lord Bless thee, and Keep thee; the Lord make His Face Shine upon thee, and be Gracious unto thee; the Lord lift up His Countenance upon thee, and give thee Peace."

And those two Commentaries upon the Readings from the Scriptures have descended to us as the Expository Sermon... the basic form from which all others derive.

*   *   *

Any competent or religiously instructed Jew of good reputation could be called upon by the Head of the Synagogue to Read the Scriptures and give the Commentaries – and Jesus, as an already known and respected Teacher, with great multitudes of people following Him, was invited to do so.

He'd be wearing no special robes, no embroidered vestments – merely a long tunic of coarse cloth with a belt of rope tied around the waist, a cloak of woven camel-hair which also served as a blanket by night, rough leather sandals, and a square of linen covering His head. And, as a faithful Son of the Law, He'd wrap His shoulders in the obligatory prayer-shawl, a large white scarf with ritual fringes and tassels.

At the invitation He ascended the steps to the raised seat, the Clerk drew aside the silk curtain of the Ark, took out the parchment Scroll of the Prophet Isaiah which contained the Reading for the Day, and handed it to Him. And Jesus unrolled the Scroll, and found the required Verses in what we know as chapter sixty-one: *The Spirit of the Lord God is upon me* . . .

The whole congregation stood to listen, and Jesus read the well-known words: "The Spirit of the Lord God is upon me, because the Lord hath anointed me to preach Good Tidings unto the poor and meek. He hath sent me to Heal the broken-hearted, to Proclaim Deliverance and Liberty to the captives, the Recovering of Sight to the blind, and the Opening of the Prison to them that are bruised and bound, the comfortless, to Preach the Acceptable Year of Pardon and Forgiveness by the Lord."

He then rolled the Scroll closed, handed it back to the Clerk, and sat down.

And the eyes of all them that were in the Synagogue were fastened on Him with a gaze of intense earnestness, for He spoke with the ring of mysterious authority.

And He began to say unto them: "This day is this Scripture fulfilled in your ears . . ."

Obviously making the claim that *He* was the Anointed One, the Messiah promised by Isaiah seven hundred years before. No, He hadn't merely read the words aloud, but, as the King's Herald, He had Proclaimed the New Age of Salvation.

Now it was the custom for the Jews of that time to give full vent to their feelings during Worship, rather like the West Indians and Pentecostalists of today, and they were at first all astonished at His blessed assurance: *they* were the poor, the sorrowful in heart, the captives of an Occupying Power, and *here* they were being granted the Year of Pardon, the Great Jubilee of the Lord their God.

But wonder soon turned to doubt, and they said, muttering among themselves: "Is this not Joseph the Carpenter's son? is not his Mother called Mary?"

And He said unto them: "Ye will surely say unto me this proverb, *Physician, heal thyself.* Let us see you do in your own country all that we have heard that you did in Capernaum."

"Is this not the Carpenter?" they said. "The brother of workmen like himself? James and Joses and Simon and Judas?"

And He said: "Verily I say unto you, A Prophet is not without honour, save in his own country, and in his own house."
"Do not his own sisters live among us?" they said. "Are they not all with us in Nazareth?"
"I tell you a truth," He said. "Many widows were in Israel in the days of Elijah, when there was a drought for three years and six months, and there was a great famine throughout all the land – but unto none of them was Elijah sent, save unto a Phoenician woman of Sidon ..."
And they were beginning to be offended with Him: "Where does he get all these Big Ideas? Even his own family do not believe in him."
"And many lepers were in Israel in the time of Elisha the Prophet," He said, "but none of them were cleansed, saving Naaman the Syrian."
What? Were *they,* the Sons of Abraham, no better than Gentiles and filthy lepers?
And all they in the Synagogue, the inhabitants of His home town, when they heard these things, were filled with wrath ... He was no longer interrupted by mutterings of disapproval, but a roar of rage.
And they rose up, tore Him down from the seat, dragged Him out, and pushed and drove Him through His own remembered streets unto the brow of the hill where Nazareth was built, that they might fling Him down headlong onto the rocks below ...
But He, passing through the midst of them, went His way.
He had come unto His own, and His own received Him not.

*   *   *

Any lessons there for our contemporary Preachers?
Well, for a start, why not sitting to *teach* rather than standing to *preach*? For to stand is to appear superior ... and who can believe any such thing before God?
And, to be thoroughly awkward, might it possibly be one Sign of Divine Grace if congregations got excited enough to make remarks about it *during* a Sermon? Even applauded afterwards?
Or if, say, the Bishop of London preached in Saint Paul's Cathedral on the Ordination of Women as Priests in the Church of England, and all they in there rose up, tore him down from that carved pulpit, dragged him out, and pushed and drove him along Trig Lane to fling him head-first into the Thames at Puddle Dock ... well, could *he* claim that he had at least succeeded in stirring them out of their indifference?
Or do we prefer to pass our time in rest and quietness?

Tongues as it were of Fire

And when the day of Pentecost was fully come, they were all with one accord in one place.

The English word "Pentecost" is a transliteration of the Greek word *pentekostos,* meaning "fiftieth."

To the Jew is was the Feast of Harvest, one of their three great yearly Festivals – being the end of the fifty days or seven weeks which started with the Offering of the First Fruits of the Barley Harvest on the second day of the Passover. It also marked the traditional anniversary of the Giving of the Ten Commandments on Mount Sinai.

So it began as a solemn Festival of the Jews, connected with the most vital fact of their agricultural life, a reminder of their utter dependence on the mercy of God, a Memorial of the Declaration of His Law on the Tablets of Stone, a Thanksgiving both for bread and Morality.

And it continues as a Christian commemoration of the Descent of the Holy Spirit.

And when was this day fully come?

The Jewish Civil and Religious Day began at sunset, and they observed their Sabbaths and Festivals from evening to evening, and *this* was fully come . . . so it would be very early morning, before the third hour summoned the Faithful to the Temple for Prayer. That is, by our reckoning, about six o'clock in the morning of a Sunday at the end of May during the year of Christ's Crucifixion and Resurrection.

And who are they, these assembled together with one accord and purpose in one place?

All the Apostles, and Disciples, and Believers:

Peter, the Little Stone, the braggart, the coward, the denier of Jesus before them all, even with an oath . . . and yet the one whose words of Faith in Christ became the Rock for the Foundation of the Church.

And James, the brother of Christ, who once thought Him mad, but who has now been made witness of the Resurrection.

And John, whom Jesus loved, and Andrew, Philip, and Thomas . . . the Thomas who had refused to believe in that Resurrection until he could put his finger into the scars of the Crucifying nails, and thrust his hand into the wounded side – but who *saw* and didn't need to *touch*, and believed, and said, "My Lord and my God."

And Bartholomew, and Matthew, and James the son of Alphaeus,

32

Simon the Patriot, and Judas the brother of James . . . and Mary, the Mother of Jesus, and His other brothers, and His sisters, and the women who had followed Him from Galilee, and Mary the wife of Cleophas, and Joanna, and Salome, and Mary Magdalene . . . with the number of the names together being about an hundred and twenty.

And what is their one accord and purpose?

To wait together and devote themselves to steadfast prayer and supplication . . . for Jesus Christ, at His Ascension into Heaven, had commanded them that they should not depart from Jerusalem, but wait there for the Promise of His Father, the Holy Spirit, Comforter.

And so they wait, united in love and prayer, still devout Jews, but with the women now gathered in that Communion where there is neither Jew nor Greek, neither bond nor free, neither male nor female, but where all are One in the Name of Jesus Christ.

And where in this place?

Jerusalem, that same city in which they had so recently watched the shame and defeat of His Crucifixion, and had been made witness to the Victory and Glory of His Resurrection.

And where in Jerusalem?

That Upper Room where they had been staying . . . even where they had shared the Last Supper. Quite unlike the ornate chambers painted by the Old Masters of Art, who served a rich Church rather than the lowly Christ: no splendid Palace or Cathedral – for these waiting Believers were also the poor, the broken-hearted, the captives, the bruised.

A few small unglazed windows, mats woven of rushes, a low wooden table, rough cushions, baskets of provisions, stone jars of water . . .

And, perhaps, a view out over the city and the Mount of Olives and the Valley of Kidron, the maze of streets and courts and passages and lanes, roofs and awnings and towers and domes . . . and the Temple itself, rising high above the levelled platform of Mount Moriah – the very Sanctuary, the Holy of Holies, the Veil of which had been ripped from the top to the bottom by the hand of God at the death of His Son.

For the Lamb of God had now been Sacrificed once and for all, the Work had been Finished, and we were now free to approach the Father without any High Priest except Christ, to Worship God in Temples not made with hands.

And the sun rises out of the Mountains of Moab and Ammon, there's the brazen clank and clatter of the Levites opening the great Nicanor Gate of that now unnecessary Temple, the trumpets call for the first Prayers of this new day . . . and then, from the courts and houses of the Sons of Abraham, the chanting of the *Shema Israel:* "Hearken, O Israel, the Lord thy God is the One and Only God, and thou shalt love the Lord thy God with all thy heart, and with all thy soul, and with all thy strength."

And the voices of one hundred and twenty True Believers raised in the beginning of a Prayer that was to turn the world upside-down . . .

And then, O *then* the Fulfilment of the Promise!

The sudden, overwhelming sound from Heaven as of the violent rushing of a mighty driving wind, filling the whole house, engulfing their souls, drowning their thoughts, mastering their minds, lifting, surging, confronting, demanding . . . and the flames of fire like many tongues, pale, but clear and intense, gathering and dispersing, settling momentarily above the head of each one of them, so that men and women alike prophesied, saw visions, dreamed dreams, were filled with the Holy Spirit, and began to speak with other tongues than their own as that Pentecostal Spirit gave them utterance . . .

*   *   *

And there were dwelling at Jerusalem many Jews, devout men, out of every nation under Heaven, and the multitude of them came together, and were confounded, because that every man heard them speaking in his own language. And they were all amazed and marvelled, saying one to another, "Behold, are not all these which speak Galileans? And now hear we every man in our own tongue, wherein we were born?"

No mere babbling this, then, sound and fury signifying nothing, no unknown tongues needing unverifiable interpretation . . . but the mystery of a miracle.

And they that heard were in doubt, saying, "What meaneth this?"

But others, mocking, said, "These men are drunk on new wine."

*   *   *

But Peter, standing with the Eleven, lifted up his voice, and said unto them:

"Ye men of Judaea, and all ye that dwell at Jerusalem, be this known unto you, and hearken to my words: For these are not drunken, as ye suppose, seeing it is but the third hour of the day.

"But this is that which was spoken by the Prophet Joel:

"And it shall come to pass in the Last Days that God will pour out His Spirit upon all flesh . . . and on His servants and on His handmaidens He will pour out in those Days of His Spirit, and

they shall prophesy.

"And He will shew wonders in Heaven above, and Signs in the earth beneath, blood, and fire, and vapour of smoke. The sun shall be turned into darkness, and the moon into blood, before that great and notable Day of the Lord come.

"And it shall come to pass, that whosoever shall call on the Name of the Lord shall be Saved.

"Ye men of Israel, hear these words: Jesus of Nazareth, a Man approved of God among you by miracles and wonders and Signs, which God did by Him in the midst of you, as ye yourselves also know ... Him, being delivered by the determinate counsel and foreknowledge of God, ye have taken, and by wicked hands have Crucified and slain ... Whom God hath raised up, having loosed the pains of death ...

"For King David speaketh concerning Him:

"I foresaw the Lord always before my face, for He is on my right hand, that I should not be moved. Therefore did my heart rejoice, and my tongue was glad. Moreover also my flesh shall rest in hope, because God wilt not leave my soul in Hell, neither wilt He suffer His Holy One to see the corruption of death ...

"Men and Brethren, let me freely speak unto you of King David, that he is both dead and buried, and his sepulchre is with us unto this day.

"Therefore being a Prophet, and knowing that God had sworn with an oath to him, that of the fruit of his loins, according to the flesh, he would raise up Christ to sit on his throne. He seeing this before spake of the Resurrection of Christ, that His Soul was not left in Hell, neither His Flesh did see that corruption.

"And this Jesus hath God raised up, whereof we all are witnesses.

"Therefore being by the right hand of God exalted, and having received of the Father the Promise of the Holy Spirit, He hath shed forth *this,* which ye now see and hear.

"For King David is not yet ascended into the Heavens, but he saith himself: *The Lord said unto my Lord, Sit thou on my right hand, until I make thy foes thy footstool.*

"Therefore let all the House of Israel know assuredly, that God hath made that same Jesus, whom ye have Crucified, both Lord and Christ."

Now when they heard this, they were pricked in their heart, and said unto Peter and to the rest of the Apostles, "Men and Brethren, what shall we do?"

Then Peter said unto them, "Repent, and be Baptised every one of you in the Name of Jesus Christ for the remission of sins, and ye also shall receive the Gift of the Holy Spirit. For the Promise is unto you, and to your children, and to all that are afar off, even as many as the Lord our God shall call."

And with many other words did he testify and exhort, saying, "Save yourselves from this untoward generation."

Then they that gladly received his word were Baptised, and the same day there were added unto them about three thousand souls.

And they continued steadfastly in the Apostle's Doctrine and Fellowship, and in Breaking of Bread, and in prayers . . .

And all that believed were together, and had all things in common, and sold their possessions and goods, and parted them to all men, as every man had need.

And they, continuing daily with one accord in the Temple, and Breaking Bread from house to house, did eat their meals with gladness and singleness of heart, praising God, and having favour with all the people.

*　　*　　*

Common people, with not a Theological Degree among them, preaching to common people . . . who heard them gladly.

Yes, in those days, when it must have been very bliss in that dawn to be alive, Christianity belonged to the poor, the broken-hearted, the captives, the bruised: the Priests had not yet complicated its simplicity, translated those tongues of fire into dust and ashes.

Raise up the stone, and you would find Christ: cleave the log, and He would be there.

See your Brother or Sister, and you would see God.

But *now* His soul grieveth over the Sons and Daughters, because they are blind at heart, and see not their poverty.

They that hath ears to hear, let them hear.

Or is our contemporary deafness *that* chronic?

Lord, lay not this Sin to their Charge

Stephen was one of the first Deacons of that Young Church at Jerusalem, a man full of Faith and the Holy Spirit, unanimously elected by the Apostles a few weeks after the Glory of Pentecost.

And, obviously being a fine and passionate advocate of this dangerously radical Sect, he naturally enough soon fell legally foul of the Orthodox Religious Leaders of the day – because, in trying to discredit him in public discussion, they found themselves quite unable to stand against either his practical wisdom or the Spiritual Power with which he spoke.

So, as is the custom of the Orthodox when they have their unholy hooks on that *other* sort of power – the Political as opposed to the Spiritual, the Temporal rather than the Eternal . . . well, they resorted to Official violence for the swift oppression of reason . . .

When was it ever different?

Had him arrested in the High Cause of Law and Order, rigged a trial with bribed witnesses, which said, "This man ceaseth not to speak blasphemous words against this Holy Temple and the Law. For we have heard him say," they said, consulting their little black notebooks, "that this Jesus of Nazareth shall destroy this Temple, and shall change the Traditions and Ceremonials which Moses delivered us."

And all that sat in the Council, looking steadfastly on him, saw his face as it had been the face of an Angel.

Then said the Archbishop, "Are these things so?"

And Stephen said: "Men, Brethren, and Fathers, hearken . . ."

And preached for less than ten minutes: first, according to the more wide-eyed Commentaries, "demonstrating by the courtesy of his demeanour towards them, and the general reverence of his language, that he was incapable of blasphemy" . . . and then leading them through a calm review of Jewish History from Abraham and Isaac and Jacob, to Joseph and Moses in Egypt, the Exodus and the forty years of wandering in the wilderness – all apparently intended to show just how wrong they were about the religious conclusions they drew from it.

The Covenant of God had *nothing* to do with the Tabernacle and the Temple and complicated observances and ceremonials . . .

"Solomon built the God of Jacob an House," said Stephen. "Howbeit the Most High dwelleth not in Temples made with hands. As saith the Most High through His Prophet: *Heaven is my Throne, and the Earth is my Footstool. What House will ye build me?* saith the Lord. *What is the Place of my Rest? Hath not my Hand made all these things?"*

In other words, as their own History should have taught them, the Children of Israel had *always* been unfaithful to the God of their Fathers, and whored after false gods, and worshipped the Golden Calf, even taken up the Tabernacle of Moloch and the Star of Remphan – which had been dearer to them than the Tabernacle of Witness and the Shechina of the Most High . . .

"Ye stiff-necked and uncircumcised in heart and ears," he said, "ye do always resist the Holy Spirit. As your Fathers did, so do you. Which of the Prophets have not your Fathers persecuted? And they have slain them which came before the Coming of the Just One, Whom those same Prophets foretold should come into the world, of Whom ye have been now the betrayers and murderers, you who have received the Law by the disposition of Angels, and have not kept it."

*   *   *

When they heard these things, they were cut to the heart, and lost their temper . . .

Lost their temper?

They ground their teeth at him in their murderous rage . . .

But he, being full of the Holy Spirit, looked up steadfastly into Heaven, and saw the Glory of God, and Jesus standing at the right hand.

And Stephen said, "Behold, I see the Heavens opened, and the Son of Man standing at the right hand of God."

But they stopped their ears, and, yelling with fury, as one made a rush, and dragged him out of the city to smash him to death with stones.

*   *   *

Stoning was always a cruel death, though (as with all such capital punishments) something was usually done to mitigate its severity and lend a superficial appearance of Judicial pomp to the essential barbarity: a chance of Appeal with (perhaps) the chance of a Reprieve, the procession of the condemned to the place of execution, Ritual Prayers, a drink to stupify the victim, and so on . . .

But *this* was a religious lynching.

The "Pit of Stoning" was a disused quarry in the side of a hill, all around lay heaps of stones and small boulders . . . the bottom covered with them, some flecked with crusted blood . . .

And Stephen was stripped, and flung into this pit . . .

And there he was, stumbling before them, an innocent man with seconds to live before the first stone was raised . . .

And he called upon God, saying, "Lord Jesus, receive my spirit."

And they started to murder him, the stones smashing down . . .

His body gouted with blood . . . he was driven to his knees . . .

"O Lord," he cried aloud, so that they all heard him, "lay not this sin to their charge."

Yes, remembering the words of Jesus on the Cross . . . and still seeing that Son of Man now standing in Glory . . .

And then fell into the sleep of death.

*   *   *

And there, formal custodian of the raiment of them that slew Stephen, consenting to his death, was a young man, whose name was Saul.

*   *   *

All a very long time ago?

The Brethren and Fathers are not like that these days?

You try telling the Dean and Chapter of any of our Cathedrals that the Most High dwelleth not in Temples made with hands, or that they ought not to have treasures of gold and silver on their Altars, or that to charge for admission at the turnstiles is to make their place a Den of Thieves.

True, they no longer have legal access to the ancient ecclesiastical methods of argument and persuasion, so you'll be in no great danger . . . least of all if the discussion is on television.

Or try reassuring the Roman Catholics of Northern Ireland when the Orange Order marches through its streets . . . or mention it to the Jehovah's Witnesses in Southern Ireland or Spain or Italy.

Or try preaching Christian Pacifism to the Royal British Legion at a Church Parade on Remembrance Sunday.

Or does *our* Most High actually dwell behind those turnstiles at Westminster Abbey?

Gentlemen of Athens

So there was the young man, Stephen, stoned to death by the Orthodox Religious Leaders of his day for preaching the Truth as he saw it . . . and there was the young man who acted as the formal custodian of the raiment of them that slew him: Saul, who thus consented to that death, and was a full accessory before, during, and after the crime – as much a murderer as all who likewise consent to such executions, even by mere silence. The most wicked stones are those you don't need to pick up to throw, that draw blood where no wound bleeds.

Saul, then, a Jew of Tarsus, citizen of no mean city, circumcised on the eighth day, of the stock of Israel, of the Tribe of Benjamin, an Hebrew of the Hebrews, and, as to the Law, a Pharisee, educated at the feet of Gamaliel.

And, while reverent men buried the broken body of Stephen, and made great lamentations over him, *this* man made havoc of the Young Church in Jerusalem, City of God, breathing out threatenings and slaughter against the Disciples of the Lord, entering into every house, dragging away anybody even suspected of being a Believer in the Risen Christ, and having them flung into prison.

By what authority?

That of the Chief Priests in Jerusalem, to bind all that called on the Name of Jesus, and deliver them unto the Sanhedrin.

And, in his own later words, he admitted that he "persecuted the Church of God beyond all measure, and tried to destroy it," being "exceedingly zealous of the Traditions of the Jews."

He was the sort of man we now know as a Religious Bigot: his mind closed, the door of his understanding slammed and bolted against any new idea, locked and barred against anything which didn't fit his preconceptions, didn't suit his narrow little orthodoxy . . . and who "proved" his Theological arguments with brute force and ignorance.

Such men have prowled through the shadows of Christianity . . . and are still there today, lurking, seeking whom they may devour with roaring words and texts hurled like stones.

Anyway, with Jerusalem cleared of Christians, and thus made safe for his restricted ideas about God, and still uttering murderous threats against anybody who dared to cross his purifying path, he made for Damascus with unlimited authority for the hunting down of heretics . . .

*   *   *

But, when he was almost there, suddenly, blindingly, a Light from the Heavens blazed around him . . . and he fell to the ground . . .

"Saul, Saul," said a Voice . . .

Remember Jesus and Mary Magdalene in the Garden on the morning of the Resurrection?

"Mary," He said . . . merely her name.

"Master," she said . . . merely the one word from her heart.

"Saul, Saul," He said now, "why are you persecuting me?"

Not: "Why are you persecuting my Disciples? Why did you consent to the stoning of Stephen? Why are you making havoc of my Young Church? Why are you flinging my Brothers and Sisters into prison?"

But, simply: "Why are you persecuting *me*?"

And Saul, blinded with excess of Light, said, "Who are you, Lord?"

"I am Jesus of Nazareth, Whom thou persecutest . . ."

*   *   *

Two warnings here for Preachers.

When Christians persecute anybody, especially those we regard as our enemies (or, worse, the enemies of God and His Truth), we may well be persecuting Christ in the least of His Brethren and Sisters . . . even Crucifying Him again as we clench our sweaty hands, scourging Him with our loaded texts, crowning Him with the thorns of Theology, hammering in the nails of creed and doctrine and dogma.

Yes, we might feel, as we usually do, perfectly self-justified.

We might have these heretics cornered in the futile mazes of our Biblical Higher Criticism, clobbered with our profound Christology, incoherent at our knowledge of the original Hebrew and Greek . . . but that poor wretch we have in our unmerciful power at the sharp end of our Sermon may be Jesus, the One we claim to love and worship.

Impossible?

Isn't *that* what Saul thought?

So, rather than risk the same mistake as Saul, why not let's declare a Close Season on those we presume to call heretics? Stop hunting the major Sects with large-bore (and largely boring) volumes? Give up tracking down the Christian Deviations through the wilderness of our pamphlets? Condemning the Cults from our own particular square-yard of intensively cultivated Creed?

Why not leave such matters to God?

41

Isn't there something written somewhere about "Author of Peace and Lover of Concord"?

And the other warning is against abstractions.

Saul only had to hear that Voice calling his name, and he answered at once: "Who are you, Lord?"

There were no clever words, and certainly not the complicated sort he went in for himself later on, no exercises in the, er, Theology of the Demands of Law as Opposed to the Freedom of Grace, no accommodations of the Gospel to the needs of these times, no Apologetics – not even any Big Appeal for a Decision as the electronic-organ dribbles away like warm treacle – but merely that Voice calling him by name . . .

*   *   *

And, trembling and astonished, Saul said: "Lord, what wilt Thou have me do?"

At *that* moment the persecutor became Paul, Apostle to the Gentiles.

A most extraordinary transformation of character: *there* he was, only a week or so before, taking part in the stoning of Stephen . . . and now *here* he is, risking that same death himself.

Why?

It's all too long ago to be clinical, to chatter about Epilepsy and Symptoms of Religious Hysteria and the Psychological Pre-structuring of the Authoritarian Personality. There's too much we don't know and can't understand, even about ourselves and our motives – least of all about the mysteries of God and the deeper workings of the human mind . . . but, perhaps, as Augustine of Hippo wrote three hundred years later, "if Stephen had not prayed, the Church might not have had Paul."

One of the questions then being whether or not the Church might not have done better without him.

But, for a start at least, the persecutor, having seen Christian forgiveness in action, had been as much broken by the Love of Christ in Stephen as ever the body of Stephen had been by the stones . . . and so the first Martyr of the Church thus helped to convert the first Missionary of the Church. Blood had been drawn where no wound bled.

*   *   *

His life from then on is so well-known as to be almost past telling: instructed by Christ to go into the city of Damascus to a house in the street called Straight, where he would be told what he had to do, three days without sight, neither did he eat nor drink . . .

Then Ananias sent by the Lord to put his hand on him so that there fell from his eyes as it had been scales, and he received back his sight at once, and arose, filled with the Holy Spirit, and was Baptised . . . but conferred not with flesh and blood, but went away solitary into Arabia. And then lived certain days with the Disciples which were in Damascus. And straightway he preached in the Synagogues, confounding the Jews, proving from their own Scriptures that Christ was the Promised Messiah, the very Son of God.

And then carried the Good News of Salvation all over most of the Roman Empire, facing death every day of his life, imprisonment in dark and stinking holes, manacles and leg-irons, food crawling with maggots, foul water, floggings, beatings, fighting against the wild animals in the gladiatorial arena at Ephesus, shipwreck . . .

And even all this was merely in addition to the usual hardships of life: hard work – for though he could have made a living by preaching, he chose to earn his daily bread by his family trade of tent-making, working in goat-hair felts . . . long hours, exhaustion, the pain of sickness and disease, nights without sleep, hunger and thirst, bitter cold and parching heat, exposure, lack of adequate clothing . . .

Was there something said about Clergy Stipends? the Salary of our Bishops? Allowances? Annual Increments? Church Investments?

*   *   *

"Small and bald," variously write the Greek Fathers, "crooked thighs, lean face, wrinkled forehead, hollow-eyed, beaked nose, stooping shoulders . . . a look as it were of wild perplexity . . . in a moment he will become flame . . . a fire in his voice . . ."

And the words of his preaching?

*   *   *

He came with Barnabas to Antioch in Pisidia, where the Disciples were first called Christians, and went into the Synagogue on the Sabbath day, and sat down. And, after the two Appointed Readings from the Law and the Prophets, the Head of the Synagogue said unto them, "Ye men and Brethren, if ye have any word of exhortation for the people, say on."

Then Paul, rather than ascend the steps to the raised seat, stood up where he was, and, beckoning with his hand for them to gather around, said: "Men of Israel, and ye that fear God, give audience . . ."

And, like Stephen before him, and using the same arguments, even some of the same words, he preached for less than ten minutes, closer to five, commenting on the two passages of Scripture they had just heard read, reminding them that they were a People Chosen by God, Who brought them out of the Land of Egypt, out of the House of Bondage, led them through their forty years of wanderings in the wilderness, delivered them into the Promised Land, and raised up Samuel the Prophet, and King Saul, and then King David . . .

"And of King David's seed hath God, according to His Promise, raised unto Israel a Saviour, Jesus, Whom John the Baptist said would come after him, Whose shoes he was not worthy to loose. Men and Brethren," said Paul, "Children of the Seed of Abraham, and whosoever among you feareth God, to you is the Word of this Salvation sent.

"For they that dwell at Jerusalem, and their Chief Priests and Elders, because they knew not this same Jesus, nor yet the words of the Prophets which are read every Sabbath day in our Synagogues, *they* have fulfilled these Prophecies by condemning Him. And though they found no case for putting Him to death, yet desired they Pilate that He should be slain. And when all the Prophecies that were written of Him were fulfilled, He was taken down from the Cross, and laid in a sepulchre.

"But God raised Him from the dead.

"And He was seen many days by them which came up with Him from Galilee to Jerusalem, who are now His witnesses unto the people.

"And so," said Paul, "we declare unto you these Glad Tidings, how that the Promise which was made unto our Fathers hath been fulfilled unto us, their Children, in that God hath raised up Jesus from death.

"As it is also written in the Second Psalm: *Thou art my Son, this day Have I begotten Thee.*

"And as concerning that He raised Him up from the dead, now no more to return to corruption, He said on this wise: *I will give you the sure mercies of David.*

"Wherefore He saith in another Psalm: *Thou shalt not suffer Thine Holy One to see corruption.*

"Yet David," said Paul, "after he had served his own generation by the Will of God, fell on sleep, and was laid unto his Fathers, and saw corruption in his flesh.

"But Jesus, Whom God raised again from death, saw no corruption.

"Be it known unto you therefore, Men and Brethren, that through this Man, Jesus, is preached unto you the Forgiveness of Sins, and by Faith in Him all that believe are Justified from all things from which ye could not be Justified by the Law of Moses."

*　　*　　*

"And when the Jews were gone out of the Synagogue, the Gentiles besought that these words might be preached to them again the next Sabbath.

And the next Sabbath day came almost the whole city of Antioch together to hear the Word of God . . . but when the Jews saw the multitudes, they were filled with envy, and spake against those things which were spoken by Paul, contradicting and blaspheming.

Then Paul and Barnabas waxed bold, and said: "It was necessary that the Word of God should first have been spoken to you – but seeing ye put it from you, and judge yourselves unworthy of everlasting life, lo, we turn to the Gentiles!"

And Paul said: "For so hath the Lord commanded me, saying, *I have set thee to be a Light unto the Gentiles, that thou shouldest be for Salvation unto the ends of the earth.*"

And when the Gentiles heard this, they were glad, and glorified the Word of the Lord . . . which was published throughout all the region . . ."

*　　*　　*

One question: Why preach for ten minutes when you can say it all so much more powerfully in five?

Yes, most Evangelical Commentators claim that all we have is the summary of what Paul actually said, the "general sense" as recommended by Thucydides to historians.

But with summaries like *that,* who needs Sermons at Evangelical length?

True, Paul wasn't always so commendably brief, because, at Troas, when the Disciples came together in the evening to Break Bread, he preached until midnight . . . three hours at least!

Though even *they* couldn't all keep awake, and one of them, a young man Eutychus, sat on a window-ledge, being sunk into a deep sleep as Paul was long preaching, fell from the third storey, and was picked up as dead.

But Paul merely went down, embraced him, and said: "Trouble not yourselves, for his life is still in him."

And then went back upstairs, had some more to eat and drink, and continued preaching until the break of day . . . another six hours!

45

Fortunately, the young man recovered . . . but it's obvious that not even Paul could hold everybody's complete attention for quite so long.

Lesser Preachers, with less first-hand experience to communicate, should keep one eye open for people with both closed.

*   *   *

Then, there being a persecution raised against Paul and Barnabas in Antioch, they shook off the dust from their feet . . . and came unto Iconium, and Lystra of Lycaonia, and Pamphylia, and eventually back to Jerusalem, and back again to Antioch, being called by the Holy Spirit from one country to another, Phrygia and the region of Galatia, and over into Macedonia . . . beaten with many stripes, cast into prison, their feet made fast into the stocks . . .

Where they prayed, and sang praises unto God.

And any of the proliferated works of scholarship will give you all the details in footnotes . . . but, eventually, eventually, they that conducted Paul brought him unto Athens, the Eye of Greece, Mother of Arts and Eloquence, the Jerusalem of the Gentiles.

*   *   *

Now as Paul walked about Athens, his spirit was exasperated beyond endurance in him, when he saw the city wholly given over to idolatry, and he felt compelled to discuss the matter in the Synagogue with the Jews, and with God-fearing Gentiles . . . and he even argued daily with the people in the open market-place at the foot of the Acropolis, where the citizens, being insatiably curious, met to exchange the latest news and debate the newest ideas: that very Agora where Socrates had taught so conversationally four hundred years earlier.

Then certain Philosophers of the Epicureans, and of the Stoics, encountered him.

And some said: "What is this charlatan trying to prove?"

Others said: "He seems to be proclaiming some more gods, and outlandish ones at that!"

And they took him, and brought him to their court, the Areopagus, where were assembled the Elders and Judges, who said: "May we know what this new doctrine of yours really is? For you bring certain strange topics to our ears, and we would know therefore what they mean."

For all the Athenians and strangers which were there spent their time in little else, but either to tell, or to hear some new thing.

Then Paul stood in the midst of the Hill of Mars, and said:

46

"Gentlemen of Athens, I perceive that in all things religious you are uncommonly scrupulous.

"Because as I passed by, and beheld your Shrines and Temples, I found an Altar with this inscription, *To the Unknown God.*

"Whom therefore you worship without knowing, *Him* I declare unto you!

"God that made the world and all things therein," said Paul, "seeing that He is Lord of Heaven and Earth, dwells not in Temples made with hands, neither is worshipped with the deeds of men's hands, as though He had necessity of any such service – because *He* gives life to all men, and breath, and every good thing. And He made of one blood all nations of men for to dwell on all the face of the Earth, and has determined the sequence of seed-time and harvest, and the epochs of our history, and the bounds of our habitation. So we should seek the Lord, in the hope that we might experience Him, and find Him – though, in fact, He be not far from every one of us.

"As your own Poet, Epimendies the Cretan, has said: *For in Him we live, and move, and have our being.*

"Again, as your Aratus the Cilician has said: *It is with God that every one of us in every way has to do, for we are His children.*

"However," said Paul, "even though we are indeed the children of God, we ought not to presume that He is to be made in gold, or silver, or stone, carved or graven or fashioned by mere human art, no matter how beautiful. Imagination is not enough.

"It is true that God has mercifully overlooked the times of this ignorance – but He now commands all men everywhere to repent. Because He has appointed a day, in the which He will Judge the whole world by the standards of this Jesus, Whom he has Ordained. Whereof," said Paul, "He has given assurance unto all men, in that He has raised this same Jesus from the dead."

But when they heard of the Resurrection of the Dead, some mocked, remembering the words of their own Poet, Aeschylus: *When the dust has soaked up a man's blood, once he is dead, there is no resurrection.*

And yet others said: "We should like to hear you expound again on this matter."

Yes, outright derision, and polite dismissal.

So Paul departed from among them, and left Athens . . .

His Holy Land was elsewhere.

*   *   *

Well, you can't win 'em all, can you?

Especially when you argue with such Philosophers on their own chosen ground, and try to counter the systems of Reason by what to them were unsupported assertions.

"How could *he* know the purposes of this god he spoke about?"

True, it would have been futile to have used his customary "proof" texts from the Old Testament to build his case, because the Athenians simply wouldn't have heard of them, let alone been impressed.

And the blatant flattery of quoting their own Poets to them was a feeble rhetorical flourish, the equivalent of a visiting American mass-evangelist mugging up a few phrases of English slang for the beginning of his first Hell Fire Sermon in a London football stadium. The techniques of Dale Carnegie may Win Friends and Influence People when you're trying to sell Life Insurance, but they are not the honourable preaching of the Gospel of Jesus Christ.

Again, he failed to argue from First Principles, as was the intellectual discipline of the various Greek Schools of Philosophy, and relied on what *he* believed was the direct Revelation of God – which was a mistaken tactic with such sophisticated minds. *They* expected demonstration by means of Reason and Logic, even experimental proofs of veracity . . . and he merely asserted what he believed to be true.

The tragedy was that they already agreed with much of what he said.

For example, his point (obviously remembered from Stephen's Sermon) that God did not dwell in Temples and Cathedrals made with hands: well, another of their own Poets expressed the same thought . . . "What house made by builders," wrote Euripides, "could contain the Divine Form of a God within enclosing walls?"

Again, had Paul spoken about the immortality of the soul, rather than bodily resurrection, most of his cultured hearers except the Epicureans would have agreed with him.

So he spoke in the wrong way about the wrong subjects to the wrong people . . . and failed.

Mind you, he did get *some* response out of them, which was better than blank indifference.

A bland Preacher, preaching "smooth things," will usually be accepted with languid tolerance . . . but once speak with passionate intensity, and almost any degree of Prophetic Truth, and you'll be confronted by the insecurity and anger of those forced to question their own assumptions, reconsider their own prejudices, look into their own hearts.

48

At Antioch and elsewhere Paul did exactly that, and helped to turn the world upside-down.

At Athens he fumbled and fudged with First Year Philosophy to a Class of Advanced Graduates, who laughed at his presumption.

He never made the same mistake again.

*   *   *

After that, to quote Erasmus, it was "thundering and lightning and talking sheer flame."

Until, according to Clement of Rome, "he at last suffered Martyrdom, and departed out of the world, and went unto his Holy Place, being become a most eminent pattern of patience unto all ages."

*   *   *

One last question: If even Paul believed that the Most High dwells not in Temples made with hands, what would *he* have to say about a certain Cathedral named after him in his Saintliness?

From Fellowship to Membership

The Church, then, began in martyrdom and continued in persecution: and those first Christians had all things in common, looked after all of their fellowship in affliction ... and did eat their meals with gladness and singleness of heart, sharing both real and symbolic bread, the cup of rough wine both necessary drink and Holy Communion, the very Feasting of Love.

Rich and poor Believers were treated alike: "Let there be no more respect paid to a rich man with goodly apparel and a gold ring than to a poor man in vile raiment," said James the Apostle. "God chose the poor of this world because they are rich in faith."

And neither were there any artificial distinctions between priests and laity, because Jesus was their sole High Priest – and *this* was a Royal Priesthood of all Believers. Even their occasional Preachers had to earn their own bread: "If they ask money, they are false."

Yes, a Vision of pure religion and undefiled: neither Jew nor Greek, neither bond nor free, neither male nor female ... merely the Children of God, praising Him, all one in Christ Jesus.

*   *   *

Within a few generations, for reasons beyond heartbreak, the Church was already in a position of power and patronage ... and the persecuted were becoming the persecutors.

And there were Treasurers and Clerics, Deacons and Overseers, Bishops and Archbishops: Priests and Laity, above and below, us and them ... Hebrew Christians *and* Gentile Christians, slaves *and* owners – and men as Masters again, with women a poor second several dutiful steps behind ... Creeds, Rituals, Forms of Words, Vestments, Altars, Sanctuaries, Temples made with hands in which to worship the Most High ... and the Cathedrals and Cardinals to come, Prelates and Popes the Princes of the Church ... the whole gold-plated and jewel-encrusted History of Christianity, divided and divisive, blood-soaked and unholy.

All we can do is trace its wandering course through the wilderness of hatred and misery, try to understand the reasons for this betrayal of the Faith once delivered unto the Saints, and remember that prayer of Jesus on the Cross: "Father, forgive them, for they know not what they do."

The trouble is that some of them knew very well what they were doing.

Mea culpa, mea culpa, mea maxima culpa.

Which, being translated, is: "Through my fault, through my fault, through my most grievous fault."

*   *   *

To return to those days of martyrdom and persecution, the early Sermons and some of the words which were shaking the foundations of the world.

According to Eusebius, the Father of Ecclesiastical History, writing at the beginning of the fourth century, the Epistles of Clement (where that quotation about the death of Paul came from) were "publicly read during assemblies of the Early Church," in both the Roman Empire of the West and the Byzantine of the East.

So, apart from those of Peter and Paul reported by Luke in the *Acts of the Apostles,* they are probably the first Christian Sermons of which we have any record.

True, they weren't preached in person by Clement himself, but *for* him by an Elder or Deacon, reading aloud from a manuscript – perhaps even in Clement's own handwriting ... and yet we can still read his translated words, hear them across the centuries in some private Upper Room of the mind, reach out and touch a man.,

Which, of course, also holds for the Epistles of the New Testament.

"I charge you by the Lord," writes Paul in his First Letter from Athens to the Christians in Thessalonica, "that this be read unto all the Holy Brethren."

And to *hear* them as Sermons kindles the print into words of fire.

*   *   *

A note in passing:

In quoting these ancient Epistles and Sermons I have remembered a few vivid phrases of Euagrius of Antioch, who was a brilliant translator from Greek into Latin.

"Direct word for word translation from one language into another," he wrote, as translated by Helen Waddell, "darkens the sense and strangles it, even as spreading couch-grass a field of corn ... so whatever the lack may be in the words, there must be none in the meaning. Let the rest go bat-fowling for letters and syllables – do *you* seek for the sense."

I have, then, tried to find translations from all manner of sources in an attempt to "seek for the sense" as I understand it, words here, phrases there, adapting, blending, even having a rough and ready go myself . . . all for the Love of Man and in Praise of God.

(In "Man" include women.)

If you prefer scholarship, please go to the scholars.

*   *   *

Roman Catholic tradition has it that Clement was the son of a Jewish freedman in Rome. When Peter arrived there, on his way to that legendary inverted crucifixion, Clement was converted . . . and eventually followed Peter by becoming Bishop of Rome – and thus the fourth Pope. And the two Clementine Epistles of the Corinthians are undoubtedly among the earliest extant Christian documents, written not later than the end of the first century, sixty years after the death of Christ.

In these letters to be read aloud, Clement commends the Brethren and Sisters at Corinth for their "excellent order and piety in the Lord" before their "recent schism broke out . . ."

Which means that the troubles Paul had warned them about in *his* two letters, thirty or forty years earlier, were still dividing them: "Now I beseech you," he wrote, "by the name of our Lord Jesus Christ, that you all speak the same thing, and that there be no divisions among you . . . Is Christ divided?"

Yes, the same old, old story of Christianity: Christ is *not* divided, but *we* are, world without end, Amen. Churches and schisms and sects and denominations and cults and prophets and evangelists and preachers and personalities, emulation, and envy, and strife . . .

"They who were of no renown," writes Clement, as much to us as Corinth, "lifted up themselves against the honourable, those of no reputation against those who were in respect, the foolish against the wise, the young men against the elders.

"Therefore righteousness and peace are departed from you, because every one hath forsaken the fear of God, and is grown blind in his faith, nor walketh by the rule of God's Commandments, nor liveth as is fitting in Christ. But every one walketh after his own wicked lusts, having taken up an unjust and wicked envy, by which death first entered into the world."

*   *   *

But Clement doesn't always nag on like that. He usually quotes the Old Testament in a more literal and less mystical way than Paul . . . and occasionally rises to simple eloquence.

52

"Let us, therefore, humble ourselves, Brethren, laying aside all pride, and boasting, and foolishness, and anger. And let us do as it is written in the Scriptures.

"For thus saith the Holy Spirit: *Let not the wise man glory in his wisdom, nor the strong man in his strength, nor the rich man in his riches. But let him that glorieth, glory in the Lord, to seek Him, and to do judgement and justice.*

"Above all, remembering the words of the Lord Jesus, which He spake concerning equity and long suffering, saying: *Be ye merciful and ye shall obtain mercy; forgive, and ye shall be forgiven; as ye do, so shall it be done unto you; as ye give, so shall it be given unto you; as ye judge, so shall ye be judged; as ye are kind to others, so shall God be kind unto you; with what measure ye mete, with the same shall it be measured to you again.*

"By this command, and by these rules, let us establish ourselves, that so we may always walk obediently to His Holy Words, being humble minded. For so says the Holy Scripture: *Upon whom shall I look? Even upon him that is poor and of a contrite spirit . . .*

"It is, therefore, just and righteous, Men and Brethren, that we should become obedient unto God, rather than follow such people as, through pride and faction, have made themselves the leaders of a detestable emulation.

"But let us be kind to one another, according to the compassion and sweetness of Him that made us.

"For it is written: *The merciful shall inherit the earth, and they that are without evil shall be left living upon it at the Latter Day, but the transgressors shall perish from off the face of it.*

"So keep innocently, and do the thing that is right, for there shall be a Remnant to the peaceable man.

"Let us, therefore, hold fast to those who religiously follow the ways of peace, and not such as with hypocrisy pretend to desire it.

"For He saith in a certain place: *This people honoureth Me with their lips, but their heart is far from Me.*

"And again: *They bless with their mouths, but curse in their hearts.*

"And again He saith: *They loved Him with their mouths, and with their tongues they lied . . .*

"Let all deceitful lips become dumb, and the tongue that speaketh proud things. For we will magnify with our tongue Him who is Lord God over us.

"Now will I arise, saith the Lord, *to ease the oppression of the poor, to answer the sighing of the needy. Yea, I will set them in safety, I will deal faithfully with them,* saith the Lord."

*   *   *

The tragedy is that all these words and wisdoms are known to us, having been spoken by God through His Prophets, and by Christ and Peter and Paul and Clement and a thousand Apostles and ten thousand Disciples and Heaven only knows how many Preachers . . . and that we take so little notice of them, preferring our own Creeds and Dogmas, teaching for Doctrines the Commandments and Traditions of men.

But let us be kind to one another . . .

*   *   *

Yet, in another part of that same Epistle to the Corinthians, that same Sermon of Reconciliation, Clement was also seeking to justify from the Scriptures the changes which were already burying the Church in its own structures, rolling back the great stone to close the sepulchre that was hewn in rock . . . the Tomb out of which Jesus Christ had Risen in Glory to defeat that Dominion of Death.

"It will behoove us," he says, "that we do all things in Order . . . and particularly that we perform our Offerings and Services to God at their Appointed Seasons, for *these* He has Commanded to be done, not whenever we choose, nor in any disorderly manner, but at certain determinate days and hours, and in certain places."

"And therefore He has Ordained by His Supreme Will and Authority, both where, and by what Persons, they are to be performed, so that all things, being piously done, may be acceptable unto Him . . ."

Clement, Bishop of Rome, remember, then draws a parallel between the Temple at Jerusalem, with its "daily sacrifices" and "Chief Priests" and "Priests" and "Levites" all in their "proper Ministries," the "laymen confined to the bounds of what is proper to laymen," and the New Church of Jesus Christ . . .

"Consider, Brethren," he says, "how much better is the knowledge that God has vouchsafed unto us" . . . and he reminds his hearers that Jesus was "sent by God" and the Apostles were "sent out by Christ," so "both were orderly sent according to the Will of God." And, "thus preaching through countries and cities by the Will of God," the Apostles themselves "appointed Bishops and Deacons over such as believed. Nor was this any new thing," he says, "for thus saith the Scripture in a certain place: *I will appoint their Bishops in righteousness, and their Deacons in the Faith.*"

Which was obviously intended to be conclusive . . . except that the verse he "quotes" from the sixtieth Chapter of the Book of Isaiah merely has *I will also make thy officers peace and thine exactors righteousness,* where the word *officers* may be variously translated as "princes" or "governors," and *exactors* as "rulers" or "task-masters." Indeed, the *New English Bible* simply has *I will make your government be peace and righteousness rule over you,* with never a whiff of Priests – let alone Bishops in full Pontificals!

And the whole alleged parallel becomes even less plausible when you remember that the Veil of the Temple had been ripped from the top to the bottom by the hand of God at the death of His Son, and that the Holy of Holies was now as empty as the Tomb . . . so that Christians were now free to approach the Father without any High Priest except Christ, to worship God in Temples not made with hands.

Though it would be an unusual Bishop to talk himself out of a job!

55

From Life More Abundant to Lust for Death

By the beginning of the second century this depressing change from simple fellowship to Ecclesiastical structure was complete. True, it would all get intricately convoluted later on, with many more assorted varieties of Ordained Priesthood and Forms of Service and other Rites and Ceremonies . . . but the foundations and columns and beams were already in place for as complicated a Cathedral of Theology as the proliferating Hierarchy cared to elaborate.

Here, for example, are a few words from an Epistle or Sermon sent to the Church at Smyrna by Ignatius, already the third Bishop of Antioch: "Avoid divisions as the beginning of evils. All of you follow your Bishop as Jesus Christ followed the Father, follow your Priests as the Apostles, and respect your Deacons as the Commandments of God. Let no man perform anything pertaining to the Church without the permission of your Bishop. The only valid Eucharist is that over which your Bishop has presided, or that presided over by a Priest your Bishop has appointed. Wherever your Bishop is, just as wheresoever Christ Jesus is, *there* is the Catholic Church. It is not permitted for any person to Baptise or hold the Feast of Love apart from your Bishop, or a Priest your Bishop has appointed. But whatever *he* may approve, *that* is well-pleasing to God, so that everything which you do may be sound and valid."

It's doubtful if Ignatius would have permitted Jesus to have taken part in the Last Supper, let alone preside over it . . . for Christ had come to give us Life, and that more abundant – while our Brother Ignatius wrote the terrible words: "I lust after death . . . Grant me nothing more than that my blood be poured out as a Libation of Wine to God."

*   *   *

Given the depressing change of emphasis inherent in this decline from the free association of loving fellowship to mere fearful membership of an authoritarian structure increasingly controlled by a celibate Priesthood, this paranoid compulsion towards martyrdom was common enough at the time. Once start despising the sexual uses of the body and you finish by despising *all* its uses . . . so why *not* put an end to your troubles in this Vale of Tears?

56

"We kill the body," said the so-called Fathers of the Desert, "for it kills us."

But with Ignatius this other sort of lust found its ultimate voice.

"Let me be given to the wild beasts in the arena of Rome," he said, "by which I shall attain God. For I am the Wheat of God, and will be ground by their teeth that I may become the Pure Bread of Christ." And his words rise to the hysteria of genuine masochism: "Come fire and cross, encounters with those wild beasts, tearing apart of bones, hacking of limbs, crushing of the whole body, tortures of the Devil come upon me . . . if only I may attain unto Jesus Christ."

That, in a terse phrase by Robert Payne, describes a man "leaping towards his own death."

And, according to *The Antiochene Acts,* Ignatius achieved his ambition when he was "fettered, taken to Rome, and thrown to the wild beasts to amuse the people."

Some of his own words are his best epitaph: *For what value is all the world? Better to die for Christ than to rule over kingdoms.*

But that voice echoed across the arena, and sounded down the dreary cloisters of the years . . .

"Be diligent," it thundered, "be sober, be God's athlete, be as the beaten anvil under the hammer of God's wrath."

It became the trumpet call of those Fathers of the Desert, the one theme of the whole Monastic Movement – which, in later centuries, tried to train men and women for the Life of the Spirit by mortifying the flesh, seeking to enter into the pleasures of Heaven by enduring the pains of Hell on earth.

*   *   *

Forty years or so after the rending of Ignatius, the aged Bishop of Smyrna, believed to have been a Disciple of John the Revelator, and perhaps even the first reader of that Epistle from Ignatius, was also a man "leaping towards his own death."

For there he stood, haled before Titus Statius, the Roman Governor, at the Annual Games, with the wild beasts already howling and slavering.

"Swear by the Fortune of Caesar," said the Governor. "Revile Christ, and I will set you free."

"I have served Him for eighty-six years," said Polycarp, "and He has done me no wrong. How can I speak evil of the King Who has Saved me?"

"Unless you repent your ways I'll have you thrown to these beasts."

"Release them into the arena," said Polycarp. "Repentance from the better to the worse is no change to be desired – but it is good to change from cruelty to justice."

"If you despise the beasts," said the Governor, "I will have you consumed by fire."

"What is that to me?" said Polycarp. "The fire burns for an hour at most, and this life is easily quenched – but you know nothing of the fires of the coming Judgement . . . Why delay? Do as you will."

He was taken to the stake, stripped naked – but, as they were about to nail him to it, he said: "Leave me as I am, for He Who enables me to enter the fire will also enable me to abide it unflinchingly."

And so he died . . . preaching in words of undying fire.

The Lord gave, and the Romans hath taken away: Blessed be the Name of the Lord. . .

And so, generation by generation, persecution by persecution, these Holy Martyrs suffered and died . . . and the Faithful gathered up their bones, which "were more valuable than jewels or gold, and laid them in safe places for memorials of them."

*　　*　　*

Until that time soon came when Christians had achieved enough temporal power to be able to persecute those other Christians who didn't agree in the minutest particulars or spiritual doctrine or dogma.

And we will hear *their* words of fire down the screaming of the years.

The Holy Feast of Life

As a necessary relief, consider another Clement – the gentle old man who believed that "all life is a Holy Feast."

True, this is more often a pious wish than an economic fact, but it's at least a sweeter Christian view than that of Ignatius.

Clement of Alexandria was born in Athens about the middle of the second century, and became a wandering scholar and teacher with a wide and deep knowledge both of Greek Philosophy and the Pagan Mysteries . . . who travelled in search of knowledge through Greece, Palestine, Asia Minor, Southern Italy, and finally Egypt . . .

"Born a Pagan," writes Robert Payne in a loving and lovely sentence, "he seems to have become a Christian as effortlessly as one crosses a country road."

For Clement the Religions of the Pagans and the Jews were merely the prelude to Christ, and what astonished him was that people could still believe in the old Gods: "Where is Zeus now?" he said. "Where the Eagle? Where the Swan? No, Zeus has grown old with his feathers. He is dead, as Leda is dead, and the Swan also, and the Eagle, and the Lover, and the Serpent."

And he preached some soaring words about the effect of belief in Christ on the Believer:

"A noble Hymn of God is Man, immortal, founded upon righteousness, the Oracles of Truth engraved upon his soul."

"For where else save in the wise soul can Truth be written? or Love? or Reverence? or Gentleness?"

"Those who have had these Divine Characters engraved and sealed upon their souls deem such Wisdom a fair point of departure for whatever journey their course is trimmed to, and this Wisdom is also a Haven of Peace and Fair Return."

"And by this Wisdom those who have betaken themselves to the Father have proved good fathers to their own children, and those who have known the Son have proved good sons to their own parents, and those who remember the Bridegroom become good husbands to their wives – and, having been redeemed from absolute slavery, they are good masters . . ."

Yes, to change the world you must first change yourself.

"Let us hasten, therefore," says our Brother Clement, "to gather ourselves together unto Salvation, in the New Birth, in the One Charity, on the pattern of that Perfect Unity that is the One Nature of God."

"For once be instructed in *these* Mysteries, and you shall dance with the Choir of Angels before the Uncreated and Eternal God, whilst the Logos will sing the Sacred Hymns with us. This Jesus, our One High Priest, intercedes for men and women, and calls aloud on them: *I summon the whole human race!*"

Clement, thy name is an ointment poured forth . . . let me see thy countenance, let me hear thy voice . . .

All manner of thing shall be well

Now I must admit that, even with the occasional Clement to lighten our darkness, these early Fathers of the Church are a specialised taste: their lives and opinions are nearly always depressing to hear about, these deniers of life in thought, word, and deed. And their writings fill volume after volume along the most awkward bottom shelves of the Reference Library . . . solid pages of baffling Greek or impenetrable Latin, polysyllabic Victorian translations, and that faint smell of dust and decay.

It needs to be raining very hard outside to drive me down to unwedge one from the jammed rows . . . and yet they are an essential strand in the knotted History of Christianity, and what some of them did to the Sermon has left it maimed to this day.

And every so often you may meet a stranger who becomes a friend.

*   *   *

I shall always remember the pleasure it gave me when I discovered that the name Origen means "born of Horus," and that his mother was probably an Egyptian. What an immediate link with the remote past, that antique land, ancient Gods and Goddesses, Mysteries, the Voices of Silence . . . and the lone and level sands stretching far away . . .

He was born towards the end of the second century, the son of a cultured Greek . . . and of all these early Fathers of the Church this Child of Horus was most of a genuine Saint, though he "thought his own thoughts about God," and so was always too dangerous a thinker for any establishing Church to leave unmolested. Everybody with an opinion worth having agrees that he was a "passionate scholar," the "acknowledged founder of Biblical textual criticism" . . . and yet, to use some more of those murmuring words, "his moral qualities were as remarkable as his intellectual gifts."

For he was also a man of joy, perhaps a bit too wilful and impetuous for his own good in a wicked world, and, like Francis of Assisi after him, he worried comfortable Christians by taking the words of Jesus in their simple literal meaning: he carried no scrip (or pack), didn't bother with money, wore only one tunic, went around barefoot, endured "cold and nakedness to the furthest extremes of poverty," and "spent his happy hours in study and preaching and prayer." And would probably never be allowed within a mile of

Westminster Abbey during a Royal Performance of Choral Evensong.

*   *   *

Like our own lovely Julian of Norwich fourteen centuries later, he
believed that "all will be well, all will be well, all manner of thing will
be well" . . . which is probably the chief reason that neither of them
have ever been formally Canonised as Saints.

"Rocks, stones, fish, tigers, Angels," he said, "all have their place
in the Divine Economy, all celebrate the Glory of God . . ."

"The Angels command all things, earth, air, fire, water, and all
alike. The Word employs them as Instruments to regulate the
movements of animals, plants, stars . . . *They* are the Virtues who
preside over the earth and the seeding of trees, who see to it that
springs and rivers do not run dry, who look after the rains and the
winds, the creatures that live on land, and those that live in the sea,
and all that is born on the earth and flies above it."

And "all desire to be dissolved, to return and be with Christ, which
is far better than our present state."

He called this "return to the original spiritual condition" of the
universe *apokatastasis panton,* Greek words meaning "a return to
stasis, stability, stillness, peace, innocence . . . universal restitution
and restoration, harmony . . ." Two words . . . but what a liberating
idea!

"By reason of God's Love," said loving Origen, "even the Devil
will one day return to his proper inheritance, Hell will be no more,
and all sinners will come at last to Heaven . . . We will enter a state of
Grace in which sin is no more, and will remain unimaginable."

Wherever there was alienation from God, there is "always the
possibility of restoration through Christ," and Origen's charitable
heart and incisive mind together believed that "Christ could not
enjoy perfect Blessedness as long as even one of His children was
ensnared by evil or was in a state of suffering." And he follows the
thought to the far reaches of mercy: "Our Saviour will enter His
definitive Glory only on the day when He delivers up His Kingdom
into the hands of His Father in an act of total submission, and this
cannot take place as long as *all* the Elect are not gathered together in
Christ and the whole world brought by Him to the summit of
perfection."

And then, typically, Origen goes on to involve the Mystical Union
of Christ with His Church, and compares it with the union of soul and
body: "For it is one single body that awaits its Redemption . . . The
eye may be without blemish, yet if the other parts of the body are

missing, how can the eye rejoice? Or what perfection will there be if the body has neither hands nor feet? or wants for other limbs? No, while we remain in sin, so Christ must remain in grief . . . and as long as we remain imperfect, His Work too is imperfect."

Behold! I show you a mystery!

"Though how Christ shall make well all that is not well," wrote our Sister Julian, gravely considering the same mystery, "what the deed shall be, and how it shall be done, there is no creature that can know it, nor shall understand until it is done."

For this generous belief in the ultimate Mercy of God, for refusing to place a limit on the Love of Christ for the world, Origen has often been condemned and damned as a heretic.

Indeed, in the fifth century there was already a famous Monastic story, which was repeated with embellishments until the end of the sixteenth, about a Vision of Hell" granted unto a "pious monk called Theophanes" – a "place of darkness and stench, belching forth continual flames, prepared for heretics and blasphemers, wherein he saw Judas Iscariot, Nestorius . . . and Origen, and certain others . . ."

So, as his Christian Brethren failed to burn him alive, they have made sure he burns for ever.

Yes, the punishing and eternal fires of Hell were obviously very necessary for the temporal well-being of the Church.

Probably still are . . . if they thought anybody would believe that *they* had any access to the keys of those clanking gates.

*   *   *

To rise above that petty-minded post-mortem burning . . .

Origen practically invented Biblical scholarship, and brought the spiritual interpretation of Biblical narrative to its first flowering.

"We do not despise the Law of Moses," he wrote, "but accept it – so long as it is Jesus Who interprets it for us. Only thus shall we understand it aright."

But the "interpretation" of Origen is never merely a commentary: it's more than an intellectual explanation or exposition, but a fulfillment.

"God," he seems to say, "reveals Himself through History. Therefore, the facts of historical reality, especially the *words* by which that reality is expressed, must be understood in as many ways as possible – for what limit can be set on the ways and means of God?"

So Origen broods as much on the words as the facts, more on the full depths of symbolic meaning than on the comparatively unimportant literal events. To him, at that time of innocent newness, the Bible wasn't simply a book recording those events, but *an event in itself* . . . an almost incarnate word within a Word, all written in the language of mystery.

And no Biblical event was too apparently trivial to have its "depths" fathomed, searched for meaning . . .

*   *   *

Here, for a simple example, is Origen preaching on three verses from the fifteenth chapter of the Book of Exodus.

And when the Children of Israel first came up out of the land of Egypt, they went three days in the wilderness of Shur, and found no water.

And when they came to Marah, they could not drink the waters, for they were bitter – which is the meaning of the name of that place, bitterness.

And the people murmured against Moses, saying, What shall we drink?

And he cried unto the Lord, and the Lord shewed him a tree, which when he had cast into the waters, the waters were made sweet . . .

Surely a plain description of primitive water purification?

Not a bit of it!

"The Old Law of Moses," says Origen, "is an exceeding bitter draught to drink . . . but if God should reveal a tree which, when cast into this bitterness, should turn it into a Law of Sweet Waters, then you might drink of it.

"More, we know the tree that the Lord has revealed, for Solomon teaches us when speaking of *Wisdom that is a Tree of Life to those that embrace it.*

"If, then, the Tree of the Wisdom of Christ be cast into the waters of the Old Law, and shew us what we are to think of Circumcision, and the obligations of the Sabbath, the distinction between things Clean and Unclean, then the water of Marah is made sweet, and the bitterness of the letter of the Law is turned into the sweetness of a Spiritual Understanding, so that we of God's Spiritual People can drink it.

"For unless we understand such things in a Spiritual sense," says Origen, "then a People which has abandoned idols and turned to the One True and Living God, on hearing of an Old Law requiring Sacrifices in the Temple, will have none of that Law, and will refuse to drink of it, finding it bitter and harsh.

"To make this water of Marah drinkable, then, God has revealed a Tree that may be cast into it, so that he who drinks of the water may neither die nor find any bitterness in it.

"Clearly, then," says Origen, "if anyone wishes to drink of the letter of the Law without this Tree of Life – that is, without the

Mystery of the Cross, without Faith in Christ, without Spiritual Understanding – then he will die of its exceeding bitterness. This is what the Apostle Paul had in mind when he wrote that it is the *letter that killeth,* plainly declaring that the water of Marah is deadly if drunk unsweetened and unchanged . . ."

*   *   *

Well, our Brother Origen started the fashion for such Sermons . . . so he has a lot to answer for when we all return to our original spiritual condition at the Latter Day of Time.

However, the symbolism, though often fetched from a far country of the mind, is nearly always beautiful.

Here's a typical example of what his School could do with a couple of phrases from one verse from a Psalm: . . . *yet shall ye be as the wings of a dove covered with silver, and her feathers with the paleness of pure gold.*

"This Dove is Scripture. By the silvery wings, outwardly shining, should be understood the Sacred Words in their literal meaning. As for the paleness of gold, it refers to the precious Mysteries of Christ, which shine with an inner radiance."

When these ingenious interpreters reached *The Song of Solomon,* with its "breasts like two young roes feeding among the lilies" and "bellies bright as ivory overlaid with sapphires," their sexual frustrations took flight into aching fantasy . . . and even Origen, otherwise the sanest of men, but a Son of his Time, felt obliged to castrate himself as the only way of subduing our Little Sister Flesh.

These fantasies soared to the heights of genuine poetry with Bernard of Clairvaux a thousand years later . . . a pleasure we will reserve.

*   *   *

Origen left us many Sermons, all of them worth more of our time than most we could hear from the pulpits of our floundering generation . . . he even left what must be Sermon Notes.

"We have learnt from Peter that the Church is the House of God built of Living Stones, a Spiritual House for a Holy Priesthood.

"Solomon building the Temple is an Allegory of Christ.

"Each of the Living Stones, according to the worth that they have acquired in this earthly life, will have its place in the Heavenly Temple.

"One, Apostle or Prophet, will be laid as the foundation to uphold all that is built upon it.

"Then another, upheld by the Apostles, will bear along with them the weaker stones.

"There will be, also, a stone within the building where are the Ark and the Cherubim.

"Another will be the stone of the Entrance Hall, and yet another the Altar Stone of the First Fruits."

*   *   *

But he's at his considerable best searching the New Testament for meanings beneath meanings, words within the Word:

Jesus was born in Bethlehem, which means the "House of Bread," because *His* House (or Church) is the only place where the True Bread of Heaven may be found.

"For in truth the water of the First Miracle at the Marriage Feast of Cana was the Scripture, and Jesus turned it into the Wine of Wisdom which we may now freely drink."

Martha and Mary represent the Synagogue and the Church, with the Church naturally having the "better part" with Mary sitting at the feet of Christ and "contemplating on the Mysteries of Truth."

When Jesus "calmed the storm on the waters of Galilee" He was "showing forth His Spiritual Coming to help the Church tossed by the storms of the world," and the boat was "our Ark of Salvation."

The ointment poured over His feet by Mary Magdalene is a symbol of "every sincere repentance."

The ass on which Christ rode into Jerusalem represents the Jewish converts, and the colt the Gentiles.

The two Thieves on either side of the Cross are the "cursing Jews" and "repentant sinners."

And the Rock Tomb is the "heart of each one of the Faithful in which He is laid away awaiting His daily Resurrection into every life . . ."

*   *   *

And here's a slightly more extended example of his method and style, from a Sermon on *The Good Samaritan* . . . in which almost every detail is made to bear an allegorical interpretation:

"The man on his way down to Jericho means Adam with the life he originally led and with the Fall caused by his disobedience.

Jerusalem means Paradise, or the Jerusalem on High.

Jericho is the world, the robbers are the powers in opposition to

66

Christ, whether Devils or False Teachers, especially those who profess to come in the Name of Christ.

The wounds are disobedience and sins.

Man is stripped of his clothing – that is, he loses incorruptibility and immortality, he is despoiled of every virtue.

He is left half-dead because Death has seized a half of our human nature.

The Priest is the Law.

The Levite represents the Prophets.

The Samaritan is Christ who took on human flesh through Mary.

The beast of burden is the Body of Christ.

The wine is the word of teaching and correction, the oil is the word of good works, compassion or encouragement.

The inn is the Church.

The inn-keeper is the College of Apostles and their successors, Bishops and Teachers of the churches, or else the Angels who are set over the Church on earth.

The two pennies are the two Testaments, the Old and the New, or Love of God and one's neighbour, or knowledge of the Father and Son.

The return from Samaria is the Second Coming of Christ."

However, it's interesting to remember that though Origen brought this sort of spiritual interpretation to its first flowering he didn't invent it – because, at the beginning of that Sermon, he quotes from an "Elder" whose own "allegory" he considers "reasonable and beautiful" . . . before then going on to embroider it even further.

As he himself was embroidered . . .

*   *   *

Here's what *The Good Samaritan* became in the pulpit of Severus of Antioch, another of these Greek Fathers:

"A certain man was going down from Jerusalem to Jericho . . .

"The use of the specific noun is to the point, because it is not merely *somebody was going down,* but a *certain man* – for the whole of humanity is in question here, inasmuch as it has Fallen, through the disobedience of Adam, from the height of the Abode of Paradise . . . aptly called *Jerusalem,* which means *Peace of God,* down to the depth of Jericho, low-lying and stifled in heat, meaning the burning lust of this world, which separates us from God and drags us down, causing suffocation in the heat of our shameful desire, and chokes us to death.

"Once humanity had gone astray in this life, and had lost his

67

balance and been drawn down, borne little by little to the lowest point of the downward path, there settled on him a swarm of savage Demons, like a band of brigands. And they stripped him of the cloak of Virtue, leaving him not a vestige of Fortitude or Temperance or Justice or Prudence, or of anything that represented the Image of God. And so they hacked at him with the repeated wounds of various sins, leaving him cut to pieces – in a word, half-dead . . .

"So while humanity was lying prostrate and all but fainting to death, he was visited by the Mosaic Law – for this, of course, is the meaning of the Priest and the Levite, since it was the Law that taught the Levitic Priesthood. It did indeed visit him, but it fell short in competence, and was not capable of a full treatment. It did not even raise the prostrate body, but went perforce, in its incompetence, on its ineffectual round of sacrifices, because it was impossible that the blood of bulls and goats should entirely take away sin . . .

"At last *a certain Samaritan who was going on a journey came to where he was* . . . Now it is also to the point that Christ, in telling this Parable, here called Himself a Samaritan – for, since he was answering a Lawyer, who prided himself greatly on the Law, Christ took care to show by His words that it was not the Priest or the Levite, who thought to model their conduct *on* the Law, but *Himself* who was come to *fulfil* the Law, and to show by actual practice who was really one's neighbour, and what it was to love him as oneself . . .

"This Samaritan, then, who was going on a journey – that is, Christ on His journey to Save us – this Samaritan came to the prostrate man.

"For Christ had, in fact, really *come* on this journey. He was not merely passing by, but was making the journey for that very purpose – to *come* to us, the People for whom He came down to earth and with whom He dwelt. And He poured wine on the wounds, the *wine of repentance* – and, since the severity of the wounds could not bear a strong astringent, He tempered it with oil, for it was *mercy* He brought, not *sacrifices* . . ."

And so on, even more elaborately than Origen, with the "beast" on which the man was taken to the Inn representing "every beastly and unclean desire," the Inn the "all-receiving Church," the two coins the "Old and New Testaments . . . that is, the one given in the Mosaic Law and the Prophets, and the one given in the Gospels and the Apostolic Constitutions, both of which are of the same God, and bear, like coins, the same Image of the same King on High, and with their Sacred Words imprint in our hearts the stamp of the same Royal Likeness."

And then, just when any further "meanings" seem impossible to find, Severus takes an even deeper breath: "And both these coins were of the same King, given by Christ to the Church together, without any distinction of value. Now, since the Pastors of the Holy Church have received these two Testaments, and developed their teachings with much labour, thus increasing their value, each of them will say when Christ has come again at His Second Coming: *Lord, Thou gavest me two coins, and I have increased their value, and multiplied Thy Flock.* And He will say in reply: *Well done, good and faithful servant, thou hast been faithful in charge of a few things, and now I will give thee charge over many. Enter upon the joy of the Lord."*

And then even Severus stops.

*　　*　　*

But let's leave the last words with Origen.

Sometimes these "meanings" extracted from the Bible by the Fathers of the Early Church are obvious enough, and, once granted the possibility that either God or the Inspired Writers intended such "depths" to be there for our "building-up into the Faith," then most Commentators agree about their "interpretation" and significance.

For example: *Jesus, when He had cried out with a loud voice, yielded up the spirit. And, behold, the veil of the Temple was rent in twain from the top to the bottom . . .*

Well, the literal meaning is that God was telling us something in a symbolic way: the veil separating the Holy of Holies was now done away with, and the people could now approach Him without the intercession of any human High Priest . . . for *now* we have the Great High Priest, Jesus Christ, Who has entered into the very Sanctuary of Heaven on our behalf.

So the rending of the veil "signified" an end to the necessity of the old Jewish Sacrificial System, and, at the same time, the manifestation of Christ's Spiritual Priesthood in the priesthood of all Believers.

Origen sees deeper than *that*, and "rends the veil" between the literal and spiritual meanings of the event: "Before the First Coming of Christ, the Law and the Prophets were not yet part of the Announcement of what actually came to pass in the Gospel, because He Who was to fulfil their prophecies and make their mysteries clear had not yet come. But once the Promised Saviour *had* come to us, and given a Body to the Gospel, *then* He effected that *all* of the Scriptures should be as the Gospel, and thus *one* Scripture – two Testaments *one* Testament."

And even *such* embroidery is only the beginning, for the event can *also* be seen as the "rending of the division between the body and soul in the unity of Christ," and even the symbolic equivalent of "defloration" during the Mystical Marriage of the Lamb and His Church . . . and so off into the wide blue yonder, where the Fire and the Rose are One and Love is the Power that Moves the Stars . . .

No, you may not always agree with Origen . . . but, once you start reading him, no rainy afternoon in the Reference Library will be quite long enough.

Words from the Fathers

As I've already admitted, these early Fathers of the Church are a specialised taste . . . and I can name a thousand books I'd rather read before I'd ever again reach down to those awkward bottom shelves to unwedge, say, Optatus or Epiphanius, Palladius or Maximus the Confessor, from the jammed rows.

But out of the darkness of their centuries there's the occasional gleam of beauty like the gold of mosaic in the Byzantine church, some phrase of terrible power, a sentence or paragraph of original thought or compassion – even simple passion itself . . . the almost tangible presence of a living man in agony or ecstasy.

*   *   *

Consider our Brother Cyprian, Bishop of Carthage in the middle of the third century . . . once a Pagan and a celebrated teacher of Rhetoric – and then, suddenly, a Christian.

"In his Conversion," wrote Pontius, his Deacon, "all things incredible met together. The threshing of the harvest anticipated its sowing, the tender grapes of the vintage anticipated the uncurling of the tendril, the ripe fruit anticipated the firm root."

To confine ourselves to Cyprian the Preacher, he was "daily in the pulpit," and the "clear, soul-stirring tones of his voice rang out like an Angel of Mercy." His words were "filled with light and music," and "bore the fire of his spirit into a thousand hearts, to set them aglow."

And what did he say in his Sermons to cause such effects?

Here's a passage about Insincere Repentance:

"Are we to believe that a man is sincere in his repentance for his sins, that he sorrows with his whole heart, if he still feasts on sumptuous repasts, and, distended with too many dainties, belches forth their unwholesome remains the day after – but never supplies the necessities of the poor with a share of his meat and drink?

"Or are we to believe that a woman is groaning and wailing over her sins, if she can still find time to attire herself in costly array – but bestows no care on that Robe of Christ which she has lost? Who could possibly put on precious ornaments and richly wrought necklaces, without shedding a tear at the loss of

71

her Divine and Heavenly jewels?

"Thou art naked, woman, though clad in foreign fabrics and silken robes. Bedizened with gold, and pearls, and gems, thou are unsightly, destitute of the comeliness of Christ. *Now,* at least, during these sorrows, stop, thou who dyest thy hair and encircles thine eyes with a line of black paint! *Now*, at least, wash thine eyes with tears . . .

"Wretched woman! it is thine own soul thou hast lost!

"The spiritual life extinct, thou hast begun to live unto thyself, and to walk about, bearing thine own corpse . . ."

From there it's an easy modulation to one of their favourite subjects, the obsession with women and cosmetics . . . which can still be met with in many a contemporary pulpit.

"The Apostate Angels taught the painting of the cheeks with dishonest tints, the dyeing of the hair with false colouring, and to make away with all truth of face. I consider," says Cyprian, "that what God has made and fashioned, ought in no wise be tampered with, whether with yellow dye, or black powder, or rouge, or any other preparation at all.

"Be such as God your Creator made you. Be what you were fashioned by your Father's hand. Tamper not with your face, keep your figure in its natural shape. Do not pierce your ears, do not encircle your arms or neck with armlets or collars, load not your ankles with fetters of gold, and keep your eyes worthy of seeing God . . .

"Conquer dress, since even you married women are spiritual virgins, and conquer gold, since you are engaged in conquering the flesh and the world. And avoid wanton feasts and sinful entertainments – for they are perilous infections."

*   *   *

Yet, when he had a subject worthy of his rhetoric, he could be genuinely eloquent.

"The Church is one, though she be expanded into a multitude by the increase of her children. For as the sun has many rays, but one light; as the tree many branches, but one vital power seated in the tenacious root; and as, when many streams flow from one source, that bounteous and overflowing abundance gives rise to the appearance of a multiplicity of waters diffused abroad – yet unity is preserved in all these.

"Try to part a ray of the sun from its orb, and the unity of light forbids this division; break off a branch from the tree, and, once broken, it can bud no more; cut off the stream from the fountain, and the stream will be dried up.

"Thus the Church, filled with the Light of the Lord, sends forth her rays all over the whole earth – the Light, which is thus diffused over all places, remains one, and the unity of the body is unbroken.

"And thus the Church expands her boughs over the wide world in the rich results of her exuberance – and scatters, with beneficent hand, many flowing streams.

"Yet is there one Head, one Source, one Mother, whose abundance springs from her own fruitfulness."

Which is as beautifully organised as a Piano Sonata by Mozart, a piece of prose Jeremy Taylor would have been proud to have written. And here, finally, is what must have been a Vision of Heaven:

"We regard Heaven as our native land . . .

"So why do we not haste and run, that we may be able to behold our country, to salute our native land?

"A great multitude of loved ones await us there, parents, brothers, children – a varied and numerous assemblage longing after us, who, secure of their own Salvation, still feel anxiety for ours.

"What a mutual joy to them and to us, to pass into their presence and to embrace! How exquisite the pleasures of those Celestial Realms, without fear of death – with an Eternity of Life! O Supreme and perpetual Bliss!

"There is the glorious Choir of the Apostles: *there* is the Assembly of Prophets exulting; *there* is the innumerable Host of Martyrs crowned for their Victory over strife and suffering; *there* are Virgins triumphant, who have overcome the concupiscence of the flesh; and *there* are the merciful men enjoying their reward, who fulfilled the works of righteousness, giving food and gifts to the poor – and, in conformity with the instructions of the Lord, transferred their earthly inheritance to the Treasury of this Heaven . . .

"To *these* let us, with eager longing, hasten!

"Let it be the portion which we desire, soon to be among them – soon to be gone to Christ."

And our Brother Clement was granted his portion of desire, being executed for his Faith – when he "ordered gold pieces to be given to the trembling executioner, bade him do his office quickly, knelt in prayer, covered his face with his hands, and calmly awaited the fatal stroke."

*   *   *

But Cyprian of Carthage left us a legacy more troublesome than any number of gold pieces ... for he spoke a few words which have caused more misery than millions of complete Sermons: religious wars, the hunting down and torturing to death of heretics, the rack, the stake, the noose and the disembowelling knife ...

Extra Ecclesiam null Salus ...

"Outside the Church is no Salvation."

True, he also expressed the idea more gently: "No man can have God as his Father unless he has the Church as his Mother." But, if he has indeed "gone to Christ," whatever will he find in his repentant heart to say to that "innumerable Host of Martyrs crowned for their Victory over strife and suffering" in persecutions urged on by his merciless words?

Will the word "sorry" be enough?

*   *   *

Around this same time there was an equally famous Preacher with a distinctive manner: Paul of Samosta, Bishop of Antioch ... who obviously annoyed Eusebius.

"This Paul courts popularity and poses to appear holy. He smites his hand on his thigh, stamps his foot to emphasise a point ... and rebukes and insults those who do not approve."

No, there's no new thing under the sun ... though I wonder what Eusebius would have made of Billy Graham in his younger "preaching windmill" days?

*   *   *

Sampson once found a swarm of bees and honey in the rotting carcase of a young lion he had slain, and did eat of the honey ... and so there's a lovely passage in praise of light by Basil of Cappodicia, a ruthless and inflexible man, who wrote the first known Set of Rules for Monastic Discipline: severe, harsh, even brutal ... and yet whose soul could mysteriously rise to passionate utterance ...

"For the heavens were enveloped in darkness, but now, suddenly, they appeared in the beauty they still wear in our eyes, and all the air was lighted up, light and air co-mingling together, and splendidly did they disperse in all directions, as far as they could reach.

"Light sprang up to the very heavens, and the width and breadth of the world were bathed in light, north, south, east, and west.

"And the waters shone, glittering, shooting forth quivering flashes of reflected light from their clear surfaces . . ."

Which at least must have brought some movement of beauty in the hearts of the monks who heard him, some glimmer of another light in the shadows of their cloisters.

And Basil, for all his Rules and the whips which enforced them, still had an eye for the dangers of the very Monasticism he helped to establish in Europe.

"If you live alone as a Hermit," he said, "whose feet will you wash in the humility of Christ?"

I hope that he did sometimes eat of honey in his aching cell.

*   *   *

And then there's our Brother Ambrose, Bishop of Milan early in the fourth century, who preached Sermons well worth our memory . . . and who left one sentence which would provide a magnificent text for a Sermon yet to be preached: "The Will of God is the Measure of All Things . . ."

He was also a delightfully practical man, who said that the Church "amounted to little if it could not protect the poor," and so he was always selling gold and silver chalices and candlesticks to buy bread for the hungry. "Which is more valuable?" he said. "Church vessels or living souls?"

I wonder would the Bishop of London care to answer that question?

And Ambrose had little sympathy for the ostentation of the rich, a "scandal crying out to Heaven for vengeance" . . . and the "savagery of the powerful showed Hell taking up its residence on earth. Nature knows no rich," he said. "We are created all alike, born alike of a woman, and we are all eventually alike enclosed in a sepulchre. What more resembles one dead man than another dead man?"

Which is a sentence that ought to be blazoned in letters of fire a foot high on the wall above the thrones of Kings and Queens, and in front of the daily eyes of Presidents and Prime Ministers: *What more resembles one dead man than another dead man?*

*   *   *

Ambrose was equally good at greater length.

"If you wish to buy a field, if you are buying a house, you take into your counsel a man of skill . . .

"But *now* the question is of your *own* purchase and price, so please consider *what* you are, and what credit you have.

"What do you stand to gain?

"Not land, money, or jewels – but Jesus Christ, to Whom no price or mere ornament can be compared.

"So take as your counsellors Moses, Isaiah, Jeremiah, Peter, Paul, and the Greatest Counsellor of them all, Jesus, that you may thereby gain so great a Salvation."

He preached in this simple way every Sunday, and the "fame of his eloquence spread far and wide." Indeed, Augustine of Hippo tells us that he was "charmed" by it at a time when he was "regarding the Gospel with the cold disdain of scepticism" . . . until his "inward exclamations" changed from "How fine!" to "How true!"

Which is probably the highest compliment ever offered by one Preacher to another . . . and certainly warms me towards Augustine.

*   *   *

One last gleam of gold from those Byzantine domes of darkness . . . our Brother Gregory, briefly Archbishop of Constantinople towards the end of the fourth century.

Called the Divine Theologian, contemporary of Athanasius, mocker of Julian the Apostate, "brilliant opponent" of Arianism, ecclesiastical politician . . . "responsible for five famous Discourses against Eunomius, in which the Unity of the Essence of Father and Son, and the Doctrine of the Trinity, are fiercely argued, and developed with great clearness, power, and conclusiveness."

As though any of that matters . . . except to Theologians.

But some of his words still abide.

"Despise not what is common, do not hunt after novelty in order to obtain a reputation with the crowd.

"Let Solomon instruct you by his counsel: *Better is a poor man who walks in his simplicity.* For the poor in words and knowledge, who confides in simple words is above the man of perverse lips and foolish heart, who shows the foolhardiness of ignorance in wordy argumentation, and makes the Cross of Christ of no effect.

"Why, when you have only feet, and not wings, will you soar?

"Why will you build a tower, though destitute of the materials for its construction?

"Why will you measure the ocean with your hand? and

Heaven with a span? and the whole earth with your grasp?

"First, know thyself, comprehend those things which are within your reach: *Who art thou?*

"Assuredly, all contentious argument is an exercise in wrangling about themes beyond our scope . . ."

Mind you, it *has* been put more succinctly: *Presume not God to scan.* Could close a few Theological Colleges.

Words from the Desert

Athanasius, Archbishop of Alexandria, once thought to have been the author of the Creed that bears his name, contemporary of our Brother Gregory, *did* at least write the preface to a book which many Christians believe has had a leprous effect on the happiness and culture of Europe – and probably the world.

It sounds harmless enough: *The Life of Saint Antony* . . . who was a friend of Athanasius, and the first of the so-called Fathers of the Desert – though fatherhood was one of the desires furthest from their minds, if not from their bodies.

"Marriage peoples the earth," they said, quoting Jerome, "but virginity peoples Heaven."

Hard luck on their own mothers and fathers.

*   *   *

This Antony was the son of wealthy parents, who died when he was only fifteen, and left him all their worldly goods. At the age of eighteen he heard a Sermon on the Rich Young Ruler, who was advised by Jesus to "go and sell that thou hast, and give to the poor," so that *then* he would "have treasure in Heaven." And when the young man heard that, "he went away sorrowful, for he had great possessions."

Well, the young Antony heard, and "went away joyful," sold his "great possessions," gave the money to the poor . . . and then "fled from the world" to become a hermit in a cave of the desert.

He lived there in poverty and prayer and near starvation and "valiant chastity" for the remainder of his long life . . . and suffered all those famous Temptations: the "assaults and onslaughts" of all those obscene monsters and demons and dragons and venomous toads, the "whisperings" of his dark sisters, the "lascivious women" with their "white and naked limbs" and "lewd dances and gestures," the birds of fire with trumpets for beaks and claws of molten brass, the blood and slime and filth and festering sores of this Honeymoon in Hell . . . all these obvious projections of his own nightmare imaginings as painted by Hieronymus Bosch . . . his own most secret sins made flesh and screaming around him in the lost years of his aching soul . . .

The key words of this book, *The Life of Saint Antony,* are these: "Let no one who hath renounced the world even begin to think that he hath given up some great thing . . . for the whole earth set over against the Eternity of Heaven is but scant and poor . . ."

Yes, the key to the iron gates of the desert, the book which "set the whole Roman world afire with Monastic vocations."

S.
HI
LAR
ION.

For that world was in decline, if not yet fallen into the ruin at its gates, the "blood-dimmed tide" *was* "loosed," and "everywhere the ceremony of innocence" *was* "drowned"... the *worst* lacked "all conviction," while the *best* were "full of passionate intensity."

And these "best" of men and women rejected the Pagan depravity of Rome *and* the growing corruption of the Church – because even if the world ever obeyed a "more excellent" Church it could still never be Christian: the only possible Christian Society was the Mystical Body of Christ.

And this depravity and corruption combined with despair and the wildest flights of hope to drive them out to the deserts as though from Sodom and Gomorrah and the Wrath of God to come.

True, they were also backing away from another sort of wilderness: all those arid controversies "about themes beyond our scope," the tens of thousands of sterile words about "one God in Trinity, and Trinity in Unity, neither confounding the Persons, nor dividing the Substance," with the "Glory equal... uncreate... incomprehensible... eternal," the "Father made of none, neither created nor begotten," the "Son of the Father alone, not made, nor created, but begotten," and the "Holy Spirit of the Father and of the Son, neither made nor created, nor begotten, but proceeding." It being "necessary to everlasting Salvation" to "believe rightly" in these and other matters " touching Perfect God and Perfect Man, of a reasonable soul and human flesh subsisting... not by confusion of Substance, but by Unity of Person," which, "except a man believe faithfully, he cannot be Saved," but must "go into everlasting fire... world without end." Amen.

As who could make an Heaven of *this* Alexandrian Hell?

*   *   *

And so during the fourth and fifth centuries there was a great Exodus out of what had once promised to be the Promised Land of the Church back into the wilderness of wanderings, and the deserts of the Middle East were almost crowded with hermits and monks: a mixed multitude of disaffected men (and fewer women) who were searching for what they believed was Salvation in the self-mortification of either total solitude or the harsher life of an isolated small community.

Within a generation the wilderness was no longer a solitary place: Pachomius had seven thousand men and women living under his Rule, there were five thousand monks on Mount Nitria, at Arsino there were over ten thousand under Serapion... and one traveller through Egypt and Palestine at the end of the fourth century reported that "there were as many monks in the desert as inhabitants of the towns." And the "inner desert" beyond Mount Nitria had been renamed "Cellia, by reason of the profusion of cells dispersed there."

And the promise of the Prophet Isaiah had been, they believed, for them: that *the wilderness and the solitary place shall be glad for them, and the desert shall rejoice, and blossom as the rose . . . shall blossom abundantly, and rejoice even with joy and singing . . .*

"There is, perhaps," wrote Edward Gibbon at his most magisterial, "no phase in the moral history of mankind of a deeper or more painful interest than this ascetic epidemic. A hideous, distorted, and emaciated maniac, without knowledge . . . without natural affection, spending his life in a long routine of useless and atrocious self-torture, and quailing before the ghastly phantoms of his delirious brain, had become the idea of a world which had known the writings of Plato and Cicero and the lives of Socrates and Cato."

*   *   *

This perverse impulse to punish the body for being human is generated in the false dualism of Paul: body *or* soul, with the soul superior . . . instead of body *and* soul, woof and warp, woven together into *one* cloth, both equally necessary and innocent.

Pull out either, and you're left with tangled threads, knots of guilt.

The Fathers of the Desert wouldn't agree.

"When thy body flourishes," said the Abbot Daniel, "thy soul withers – but when thy body withers, then thy soul putteth forth her tender grapes."

"Our minds are hampered," said Theonas, "and called back from the contemplation of God, because we are led in captivity to the passions of the flesh."

"I cannot be with God *and* men," said Arsenius. "So I send men away from me because I cannot send away God."

Once they had accepted Paul's mistaken condemnation of the flesh as the same Gospel Truth preached by Jesus, and this duality between body and soul had become an integral part of Christian understanding, it was almost inevitable that these desperate people should declare spiritual war on their own flesh . . . especially the sexual bits of it.

The simple human truth is that intense spirituality and passionate sensuality often walk (even scamper) hand-in-hand, and it's stunting both to body *and* soul if you believe that you have to suppress the enjoyment of your senses before you can enjoy the fruits of the spirit: love, joy, peace, patience, gentleness, faith, meekness, temperance.

As even *The Song of Solomon* demonstrates when innocently read, you can use the sexual love between a man and a woman as a symbol of the Love of Christ for us . . . or, equally, you can use the Love of Christ to show us what the sexual love can be like at its best . . . *until the day break, when we come into our garden, and eat our pleasant fruits.*

Indeed, at the peaks of human experience, you can't fulfil the body without the singing of the soul – and the soul cannot sing when the body languishes for lack of loving. Most great artists and writers and musicians combine magnificent spiritual aspirations with the liveliest interest in the pleasures of the flesh. Dante, for one, trod the very pavements of Hell *and* soared to the heights of Paradise . . . while keeping both feet firmly on the earth – where he loved and was loved.

And so the Fathers of the Desert were wrong from the start, and went from bad to worse, and worst. Yes, deny the soul, and you wallow in the gross materialism of consumer-goods . . . but deny the body, and you sweat in futile attempts to suppress your loving sexuality.

"We kill the body," they said, "for it kills us."

And most of them ended by killing the body right enough . . . but at what cost to the soul is only for God to know.

*　　*　　*

These men were either strict hermits, who avoided all human contact, or part-time hermits, who met occasionally for "mutual support and worship." And, slowly, there developed groups of *semi*-hermits, living in twos or threes . . . and, thus acknowledging the obvious need for at least *some* sort of companionship, these gatherings became small communities, with the Elders or Abbots exercising an informal authority.

Christian Monasticism derives from this necessary mitigation of the original impulse to the solitary life . . . and the words "monk" and "monastery" still bear the scars of the Greek *monos,* "alone," revealing the dry roots in that spiritual waste land of sixteen hundred years ago.

Where *shrieking voices always assailed them . . . mocking, or merely chattering . . . most attacked by voices of temptation . . .*

*　　*　　*

Even naturally sympathetic Roman Catholic scholars are obliged to admit that the "astonishing physical mortifications" practiced by these "athletes for God" were "uncontrolled and encouraged by emulation," and thus became "competitions in feats of endurance." And it is almost impossible for any normal person to imagine how the human body could survive such self-inflicted tortures as these sexually frustrated men and women devised to deny the undeniable.

First they had to learn how to exist in the deserts at all.

"So terrible a place," said one, "can only be endured by those of absolute resolve and supreme constancy."

The sun scorched and parched by day, water was "hard to find" and of a "dire odour," food was scarce and basic – a few dried figs, stale barley bread . . . and their Dark Night of the Soul was bitterly cold.

Even then they denied themselves proper shelter, ate as little as would sustain the merest minimum of life, often fasted entirely for days or weeks, drank once in the morning and only sometimes in the evening, wore thin and torn rags, hair-shirts, went without sleep, and scourged themselves and each other with knotted cords or whips of leather.

According to Jerome (who studied and wrote in the luxury of a cave), one Brother "lived down a dried well on five figs a day," and another "glorified God on barley bread and muddy water for thirty years."

And Jerome calls this the "life of Heaven on earth"!

Another "ate naught but dry bread and salt," and another "persevered for seventy weeks fasting, eating but once a week."

Abbot Zeno "stood in the hot sun for five days and roasted his body to experience the torments of the condemned . . ."

And Abbot Macarius, a Disciple of the Antony who started it all, hearing that one Brother ate only one pound of bread a week, "himself was content to nibble a handful of crusts." When another "did eat no cooked food for the Forty Days of Lent, raw herbs became his diet for seven years." He then noticed that "one Brother fasted until Vespers, another for two days, another for five, how one stood up all night and sat weaving mats all day," so Macarius "stood weaving mats for forty days and nights, neither eating bread nor drinking water, nor kneeling nor lying, nor sleeping nor speaking . . ."

Abbot Agatho "kept a stone in his mouth for three years until he learned to be silent."

And they welcomed dirt, rarely washed, never bathed, regarded lice as the "pearls of Heaven," and even wallowed in their own excrement like the deranged. And a woman penitent was "sealed up" by Paphnutius in a "doorless cell" for three years "since her filth would be a match for her sins . . ."

Thinking, poor fools, wrote Rutilius, a contemporary Roman Poet, *that Heaven feeds on filth.*

While the stories of their incessant scourgings are best reserved for the back market in pornographic flagellation.

Because by *His* stripes are we healed.

*   *   *

All of which meant that instead of being able to dedicate their days to spiritual contemplation, they had to waste most of their energies in struggling against their unappeased carnal desires.

As poor Jerome said to his pupil, Eustochium: "I, who for fear of Hell condemned myself to such a prison, the companion of scorpions and wild beasts . . . was there watching naked girls in their dances. My face haggard with fasting, my mind burnt with the desire in my shivering body, and the fires of lust leaped in the cold flesh I thought was dead."

Because they failed.

"I am still sorely harassed by the demons of lust," said one old man, after a lifetime in a solitary cell, "harried by the worst of such sinful thoughts."

Because, though they tried to "subdue every fleshly appetite," food, water, sleep, comfort . . . woman was the worst of filth, the most sinful of all thoughts, the first and last temptation.

One monk merely saw some "handmaids of the Lord" coming along in the distance, so "gave them a wide berth" . . . but was admonished, because had he been a "perfect monk he would not even have looked close enough to see that they were women."

Another had to carry his old mother across a river in an emergency, so he took off his cloak and wrapped it about his hands, lest he should in any wise touch the body of his mother, saying: "The body of a woman is fire, and she has already made me remember other women."

And one hermit, "of holy memory," once allowed a woman to shelter in part of his cell while a storm raged outside . . . and spent all night "fighting the fires of lust by burning his fingers to the bone in the flame of a lamp, one by one, to remind himself of the fires of Hell."

And that they *did* fail is miserably witnessed by their own broken admissions to the Elders and Abbots: ". . . sorely harassed by the demon of lust . . . thoughts of lust do harry me . . . having to endure the assaults of the adversary . . . the fire that still leaps in my nature . . . imaginations of lust . . . bound by the demons of lust . . . stings of lust . . . beset by thoughts of carnal passion . . ."

So they failed, failed utterly . . . and there, like Jerome, they would "sit solitary, full of bitterness," their "disfigured limbs trembling in sackcloth . . . aching on the naked earth . . ."

*   *   *

Thomas Merton believed that these Fathers of the Desert had a "wisdom as pure as the taste of clear water," and recommended that we should "follow the brook to its source."

But then that's Thomas Merton the Trappist Monk speaking, telling us that the fox is better off without a tail.

Yet, for all that, they *did* distil a few cups of clear water from the brackish depths of their suffering.

"Because of the work done by Martha, Jesus was able to praise the meditations of her sister Mary."

Which would make a useful text for a Sermon to a Convent of Enclosed Contemplative Nuns.

"Not all works are alike," said Nisteros. "Scripture says that Abraham was hospitable, and God was with him. Elias loved solitary prayer, and God was with him. Therefore, whatever you see your soul to desire according to God, do *that* thing, and you shall keep your soul safe."

"Do not judge a fornicator, even if you are chaste. For He Who said *Thou shalt not fornicate,* also said *Thou shalt not judge.*"

"It is better to eat flesh and drink wine," said Hyperichius, "than to eat the flesh of your Brothers and Sisters by saying behind their backs what you are not prepared to say to their faces."

*   *   *

No, they were not given to many words, and sometimes their Sermons were visual.

A Brother was found guilty of some offence, and his Brethren gathered to punish him . . . but their Abbot at first refused to come. So they insisted . . . and he eventually came into that severe assembly dragging an old basket filled with sand – but fast emptying.

"Father," they said, "what is this?"

And he said, "My own sins are running out like sand behind me, and here I am, come to judge the sins of my Brother."

And they heard him, and forgave their Brother.

*   *   *

But John Cassian, who spent the last ten years of the fourth century in the desert, occasionally reached eloquence. He used to talk for hours with some of these old men, and sometimes a little of their hard-won wisdom filters through that drifting sand . . . and you can hear an unknown man speaking, and know him for a Brother.

"Prayer at its highest reaches beyond sound of voice or movement of tongue or any word uttered, because then the mind is no longer narrowed by the limitations of human speech. But all the senses gather around in one fusion, and the soul soars like fountain toward God, discovering in one moment of time such mysteries as cannot easily be spoken, nor can the mind understand again when it returns from its voyage to Heaven back upon itself. And the purpose of this prayer is achieved when all love, all longing, all desire, all seeking, all thoughts, all that we see, all that we hear, all that we say, all that we hope, shall be God."

Or, as our Brother Antony said: "Prayer is perfect when you no longer know yourself to be praying."

*   *   *

Such were the fruits of the desert . . . which can be described in the sort of story told about the Fathers:

A certain monk was given a bunch of fresh grapes by a passing traveller, but, in humility, he gave them to another – who thought himself unworthy of such a gift. And so he gave them to another . . . and so on, until that same bunch of grapes, having been round the desert from monk to monk, came back to the first monk again – withered, and almost uneatable.

*   *   *

And here, finally, are some moving words by our Brother Jerome, from the end of his *Life of Paul the Hermit:* "I pray you, whoever ye be who read this, that ye be mindful of Jerome the sinner, who, if the Lord gave him his choice, would rather wear the tunic woven out of palm-leaves for himself by Paul in the desert, than the purple of kings on their thrones."

*   *   *

By the end of the fifth century the "trackless places" so beloved by the early Fathers had become "thoroughfares," and the small communities had grown into a Monastic Empire.

"The Romans have ruined Rome," said one, "and the monks have ruined the desert."

And three whips hung from a post outside each church: "to punish monks, to punish thieves, and to punish vagrants."

A few bones whitened in the sand beneath that merciless sun . . .

Yes, let us be "mindful" of our Brothers.

The Man with the Golden Tongue

The most famous Preacher of the fourth century was John of Antioch, better known as John Chrysostom . . . that being his Greek nickname, John of the Golden Tongue, the "golden-mouthed" orator.

So he had an almost impossible reputation to live up to: how could anybody be *that* good?

Yet the most beautiful prayer of the five at the end of Morning and Evening Service in the Church of England is by him:

"Almighty God, who hast given us Grace at this time with one accord to make our common supplication unto Thee, and dost promise that when two or three are gathered together in Thy Name Thou wilt grant their requests: Fulfil now, O Lord, the desires and petitions of Thy servants, as may be most expedient for them, granting us in this world knowledge of Thy Truth, and, in the world to come, Life Everlasting."

Amen, Brother John, your tongue still speaks words of pure gold.

Yes, scholars believe that "it is improbable that it was written by him," and the umpteenth Revised Order of Service has very likely left it out altogether . . . but the language of fire and roses abides their twiddling and twittering.

*   *   *

He was born into a wealthy Greek family at Antioch in the middle of the fourth century, was privileged, well-educated, and made a special study of oratory with the best private tutors of the day.

When John was in his early teens the Emperor Julian removed himself and his court from Constantinople, the old capital of the Byzantine Empire, to the new one of Antioch – which thus became the Metropolis of the Classical World: the usual mixture of great riches and miserable poverty, high culture and festering depravity . . . where, as the Emperor said, "all the vices were practised with impunity."

Babylon, Athens, Rome, Alexandria . . . Paris, Berlin, London, New York, Los Angeles, Las Vagas . . .

When has it ever been much different?

At John's conversion to the Christian Faith at the age of twenty-three he soon discovered that the Church was as corrupt as the Empire, with its Priests "voluptuous and licentious . . . given over to vain speculations," and so he decided to "renounce this pit of iniquity" . . . and began the bodily "austerities" he inflicted on his innocent flesh for the rest of his life: lack of proper sleep, constant fasting and perpetual abstinence, and regular self-flagellation – all in futile attempts to "curb his animal lusts."

He got desperate at his "failure," joined the Exodus to the deserts, and was soon a hermit in a remote cave, never washing, eating and drinking less and less, trying to deny himself all sleep, lashing his tortured body harder and more often . . . six years of complete solitude, and endured the last two without once lying down.

Not surprisingly, he ruined his health, and remained a wreck of a man. From frescoes and mosaics we can see that he was small, emaciated, with the sunken cheeks and drained face of a corpse. And from contemporary accounts we know that he was passionate and yet often gentle, domineering and yet sometimes humble . . . the victim of his own wicked temper.

For all manner of sordid political and ecclesiastical reason he was eventually made Patriarch of the Greek branch of the Church back at Constantinople . . . was then banished to a remote Armenian village on the edge of nowhere, and died at the age of sixty on his way to even deeper exile on the shores of what is now the Black Sea.

*   *   *

Enthusiasts claim that "no man ever entered the pulpit more thoroughly equipped for his vocation." His mind was "enriched by Classical learning," he had "studied the art of moving people by the powers of speech," and he had "communed for six years in prayerful solitude with his heart, his Bible, and his God."

Which, I suppose, is one way of putting what he had actually been doing in the desert.

Even given the demented response of these Early Fathers to the moral and sexual excesses of their time, he was obviously no lover of women – still less of cosmetics.

"Look at painted women," he said, transparently obsessed by what he condemned, "their lips are like a bear's mouth dyed with blood, their eyebrows are blackened with kitchen soot, their cheeks are whitened with dust like the walls of a sepulchre . . ."

Yet he obviously had the gift of eloquence about more important subjects, and was a master of every device of Rhetoric:

"Behold the sky, how beautiful it is, and how vast, all crowned with a blazing diadem of stars! For how many ages has it existed? Already it has been there for thousands of years, and shows no signs of decay. Like some young creature full of sap it preserves all the shining and the freshness of an earlier age, and manifests the beauty it possessed in the beginning, and time has not wearied it.

"And this vast, beautiful, ageless sky, unchangeable and gleaming, with all its stars, has existed through countless ages – and our Almighty God, Whom some profess to be able to see with mortal eyes and comprehend with their own pitiable intelligences . . . this same God created it as easily as a man builds a hut with branches.

"This is what Isaiah meant when he wrote: *God stretches out the Heavens as a curtain, and spreadeth them out as a tent to dwell in.*"

And he was capable of soaring ecstasy as he preached: "I exult, I am mad, and my madness is greater than wisdom! Flying and dreaming, I am borne on high! I am drunk with spiritual delights!"

*   *   *

But, again and again, as in that phrase, "young creature full of sap," his tormented mind returns to sexual imagery in daring attempts to reconcile his "animal lusts" with his passionate spiritual love of Christ:

"God desired an harlot, and how doth He then act in His desire for this unclean thing?

"He doth not send her Angels or Archangels, Cherubim or Seraphim.

"No, He Himself draws near to the one He loves – though He does not take her up into Heaven, for He could not pollute Heaven with an harlot.

"Therefore He Himself comes down to the Earth, to the harlot, and is not ashamed. He comes even to her secret dwelling place, and beholds her in her fornication.

"And how does He come?

"Not in the naked essence of His original nature, but in the guise of one whom the harlot is seeking, so that she might not be afraid when she sees Him, and will not run away to escape Him.

"No, He comes to the harlot as a Man.

"And how doth He become a Man?

"He is conceived in the Womb of the Virgin Mary, groweth little by little, and has intercourse with human nature.

"And He finds this harlot covered with sores, and oppressed by the canker of sin.

"How doth He act?

"He draws nigh unto her.

"She sees Him, and flees away.

"He calleth the three wise men, saying: *Why are ye afraid? I am not a Judge, but a Physician, come not to Judge the world, but to Save it from death.* Straightway He Saveth these wise men, for are not they the immediate First Fruits of His Coming? And they worship Him.

"And then the harlot herself comes, and is transformed into a Virgin . . .

"And how doth He act?

"He taketh the sinner, and espouseth her to Himself, and giveth her the signet-ring of the Holy Spirit as a seal between them . . ."

Poor Brother John . . . he'd have done better with a real woman to "draw nigh unto" and love in simple humanity.

*   *   *

Yet, despite the damage done to his mind and soul by the "austerities" of his body, our Brother John was obviously a True Believer.

"Today," he said, in a Sermon preached on a Good Friday, "we hold a Festival and an Assembly, Beloved, for our Lord is fixed with nails to the Cross. And think it not strange that so sad an event should be the occasion of a Festival Celebration, for such as Spiritual things, contrary to what ordinarily happens in human affairs.

"To show this clearly, consider that the Cross was once the symbol of condemnation and punishment, but has now become an object venerable and dear. The Cross was once the theme of ignominy and doom, but has become now the means of Glory and Honour.

"That you may learn that the Cross is Glory, listen to the Saviour's words: *Father, glorify Thou Me with the Glory which I had with Thee before the world was.*

"Here He calls the Cross Glory, for it is the summit of our Salvation, the foundation of countless blessings.

"Through it we, who before were dishonoured and cast off, are now raised to the rank of Sons. Through it we wander no longer in error, but have attained the knowledge of the Truth. Through it, we who worshipped stocks and stones, now know the Creator of all. By it, we who were slaves of sin, have been brought into the freedom of Perfect Righteousness. And, through it, the earth has become, and will henceforth be, Heaven.

"Through it there is no longer the smoke and smell of the shedding of the blood of beasts, but everywhere Spiritual Service – hymns and prayers and love between Brethren.

"It has become the abolisher of war, and the safeguard of peace.

"You see of what blessings the Cross is the cause.

"With reason, then, we keep a Festival."

*　　*　　*

Like Ambrose, he repeatedly told his hearers to read the Bible for themselves, thus anticipating the Protestant Reformation by a thousand years: "Hear, I adjure you, all secular folk, get yourselves Bibles, which are medicine for the soul. Or, if you will do no more, get yourselves the New Testament.

"For Christ, referring the Jews to the Scriptures, sent them not to a mere reading but to accurate examination. He did not say *Read the Scriptures,* but *Search the Scriptures.* So He commands us to dig with exactitude, in order that we may find those things that lie deep.

"Even as a safe and strong door, so doth the Bible shut out heretics from entrance, setting us in safety concerning all the things which we desire, and not permitting us to go astray."

Words which would satisfy the most rigorous Evangelical, surely?

Yet, for all his faith, he always carried the darkness of the desert with him: "Christ is recorded to have wept for Lazarus, to have wept over Jerusalem, but never to have laughed. And He is now Crucified, and thou dost laugh?"

*　　*　　*

But he once preached the ultimate Sermon on the vanity of kingship and all temporal power, dressed in his full Pontifical robes, and the Consul of the Byzantine Empire shivering with fear beside the altar . . . and at these words the world indeed shook.

"Where now is the Pomp and Circumstance? Where are the blazing torches? Where are the dancers and the music? And the Festivals? Where are the garlands and the shows? Where is the applause, the cheering, the wild adulation which greeted him in the city?

"They have all gone like visions of the night, dreams which vanish with the dawn of day, spring flowers withering on their stems with the coming of summer, no more than fleeting shadows or bubbles which have burst, or the torn threads of spider webs.

"Therefore, let us sing this Spiritual Song: *Vanity of vanities, all is vanity!"*

I wonder will we ever hear a Sermon like *that* preached in Westminster Abbey? or in any of our Cathedrals? or even the least of our parish churches?

For what could we do with such a "troublesome priest" except banish him to the remote edge of nowhere?

*　　*　　*

91

Fire and Intricacy

And then, of course, there's Augustine, Bishop of Hippo, with Ambrose, Jerome, and Chrysostom his contemporaries, and his writings in ten fine fat folio volumes along those bottom shelves.

According to the catalogue there should be twelve, but two of them, *The Confessions* and *The City of God,* are out in general circulation.

"All fire and intricacy," says Robert Payne, "the most wanton of the Saints, the man with the clearest mind, the most exalted opinion of himself," who wrote and quarrelled vehemently like a "flame burning everybody he touched."

And everything Augustine wanted us to know about the secrets of his soul he "confessed" in those famous *Confessions:* the first "modern" autobiography . . . though apparently addressed to God, starting, "Great art Thou, O Lord," and continually stopping for private prayer.

Well, on Augustine's own beliefs, God already knows even the deepest secrets of all souls, and so the book is obviously intended for a far wider readership.

It was written during his middle-age in the early years of the fifth century, at the "request of friends" to whom he "had often spoken of his past life," and it's considered by enthusiasts to be the "most famous of Christian Writings outside of the New Testament."

I prefer Thomas Traherne any day of the week, especially on Sunday.

Because there's a supposed humility in Augustine that sets my aching teeth on edge.

For example, about his education he tells us that "whatever was written on every subject, either Rhetoric or Logic, Geometry, Music, Arithmetic, I understood without much difficulty or any instruction." Which is fair enough as the self-confidence of a supremely accomplished intelligence – except that he then goes on: "Because, as Thou knowest, O Lord my God, both understanding and acuteness in any discerning are Thy gifts."

As Hensley Henson dryly observed in a slightly different context, this sort of "total prostration of the individual soul before the mandates of God" implies "assumption of plenary and direct inspiration," and "discloses and fosters a spiritual arrogance none the less morally disintegrating because it is unsuspected" . . . and he calls this overwhelmed humility the "worst and most dangerous form of spiritual pride."

And, in what should have been humiliating fact, Augustine's self-vaunted abilities didn't amount to more than a few A-levels at a grammar-school.

"His education had been of a poor standard," says Dom Roger Hudleston, a Benedictine scholar, "and he was worse than ignorant of the teaching of the Church," being "positively misinformed about it."

Exit one Early Father, feathers ruffled.

*　　*　　*

Mind you, I warm to my Brother Augustine for his human cry: "Give me chastity, O God – but not yet!"

And I love him for his love of his mother, his mistress, and his son . . . though, again, he's far too melodramatic about his "multiplied sins" of "sensuality" and "slavery to lust" with his mistress: doubtless on the old principle, still as new as yesterday's Testimony at any American mass-evangelist's Rally, *The blacker the sin, the more miraculous the conversion, to God be the Glory! Halleluiah!*

And his prose is often, almost literally, out of this world:

"But what do I love, when I love God?

"Not beauty of bodies, nor the fair harmony of time, nor the brightness of the light, so gladsome to our eyes, nor sweet melodies of varied songs, for the fragrant smell of flowers, and ointments, and spices, not manna and honey, not limbs acceptable to embracements of flesh.

"None of these I love, when I love my God.

"And yet I love a kind of light, and melody, and fragrance, and food, and embracements, when I love my God – the light, melody, fragrance, food, and embracements of my inner man . . . where there shineth unto my soul what space cannot contain, and there soundeth what time beareth not away, and there smelleth what breathing disperseth not, and there tasteth what eating diminisheth not, and there clingeth what satiety separates not.

"This is it which I love when I love my God."

*　　*　　*

"Christ came when all things were growing old, and made them new.

"As something fashioned, created, perishable, the world was

declining to its fall. And so it was inevitable that there should be miseries.

"He came to console thee in present troubles, and to promise an everlasting rest.

"Choose, therefore, not to cleave unto this ancient world, nor be unwilling to grow young in Christ, Who said to thee: *The world is perishing, the world is growing old, the world is failing, the world has the laboured breathing of old age.*

"Fear not: *Thy youth shall be renewed as an eagle's.*"

* * *

And here's an extract from one of his less famous Sermons:

"The root lives, but in Winter the green tree is like the dry.

"In the Winter the tree which is dead and the tree which is full of sap are both alike destitute of leaves, alike lacking fruit.

"But the Summer will come, and show the difference between the trees.

"The living tree produces leaves, and is covered with fruit – but the dead tree will remain as bare in Summer as in Winter.

"And so the storehouse is prepared for the one, and the axe is applied to the roots of the other, that it may be cut down and cast into the fire.

"Thus our Summer is the Advent of Christ, our Winter is His absence in Heaven. Our Highest Summer is the Revelation of Christ.

"So the Apostle addresses these words to good and faithful trees: *Ye are dead, and your life is hid with Christ in God.*

"Certainly dead, but dead in appearance only, for you are living at the root. Fix you eyes on the Summer that is to come, for *When Christ, Who is your life, shall appear, then shall ye also appear with Him in Glory.*"

* * *

Again, for the sheer pleasure of his thought and language, here's an extract from a Sermon on a much neglected teaching of Jesus: *Love your enemies, bless them that curse you, do good to them that hate you, and pray for them which despitefully use you, and persecute you . . .*

"Frequently in the Gospel, Very Dear Brethren, we have heard the Lord saying, *Love your enemies, do good to them who hate you.*

"But why should our Lord have said, *Love your enemies,* if we were not to have enemies to bear with?

"And some say, *Who* can love enemies?

"Before this, your God, though opposed to all sin, yet loved you in your sins. And though you are no longer sinners, yet you were once – because no one becomes just except by first being a sinner.

"If you ask, then, who has not committed sin, you will find none.

"Whence, then, shall any one be blessed except by forgiveness?

"So if your sin has already been forgiven, he who is not yet forgiven is he who persecutes you. And you, before you were forgiven, persecuted others. You were lost and were found.

"And he who persecutes shall be found, and shall no longer persecute.

"And, by considering well, you will see that God is able to forgive him whom you now hate, even as He forgave you.

"But, perhaps, he who today is your friend may be guilty of such sins that he cannot be with you in Eternal Life. For you do not know what a day may bring forth.

"And, on the other hand, he who was your enemy may happen to be so turned to repentance as to be worthy of being your fellow-citizen in the Heavenly Jerusalem – and may even be made greater than you.

"Let not this seem impossible.

"Interrogate the Scriptures, and in them we shall be able to recognise this more clearly.

"Paul the Apostle was formerly a wicked enemy of the Christians – he seized, he wasted, he raged.

"When?

"When the Martyr Stephen was stoned, his own hands were not enough – he stoned with the hands of all. For, in order that they might throw stones with free hands, he kept the garments of all, and thus perpetrated that crime with the hands of all.

"But see him, with one word from the Lord, from a persecutor become a Preacher . . . for Man and Sinner are merely two names.

"In these two names ask what God has done, and ask what the Devil did.

"Man was made by God, sin was committed by man at the persuasion of the Devil.

"Which of these two persecute you?

"If you live in Faith, only the Devil will persecute you.

"It is not, then, the man, but the sinner that persecutes you.

"So pray for the man, the sinner, that God may forgive the

sin . . . and you will no longer have an enemy."

*　　*　　*

Finally, from Augustine's priestly journal, *Ennarations in Psalmos,* his "daily contemplations" on the Psalms, and the "source of many of his Sermons," here's a prose anthem in praise of the God Who dwelt in the most secret place of that fiery and intricate soul.

"In Creation I find the sky good, the moon good, the stars good, the earth good, the things which are brought forth from the earth and are rooted here, all good. And all that walks and moves is good, and all that flies in the air and swims in the waters is good.

"And I say that man is good, for the *good man out of the good treasure of his heart bringeth forth good.*

"I say, too, that the Angels are good, if they have not fallen by reason of their pride and become Devils – they are good if they remain obedient to Him Who Made them.

"I say all things are good, and when I turn toward God I think I can describe this in no other way than by saying *He is good,* and I remember that the Lord Jesus said, *No one is good, save God alone.*

"So all this goodness must spring from the goodness of God."

Yes, let our Brother Augustine be praised "with the hands of all."

The Misery of Glory

Benedict, the Father of Western Monasticism, was born in the Umbrian Appennines at the end of the fifth century, and, as they say, "educated" in Rome. Though, according to Gregory the Great, his first biographer, he "despised the literary studies, and departed, knowingly ignorant and wisely unlearned." And then, "sickened by immorality and licentiousness" and inspired by popular accounts of the "heroic sanctity" of the monks of the desert, began a "solitary life" of austerity in a "remote cave" high along the wilderness of the Sabine Hills.

Where he soon "earned a reputation for grace, piety, and devotion."

There being a question which may be asked of all these hermits and many of those Fathers of the Desert: If they *were* "solitary," how did so many people get to hear quite so much of what went on in their caves?

Chrysostom, for one. There he was, "six years of complete solitude," enduring the "last two without once lying down."

Who was there to make sure?

Who counted exactly *how* many figs our Brother down that dried well ate every day? or the number of years our other Brother lived on his "barley bread and muddy water"?

Who else *ought* to have known about any of this allegedly "heroic sanctity" except God?

So, for me, it's all vaguely suspect. I'm not really doubting that they did these fearful things to their innocent flesh . . . but I'm wary of too many self-authenticated Public Relations handouts.

Anyway, Benedict up in his lonely cave paid for his reputation at the usual cost in sexual misery – because he was "tormented by the memory" of a "beautiful girl" he'd known in Rome.

"Wherefore, seeing many thick briers and nettle-bushes to grow hard by, he cast off his apparel, and threw himself into the midst of them, and there rolled so long, that, when he rose up, all his flesh was pitifully torn . . ."

After a few years he'd founded twelve small communities in those "wild regions" for men who "desired to follow his penitential example" . . . and then went on to establish his most famous monastery at Monte Cassino, about halfway along the great high road from Rome to Naples.

Where he wrote his *Rule* for the conduct of his monks.

"If any man will enquire more curiously into his character and his life," wrote Gregory about fifty years after Benedict's death in the middle of the sixth century, "he may find every act of his governance in that *Rule* which he instituted, for the Holy Man could not teach otherwise than he lived."

And Gregory had been a Bendictine monk before he became Pope, so he "knew whereof he spoke . . ."

*   *   *

This famous *Rule* of Benedict reads like the Daily Routine Orders of a "crack" Infantry Regiment, exact, detailed, demented – but, briefly:

There are the "Three Perpetual Vows of Religion, Obedience, Poverty, and Chastity."

"Labour, Prayer, and Self-Denial . . ."

The work was to be "steady" and "hard," in the "kitchen, and gardens, and the fields," for "even the Elect need to be wearied with service . . ."

Seven times during the day and the night the monks chanted Psalms, getting through the entire Biblical Psalter in a week, this being the *Opus Dei,* the Work of God – which, modified and elaborated, eventually became the Divine Office.

The monks were to read "Spiritual books" for "three hours" every day, longer on some days.

Little food and less drink, no meat, occasional fish and eggs.

Total silence for most of the time, and "never were jests or any laughter welcome . . ."

Baths were a "rare concession, except to the sick," with Jerome the authority: "Dost thou complain that thy skin, without washing, is rough and wrinkled? But when a man hath once been washed in Christ, there is no need that he should ever wash again."

Corporal punishment for even minor infringements of the *Rule* was a "standard institution," so "ordinary" that it was called the "regular discipline." If "neither rebuke" nor "threat of separation from the society of the Brethren amend a Brother," then "let the vengeance of stripes fall upon him." For one typical example, "a monk to have spoken alone with a woman was an offence of which the statutory penalty was fixed at from one hundred to two hundred stripes."

With "penitential" self-flagellation an equally "regular" activity, the monks often "assisting" each other for "more thorough discipline."

Christ have mercy upon us, who have so little mercy on ourselves.

The whole *Rule,* of course, developed as it was from the stories and legends of the Desert Fathers, with Benedict even prescribing that their "Words" should be read aloud before Compline, was based on a perverted hatred and pathological fear of the human body . . . with inevitable results: lassitude, apathy, debility, illness, sexual frustration, and mental aberrations to the gibbering edges of paranoia.

Pornographic "temptations" to rival those of Antony in the Desert were common enough, and the cells of the monks were apparently alive with "naked white limbs" and "flaunting breasts and lewd bellies" . . . but "Satan" was also "omnipresent," and would "often make the night hideous" by "imitating a chorus of wild and unclean beasts . . . the roaring of lions, bleating of sheep, braying of asses, hissing of snakes, grunting of swine, squealing of mice and rats . . ."

And our poor Brother Benedict was "always and especially tormented" by the "Master of Iniquity himself fighting openly against him," often "appearing visibly unto him most fell and cruel" with "fiery mouth and flaming eyes" . . . or, on his "nightly rounds," he'd see "devils creeping forth all foul from the depths of the latrines . . ."

What an Hell is an unquiet mind.

*   *   *

Indeed, Hell was becoming an increasingly important feature in the Cosmology of the Monastic imagination, with Demonology its Science.

These days we have often made our own Hell on earth: the killing fields of Flanders in the First World War, the German Extermination Camps . . . Auschwitz, Dachau . . . and then Hiroshima and Nagasaki . . . and Viet Nam . . . the Gulag . . .

Even our televised reality overwhelms all mere imaginings.

But the Church in those early centuries was organising Christianity into a morality of Sin and Punishment, Virtue and Reward . . . Eternal Bliss or Eternal Vengeance as the daily choice of all men and women, so that all were haunted by the Four Last Things to be Ever Remembered: Death, Judgement, Heaven, and Hell.

And, for obvious reasons, intimately meshed with the unnatural lives they led, our frustrated Brothers brooded rather less on the pleasures of Heaven than on the punishments of Hell.

They commonly believed that the "sun was red at evening for it goeth toward Hell," and the "flame of that dread place is visibly belched forth" from volcanoes. Indeed, Gregory the Great, good monk that he remained during his reign as Pope, was convinced that the "End of the World and the Last Judgement draweth nigh" because "Mount Etna was growing in intensity and opening her fiery jaws wider from day to day . . . the more openly that these places of eternal torment may be seen to gape for the reprehension of those who live in this world, in order that faithless minds which believe not in the tortures of Hell will see with their own eyes the very torments which their ears refuse to believe."

And they mapped Hell with obsessional complexity: entrances, caves and caverns and adamantine vaults, circles and galleries and pits and rivers and lakes of fire, cauldrons of boiling slime and glaciers of frozen blood . . . and they filled it with the tortures of the damned.

Most civilised people regard torture as the ultimate earthly injustice, and many penal codes expressly forbid it in principle – if not always in brutal practice . . . but *they* praised it as the "perfection of Heaven's Righteousness," the "Sentence of the Absolute Judge."

And so Hell was meticulously arranged for the appropriate torture of each and all of the bodily senses they were seeking to destroy in themselves: "utter darkness" to punish the sins of the eye, "thunderings and roarings and shriekings" to punish the sins of the ear, "filthy and intolerable smells" for the nose, "vile ordure" for the mouth . . . and a nightmare of pains for the "manifold sins of the flesh," scourging and flaying and crushing and tearing and breaking on spiked wheels, immersion in burning pitch or molten lead, roasting, impalement from anus to mouth, strangulation, disembowelling . . .

Yet, miraculously, the "damned remain so utterly bound that they are not even able to remove from the eye the worms that gnaw it" . . . and each is "tormented according to the nature of the sin" for which "both soul and body will be punished for all eternity," with "blasphemers hung up on hooks by their tongues," the "perjurers biting off their own lips" . . . "women, who had adorned themselves for adultery, hang naked by the tender nipples of their breasts over the boiling slime of lust that bubbles there," while the men "who had coupled with them were hanging by their privy parts . . ."

All flesh is "scabbed with the sores of leprosy," ulcerated and suppurating, channered by the "loathesome worms that never cease and will never die," snakes bite with "venomous fangs," toads and leeches "suck at every orifice" . . . and devils and demons, "the next even more terrible than the one before," are "for ever roaming these regions in their hatred," with claws and fangs and gaping mouths "ready to rend and devour . . ."

And with those "eternal fires ever burning more intensely," yet never consuming, never destroying: "the blood seethes and boils, the brains boil in the skull . . . the bowels a red-hot pulp of liquid pain, the tender eyes searing in their aching sockets . . ."

Hell as a charnel-house, the dungeon of the universe . . . an unholy sewer into which they poured their sado-masochist fantasies.

Even the much more rarely described "pleasures of Heaven" still seemed to involve the "punishments of Hell" . . . for our Brothers found one vindictive verse in the Psalms, and enshrined it as an absolute truth: *The just shall rejoice when he shall see the revenge.* And off they went.

The "Bliss of the Saved" depended to a certain extent on the "agonies of the Damned," and the "Saints will be in no wise disturbed at the sight of the sufferings of their parents and friends," for they "can be touched by no trouble or grief."

To Augustine it was "very absurd" that "sentimental Christians" should "hope for any end to the agonies of the Damned" . . . and, later in this demented search for greater theological precision, Thomas Aquinas pointed out that "even to commiserate with those in Hell would be a grave sin," as "casting doubt on the Justice of God."

Tertullian stated that the "Saints shall actually gain added bliss through the sights and sounds of those torments" . . . and Bernardino of Siena, Disciple of the "gentle" Francis, capped the horror: "All musical harmony needs not only soft but also deep and stern voices – and so God's Harmony of Heaven could not be complete without the bellowing of the Damned in their torments."

These are some of the words which held their world in terror.

*   *   *

Yet, despite this depressing denial of life and love for the "good gifts
of God," our Brother Benedict was reported to be an "excellent"
Preacher, and in some of his surviving Sermons we can hear him
talking to his monks. "From these passages," wrote G. G. Coulton,
certainly no enthusiast of the Monastic life, "we may take a measure
of Medieval Religion at its best."

"First," says Benedict, "pray most earnestly that thy loving
Father may perfect all that thou beginnest of good, in order
that He, Who hath now vouchsafed to count us among His
children, may never be grieved at our evil deeds . . .

"What could be sweeter, dear Brethren, than this Voice of
the Lord inviting us? Lo, in His pity He showeth us the Way of
Life. Let us therefore gird our loins with Faith, and let us follow
in His ways as the Gospel leadeth us, that we may deserve to see
in His own Kingdom Him who hath called us.

"But, if we will dwell in the Tabernacle of His Kingdom, we
can by no means come thither except we walk in good
works . . .

"The Lord expecteth daily that we should answer with our
deeds to His Holy Warnings . . . Therefore, my Brethren, we
must prepare our hearts and bodies to fight for the Holy
Obedience of His Commands . . . for if we wish to flee the
pains of Hell and to attain unto Life Eternal, we must so run
and work now, while there is yet time and we are free to fulfil all
these things by this Way of Light, that it may be to our
everlasting profit and happiness.

"For none can enter there upon but by a narrow beginning
. . . but as our hearts open wider, then do we walk in the Way of
God's Commandments with unspeakable sweetness of love . . ."

*   *   *

This, then, was the "narrow beginning" of Monasticism, the
stultifying mixture of perverted sexuality and genuine Mysticism
which became the dominant form of religious life and practice for the
next thousand years . . . and still lingers in the curious respect with
which many people regard monks and nuns and celibate priests.

"Must be *something* in it, mustn't there?"

Only the heretics ever dared to doubt that *this* was the Way of
Truth into Life Eternal . . . and the History of Christianity almost
turned into the History of the Monasteries.

Until the Protestant Reformation began to ask some of the

Christian questions . . . and went to the other extreme by turning the Story of Christ into Biblical Exegesis.

In those classic words: *We have followed too much the devices and desires of our own hearts . . .*

*   *   *

One last heretical thought about Monasticism.

Jerome can be said to have worded the "device" which these monks had embroidered on their Spiritual Banner: *Christum nudus nudum sequere . . .* "Follow, naked, the naked Christ."

What a difference it would have made to our Brothers and the History of the Church had they taken this, not symbolically, as a recommendation to poverty, but also *literally* . . . so that they could have seen their bodies as innocent sources of beauty and pleasure, worthy of respect and care and love.

What a Second Garden of Eden we might now be enjoying.

What an Heaven is a mind without sexual guilt.

Save us, Lord, from such a Doom

At the end of the sixth century the Day of Wrath and Judgement was already in rehearsal at Rome, the Decline now a Fall, the flames consuming its glory . . . "the taste of ashes in the air . . ."

And Gregory, biographer of Benedict, a "true monk" in the "Voice of his Calling," the Great Pope himself, preached one of the Great Sermons of the Western World . . . a prose *Dies Irae* . . .

*　　*　　*

"Everywhere we see sorrows, everywhere we hear lamentations.

"Cities lie destroyed, fortresses overthrown, harvests ravaged, and the land is brought to desolation.

"No farmer in the fields, scarcely a dweller is left in the towns. Yet even these few remnants are still smitten unceasingly.

"The scourges of Heaven's Justice have no end, for not even through these scourges are guilty actions put right.

"Some of our people we see led away prisoners, some mutilated, some slain with the sword.

"What, then, is there to please us in *this* world, my Brethren?

"If even thus we still love it, we love now not its joys, but its wounds, its sorrows.

"Rome herself, once Mistress of the World, how do we now see her?

"Worn out with mighty griefs, bereft of her citizens, trodden down by enemies, full of ruins.

"Where now is her Senate? Where her people?

"Their bones lie rotting, their flesh consumed, all the pride of her worldly glory is dead and gone."

*　　*　　*

The same Gregory whose four books of *Dialogues* are "one long anti-diabolic epic," full of devils and demons and the threatened pangs of Hell . . . and who made an original contribution to that demented search for greater theological precision about Damnation.

"We know for certain that at the World's End, when the number of the reprobate is consummated, there will be many more evil men than demons. For one tenth part of the Angels fell from Heaven – and *these* are the demons. Now just so many good men shall enter Heaven as the number of the Angels who remained faithful, whereby we may reckon that the number of the Elect shall be nine times greater than the number of the demons.

"It is indubitable that evil men are beyond all comparison more numerous than the good.

"Yet let evil men take no consolation from this, that they shall so far out-number the demons, for these are of so great natural power, of so concentrated malice, of such exquisite skill in torments, that one may well suffice to torture many thousand men."

Why, *this* is Hell, nor is he out of it.

The Temple built upon a Sewer

Odo, Abbot of the Cistercian Abbey near Cluny in France, the greatest Monastic authority of the time, preaching to his Monks at the beginning of the tenth century, repeats the ancient cry of every generation of Elders and Moralists as they approach middle-age . . . when the stairs get steeper, the Novices younger, and the wickedness of Youth ever more wicked and reprehensible.

"Increasing wealth has brought decay, full bellies are prone to worse fleshly lusts, and chastity is only too rare . . . We must justly mourn that Christianity, which ought to have grown stronger with all its advance in age, is on the contrary so twisted aside from the right Way, that all the observances thereof seemeth to have failed. For we are all hastening headlong to evil and Hell."

True, he's talking about the specific corruption of the monasteries, which Bernard of Clairvaux was later to reform, but the tone is all too familiar: listen to any contemporary mass-evangelist . . . though Odo is more eloquent.

"Some do so set to nought the Virgin's Son, that they commit fornication in His very Courts. Nay, in those very Inns which the devotion of the Faithful hath built in order that chastity may be kept more safely within their precincts, they do so overflow with lust that Mary hath no room wherein to lay the Child Jesus."

Which, despite its sexual obsession, remains a moving image: the monastery as the Inn of the Nativity.

"We are become a laughing-stock both to Angels and to men. What will we say at the Day of Doom? Let us look to our hidden deeds, whereof I am ashamed to speak . . ."

Though, of course, like most such Preachers, he seemed to relish his own shame, and used his pulpit to authenticate his enjoyment of his own self-disgust.

Here he is, obviously elaborating on Tertullian's famous opinion that *Woman is a Temple built upon a Sewer* . . .

"Bodily beauty is but skin-deep," says our Brother Odo. "If men could see below the skin, then the sight of a woman would be nauseous unto them. For all that beauty consisteth but in phlegm and blood and gall and filth. If a man consider that which is hidden within the nose, the throat, and the belly, he will find filth everywhere.

"So, if we cannot bring ourselves, even with the tips of our fingers to touch such phlegm or dung, wherefore do we desire to embrace this whole bag of filth itself?"

What was *he*? A whole bag of violets?

*   *   *

Matters were little better in the monasteries at the beginning of the eleventh century.

"Shame hath perished," said Peter Damian, Cardinal and Monk, "honesty hath vanished, Religion is fallen, and the whole multitude of the Holy Virtues hath as it were assembled in one flock and taken flight together. For all seek that which is their own, and, scorning the desire of Heaven, gape insatiably after earthly things."

And the passionate Peter Abelard, preaching to his own Monks, was obliged to agree that the "fervour of Religion is grown cold – nay, is almost extinguished . . . We do now follow after idleness, the enemy of the soul . . ."

Though not everybody took such a doomful view . . . and here, as a necessary change from the punishments of Hell, is a description of the pleasures of Heaven to come. It's by Johannelinus, Little John, Abbot of a monastery in Normandy at the beginning of the eleventh century: the magnificent peroration to a Sermon on the Vision of the New Jerusalem in *The Book of Revelation.*

"O thou most happy life, O Kingdom which art blessed indeed, which lacketh death, which art without end, no time doth successively pass at any time in thee.

"Whereas continual day without night knoweth no time, whereas that captain and conqueror is accompanied with those Choirs of Angels, singing of Hymns and Songs, they sing unto God without ceasing the Song of Songs of Zion.

"O most Noble Head which art compassed about with a Perpetual Crown, O that pardon and forgiveness of my sins were granted unto me, and then immediately this burden of my flesh laid away, that I might enter into thy joys to have true rest.

"And that I might enter within the goodly and beautiful walls of Thy City to receive a Crown of Life at the hand of our Lord, that I might be amongst these most Holy Choirs, that I might stand with the Most Blessed Spirits of the Creator of Glory, that I might see presently the Countenance of Christ, that I might behold always that Most High and Unspeakable Light . . .

"And so I should not only be out of all fear of death, but also I might rejoice always at the Gift of Everlasting Incorruption."

Yes, I can see Little John there amongst those most Holy Choirs, singing louder than anybody.

Standing on the very tips of his toes.

107

The Last of the Fathers

And so, century by century, the Monasteries grew more corrupt, more lavish and grand, the Monks even more idle and dissolute. They lived in comfort, fed well, and fornicated with each other and with women as though Benedict had never been born. The "war against the world, the flesh, and the Devil" had been won . . . by the world, the flesh and the Devil.

Until, at the end of the eleventh century, twelve years after the death of Little John, there arose yet another reformer: Bernard of Clairvaux, the Burgundian nobleman who became a Cistercian Monk . . . and fell on his unregenerate Brethren like a hawk on field-mice.

His "reformation" was a successful imposition of his own revision of the ancient but neglected *Rule* as an introduction to the Mystical Life: the Three Perpetual Vows, the traditional bodily austerities, simplicity, and the scourge . . . all of which had obviously failed to maintain even the rudiments of the primitive ideal.

Many enthusiasts claim that this asceticism is merely "some set efforts at self-denial, beyond what is strictly required to work out our Salvation" . . . but few have been more eloquently misleading about it than Bernard himself.

"Warm and comfortable furs, fine and precious cloth, long sleeves and ample hoods, dainty coverlets and soft woollen shirts do not make Saints. They who wear soft raiment live in the houses of kings. Wine and white bread, honey-wine – these benefit the body, not the soul . . . which is not fattened out of frying-pans. Spices may please the palate, but inflame lust. Salt with hunger is seasoning enough for a man to live soberly and wisely."

The sado-masochist reality of daily life under the *Rule* was a different cloister of frustrated souls entirely, so it was!

But Bernard is pleading a special case: his own.

Because, like Benedict before him, he was "long haunted by the memory of a girl he had once loved." So the "salt with hunger" and the lashing whip had less to do with the spontaneous love of God than the same old futile attempts to suppress the truly human impulses of loving and cherishing another, and with your body thus worshipping, rendering true worth to your Beloved.

*　　*　　*

However, I'm not so much concerned with Bernard the Reformer, because, in my opinion, Monasticism was (and is) beyond reformation: it needed (and still needs) Redemption.

But Bernard the "many-sided and complex character," the "exceptional among the exceptional," Mystic, administrator of considerable ability, the Mellifluous Preacher . . . well, *there* is a Brother to love as a *man*, "take him for all in all," we "shall not look upon his like again."

From contemporary accounts we know he was a sick man, an "implacable ascetic" who "had almost forgotten how to eat," his "whole body meagre and emaciated by fasting and nightly vigils," welted and "scarred" by "penitential discipline . . ."

Even at the peak of his immense fame, with postulants and prelates coming from all over Europe to visit him, he lived in a "mean cell, like unto a leper's hut."

He saw his duty as "not to teach, but to mourn" . . . and yet, despite this, and against the knotted grain of his sexual problems, his Sermons are masterpieces of simplicity and spiritual passion.

"The Grace of God Who had possession of this frail man," wrote Thomas Merton, "burst like flame into the hearts of all who heard him speak."

And Bernard preached most of these Sermons to his Monks in the Chapter Hall of the Abbey he'd founded in a valley along the River Aube, on the borders of Burgundy and Champagne in France: waste land, Vallis Absinthialis, "Vally of Wormwood" . . . which soon became known as Clairvaux, "Valley of Light . . ."

* * *

We get lovely little pictures of his preaching, warm and human, like illuminations in a manuscript.

In the middle of a Sermon some unexpected guests arrive . . .

"Brethren," says Bernard to his Monks, "it is good for us to be here, but lo! this calleth us away . . . I will go forth unto these guests, lest anything be found lacking in that love whereof I am even now discoursing unto you, for perchance it may be said of us: *They say, and do not.*"

Merely in passing, we mustn't make the mistake of believing that the "sacred silence" in which our contemporary clergymen expect to preach was customary even for the incomparably greater preaching of Bernard. As in the Synagogues of Christ's day, to listen in such silence was not the convention . . . and there's often a "running fire of interruptions from the hearers and rejoinders from the Preacher."

And so we find Bernard commenting on the "grunts" or "deep groans" of his listening Brethren, their "fallen faces" or "murmurings of vague disapproval" . . . even, on occasion, their complete lack of attention: "For indeed I see some yawning, and some already asleep."

Which, suddenly, fills that Chapter Hall with *men,* "in all points tempted like as we are . . ."

Anyway, according to G. G. Coulton, these Sermons "were doubtless written down by his Monks, with the help of his preaching notes."

And all we can do is "summon up remembrance of things past . . ."

*   *   *

"Do you see how Saint Paul the Apostle makes the fruit and utility of knowledge consist in the *way* we know?

"For there are some who seek knowledge for the sole purpose of knowing, and this is unseemly curiosity.

"And there are some who seek knowledge in order to be known themselves, and this is unseemly vanity . . . and there are also those who seek knowledge in order to sell it for money or for honours, and this is unseemly quest for gain.

"But there are those who seek knowledge in order to teach, and this is love . . . and there are also those who seek knowledge in order to be taught themselves, and this is wisdom."

How easy to hang contemporary names on those gentle hooks.

*   *   *

Given that he was a Monk under his own *Rule*, his bread-and-butter Sermons are not buttered very thickly, but the bread is the good thick wholemeal variety.

"On this Easter Sunday, our chief solemnity, we should seriously consider what is set before us: that is, a Resurrection, a Passover, a passing-over, a change of dwelling.

"For today, my Brethren, Christ did not remain lying dead, but He rose up. He did not come back, but passed over. He did not establish Himself afresh, but He raised His dwelling-place aloft.

"And, in truth, this Pasch that we are celebrating does not mean Return, but Passing Over – and that Galilee, in which He Who rose up promised to let us see Him, does not mean that He stayed behind, but that He had changed His dwelling.

"And it is to *that* place, so it seems to me, that the minds of many among you have gone before me, surmising rightly where my words would lead you.

"For if Christ the Lord, after the consummation on the Cross, had lived again to return once more to our mortal nature and the sufferings of our present life, I should say most certainly, my Brethren, that He had not Passed Over, but that He had come back – that He was not now established in a higher state, but that He had taken up His pilgrimage again in His former state.

"On the contrary, He is now raised up to a New Life, and that is why He calls us, as well, to the Passing Over – calls us into Galilee."

*   *   *

But Bernard was at his best on the Blessed Virgin Mary, and had a "most special Devotion" to Her.

To those of us who regard Mary with love and affection as another human-being, "handmaid of the Lord," truly "blessed among women" in that the "Holy Spirit came upon her" and she "conceived in her womb" and "brought forth a son," even Jesus, the "Son of the Highest" – but was also married in the normal holy and beautiful way to Joseph, and had other sòns, and several daughters, all born in the usual miraculous way, and all known and named in the New Testament . . . well, it remains a mystery to us why anybody should want her to be any more lovely than any happily-married woman, any more whole and holy than any loving mother.

But very soon in the History of the Church, certainly by the fourth century in the Byzantine, Christ the Mediator became Christ the

Judge. So, as Christ had stood between the sinner and God the Judge, somebody must now stand between the sinner and Christ. "Jesus taught the Love of the Father," said the Theologians, "and it now became the Mission of the Blessed Virgin Mary to teach the Love of Christ."

And off they went in all Doctrinal directions . . .

"I counsel thee to invoke, before all others," wrote Vincent of Beauvais, "Mary the Mother of Jesus, and serve Her with perpetual prayers. For She is the single hope of man's reconciliation, She is the Prime Cause of man's Salvation."

And Thomas of Cantimpre reports the Sermon of a "certain Holy Monk, speaking about Mary in wondrous fervour" and "gushing tears," who said:

"Know ye not that all sinners, without exception, when they begin to rise from their fall into sin, fear the God of Vengeance and the Lord Christ of the Universe, and flee to His Mother as to a Fount of pity and propitiation, clinging the more dearly to Her as their True Reconciler. Nor need we to wonder, for She ceaseth not in Her constant service and striving until She hath reconciled these prodigal sons to the Father of Life . . ."

And She slowly acquired a Litany and Liturgy of Her own, an impressive list of Chivalric titles by which She was addressed: *Holy Mother of God, Holy Virgin of Virgins, Mother Most Chaste, Virgin Most Powerful, Virgin Most Merciful, Mirror of Justice, Throne of Wisdom, Spiritual Vessel, Singular Vessel of Devotion, Mystical Rose, Gate of Heaven, Morning Star, Refuge of Sinners, Help of Christians, Queen of Angels, Queen of Apostles, Queen of Martyrs, Queen of Virgins, Queen of All Saints . . . Queen Conceived Without Original Sin . . .* and culminating with the triumphant *Saint Mary Virgin, Queen of Heaven, Lady of the World, and Empress of Hell . . .* "Pray for us, who have recourse to Thee."

However, apart from Her often beautiful Liturgical and Theological functions, She also served in what by now was an urgent secondary way: as the sublimated "spiritual" focus for the sexual needs of a growing army of would-be celibate Monks and Priests . . . and the literature is rich (if that's the word) with desperately erotic prose and verse ostensibly in Her religious praise.

To confine a possible anthology to one example, Bernard was believed by his contemporaries (with himself as the only possible source for the information) to have "had Her as his constant Companion," when, "from Her sweet breasts oftentimes She feedeth him bodily, to moisten his lips with Her Virgin Milk . . ."

And so, perhaps not surprisingly, he preached many Sermons on Her.

Though how much more lovely, had those "sweet breasts" been those of the "girl he had once loved."

*　　*　　*

Here's a passage from one of these Sermons . . . "than which there is none more beautiful," says Pope Pius the Twelfth, another man with a "special Devotion" to Mary, "none more impassioned, more apt to excite love, more useful for stirring imitation of Her virtuous example."

"The title *Star of the Sea,*" says Bernard, "admirably suits the Virgin Mother, for there is indeed a wonderful appropriateness in this comparison of Her to a star, because as a star sends out its rays without detriment to itself, so did the Virgin bring forth Her Child without injury to the integrity of Her Perpetual Virginity. And as the ray emitted does not diminish the brightness of the star, so neither did the Child born of Her tarnish the beauty of Her Virginity.

"She is, therefore, that glorious Star, which, according to Prophecy, arose out of Jacob, Whose rays illumine the entire earth, Whose splendour shines out conspicuously in Heaven, and reaches even unto Hell . . .

"She is, I say, that resplendent and radiant Star, placed as a necessary Beacon above life's great and spacious sea, glittering with merits, luminous with examples for our imitation.

"Whosoever thou art that perceivest thyself during this mortal existence to be drifting in the treacherous waters, at the mercy of the winds and the waves, rather than walking secure on the stable earth, turn not away thine eyes from the splendour of this Guiding Star, unless thou wishest to be submerged by the tempest!

"When the storms of temptation burst upon thee, when thou seest thyself driven upon the rocks of tribulation, look up at the Star, call upon Mary!

"When buffeted by the billows of pride, or ambition, or hatred, or jealousy, look up at the Star, call upon Mary!

"Should anger, or avarice, or carnal desires violently assail the little vessel of thy soul, look up at the Star, call upon Mary!

"If troubled on account of thy heinous sins, confounded at the filthy state of thy conscience, and terrified at the thought of the awful Judgement to come – when thou art beginning to sink into the bottomless gulf of sadness, and to be absorbed in the abyss of despair . . . *then* think of Mary.

"In dangers, in doubts, in difficulties, think of Mary, call upon Mary.

"Let not Her Name depart from thy lips, never suffer it to leave thy heart . . . neglect not to walk in Her footsteps.

"With Her for Guide, thou shalt never go astray. Whilst invoking Her, thou shalt never lose courage. So long as She is in thy mind, thou art safe from deception. Whilst She holds thy hand, thou canst not fall. Under Her protection, thou hast nothing to fear. If She walks before thee, thou shalt not grow weary. And if She shows thee favour, thou shalt reach the goal."

*   *   *

Even more obviously erotic are his eighty-six Sermons on the first two Chapters of *The Song of Solomon* – surely the most obsessional set of meditations on lost human love ever written . . . the barely disguised lamentations of a man denying himself the lovely and holy pleasures of a living woman to talk to and walk with and hold by the hand . . .

Bernard was too intelligent a man not to suspect the truth about himself: "Take heed that you bring chaste ears to this discourse of love," he says, "and when you imagine these two lovers, remember always that it is not a carnal man and a woman to be imagined, but

114

Christ and the soul, Christ the Bridegroom and His Bride the Church."

But that's the authentic voice of celibacy talking, and he works at and worries these sensual Jewish love lyrics into the most extraordinary structure of allegory and symbolism.

Let him kiss me with the kisses of his mouth, for my breasts are better than wine, surely a delightful invitation to a most fortunate human lover, becomes a strained image of the Church as the Bride, whose "twin breasts" are the Old and New Testaments, "from which her children suckle a nourishment sweeter than wine" . . . and so on into Bernard's memories and yearnings and desperate imaginings . . .

Though he often rises above his own repressions.

*　　*　　*

"Love is sufficient of itself, it pleases of itself, and for its own sweet sake. It counts as merit to itself and is its own reward. Besides itself love requires no motive, and seeks no fruit apart from its own enjoyment of itself.

"I love because I love, and I love for the sake of loving . . .

"Amongst all the emotions, sentiments, and feelings of the soul, love stands distinguished in this one respect: that in this case alone has the creature the power to make a return to the Creator in kind . . . to return love for love."

Not that he ever manages to remain for long in this "world of speculation" where "what might have been is an abstraction" . . . because his memories and yearnings are rarely far beneath the surface.

"Happy is the soul," he goes on, "to whom it has been given to experience an embrace of such surpassing delight!

"For Christ's Spiritual Embrace is a chaste and Holy one, a love sweet and pleasant, a love perfectly serene and perfectly pure, a love that is mutual, intimate, and strong, a love that joins two, not in one flesh, but in one spirit, that make two to be no longer two but one undivided spirit . . . because he who cleaves to the Lord is one in spirit with Him."

*　　*　　*

Yes, he was obviously a man capable of intense human love.

"Though thou shouldest walk on the wings of the wind," he wrote to a former student, Eugenius, newly made Pope, "yet shalt thou not escape from my affection. I have lost the duty of a mother towards thee, but no man shall deprive me of the mother's love. Thou wert

115

part of my very bowels – not so easily shalt thou now be torn from me."

But he was equally capable of the most intense love for God.

"Every soul, though it be in despair, can find within itself not only reasons for yearning after the hope of pardon and the hope of mercy, but also for making bold to aspire after Spiritual Marriage with Christ ... not hesitating to establish a Union with God, and not being ashamed to be yoked in one sweet bond of love along with the King of the Angels.

"What will the soul not dare with Him whose marvellous image it sees within itself, and whose striking likeness it recognises in itself?

"And by this conformity of loving ... the soul is wedded to Christ, when, loving even as she is loved, she reveals herself with her desires conformed to Him in Whom she is already conformed in her nature.

"Therefore, if she loves Him perfectly, she has become His Bride.

"And what can be more sweet than such a conformity?

"What can be more desirable than this loving, whereby thou art enabled to draw nigh with confidence to Christ, to cleave to Him steadfastly, to talk with Him familiarly, and to be as audacious in thy desires as thou art capacious in thy understanding?

"This is, in truth, the alliance of holy and spiritual marriage.

"But it is too little to call it an alliance, for it is an embrace ... since love knows nothing of fear ..."

My heart aches for the Bernard whose heart ached for God ... because there was no Heavenly reason why he couldn't have loved his earthly Beloved as well.

*　　*　　*

If he was at his beatific best on the Blessed Virgin Mary and the Church as the Bride of Christ, he was at his baleful worst when he Preached the Second Crusade as a Holy War to restore free access to the "places made Sacred by the Presence of the Lord in the Holy Land."

This was the man who had written that the "only fruit of secular warfare is that both the killer and the killed end in Hell" ... but, with a "sublime disregard for political circumstance," he believed that every Crusader would follow the Cross of Pilgrimage in a faith as pure and ardent as his own.

The Truth of Christ is that even if it had been fought by genuine

Saints it would have still been morally wrong – because "enemies" are there for loving not killing ... but it was waged by treacherous murderers, rapists, looters, and mercenaries.

Yes, it *is* Theologically possible in the comfort of the Library for there to be postulated the "correct" circumstances for the moral conduct of the theoretical "Just War" ... except where are the "Just" to conduct it? With Bernard at Clairvaux? My Lord Bishop at Oxford?

He that is without sin among you, let him first cast a stone ... or pull the trigger, or press the button.

Though Bernard's words were stirring:

"O ye who listen to me! Hasten to appease the anger of Heaven! No longer implore God's mercy by vain complaints!

"Clothe yourselves with your impenetrable bucklers, for the bearing of arms, the dangers, the labours, the fatigues of war are the penances God now imposes on you.

"Hasten, then, to expiate your sins by Victory over the infidels, and let the deliverance of our Holy Places be the reward of your repentance.

"Let a Holy rage animate you in the battles, and let Christendom resound with the words of the Prophet: *Cursed be he who does no staining of his sword with blood."*

Yes, stirring ... but read the History of the Second Crusade for what emotions and deeds it stirred.

And weep.

True, to what I hope is Bernard's eternal credit, he afterwards protested at the massacres of the Jews and "infidels" which marked popular enthusiasm for the Crusade ... but by then it was too late.

It's always too late afterwards.

*   *   *

There's one curious feature about his preaching: he seemed to have the Gift of Tongues – not the happy babbling which needs "interpretation" to be understood in all its banality ... but the genuine Apostolic sort as at Biblical Pentecost.

For "preaching in French to Germans who were utterly ignorant of this language," he "moved them to such devotion" that "their hard hearts were softened to the shedding of tears" ... yet these men had been "altogether unmoved by the interpreters who faithfully rendered his Sermon into their own language."

Yes, it might well be the usual hagiography, giving the painted plaster another pious touch or two of best gold-leaf ... but, somehow, it has the ring of truth.

117

*   *   *

Let's leave our Brother Bernard a few of his most beautiful words:
"It does not behove thee, O man, to cross the seas, to fly above the clouds, to climb the Alps in search of God.
"No great journey is necessary for thee.
"Seek no further than thy own soul: *there* wilt thou find thy God!"

How Pleasant it is for Brethren to Dwell Together in Unity

Another Monk of those days whose Sermons are glowing with barely suppressed sensuality was the Northumbrian, Aelred, first the Novice Master and then Abbot of the Cistercian Abbey at Rievaulx.

He lived during the half-century or so before the Norman Conquest of England, a small and frail man, reported to be "handsome," who "loved to have handsome Novices around him..."

Indeed, sexual desires obviously tormented him, for he had built a "small chamber of brick beneath the floor of the Novice House, like a little cistern, into which water flowed from underground streams"... and when he was "alone and undisturbed" he'd "enter this place, and immerse his whole body in the icy water and so quench the heat in himself of every lust."

That, at least, was the intention – except that his own words tell a more human story.

"The other day," he said in one of his Sermons, "as I was walking round the Cloister Garth of our Monastery, the Brethren were seated together like a crown that is most dear to me.

"It was as though I were amid the liveliness of Paradise, and I kept admiring the flowers and the fruit of each of the trees, the Brethren being that living grove, and I found no one in that multitude whom I did not love and by whom I was not confident that I was loved.

"And I was suffused with a joy so great that it surpassed all the delights of the world. For I felt in spirit transfused into all, and that the affection of all had passed over into me, so that I said with the Prophet: *Behold, how good and how pleasant it is for Brethren to dwell together in unity.*"

*   *   *

And there is a passage from a Sermon on *Jesus at Twelve Years Old,* in which his warm sensual imagination enjoys the very thought of Jesus as an adolescent boy ... even, perhaps, as a Novice at Rievaulx.

"*And it came to pass, that after three days Joseph and His Mother found Him in the Temple ...*

119

"Where wast Thou during those three days, O good Jesus?

"Who gavest Thee food and drink? or a bed to sleep on?

"To whom was given the great privilege of untying the latchets of Thy sandals? For even John the Baptist thought himself unworthy.

"Or who was allowed to prepare baths and oils for Thy youthful limbs?

"Sweetest Lord, I do not know, but I *do* know that thou wert able to assume our weakness just as Thou wert able to assume Almighty Power.

"So it seems to me that Thou didst go about begging like a Mendicant from door to door, thus sharing in our poverty, and assuming all the lowliness of our human nature."

* * *

Which is all very beautiful and moving until you remember what Monks believed about the "sanctity" of dirt and bodily filth . . . and the depressingly regular activity with the "youthful limbs" of boys and Novices was not to bathe and oil but to scourge, using "smooth and supple osier rods kept for this purpose . . ."

Always the channering worm at the heart of the Monastic rose.

And Aelred himself knew just how corrupt his own Monks often were, and told them in words which can still sear:

"The Brethren who complain of the heaviness of Christ's yoke are those who, like dogs returning to their vomit, make unto themselves a belly-god under the garb of abstinence.

"Under the penitent's cloak they pant after worldly glories and honours.

"Under the Holy habit of continence they are defiled with fleshly filth.

"Under the lamb's fleece they hide wolfish minds.

"Seething with insatiable greed, they spare not the widow, nor are they compassionate to the orphan, and the poor man's patrimony they claim for themselves.

"And are tortured with continual cares, inflamed with hatred, distracted with anxious thoughts . . .

"Whereas the Lord's yoke is sweet, and His burden light."

Yes, walk around the remains of Rievaulx, those "bare ruined choirs where late the sweet birds sang" . . . and remember the songs they were singing, the imaginations of their hearts.

*   *   *

Words starting to go Mad

As we have seen, one of the most over-worked rhetorical devices in the Sermons of these times was the elaborating of symbolism and allegory into the remotest ramifications of exhaustion and sterility.

Here, for an example, is a very short extract from a Sermon by Master Simon, a Theologian and Preacher in the twelfth century . . . with him embroidering away on the "meaning" of the bread and wine used in the Communion of the Roman Catholic Mass.

"Why is Christ received under the form of bread and wine?

"It may be said that in the Sacrament of the Altar there are two things involved: the True Body and Blood of Christ, and what they signify – namely, His Mystical Body, which is the Church.

"Now as one loaf is made of many grains, which are first wetted, then milled and baked to become bread, so the Mystical Body of Christ, that is to say the Church, formed by the gathering together of a multitude of persons, like to many grains, is wetted in the Water of Baptism.

"It is then crushed between the two millstones of the Old Testament and the New, or between fear and hope . . .

"And, in the last place, it is baked in the fire of passion and sorrow that it may be made worthy of the Body of Christ. In truth, the Blessed Martyr Ignatius wished to be united with this Body in fullest reality when he said: *I am the wheat of Christ – let me be crushed by the teeth of the wild beasts to become the Bread of Christ.*

"Likewise, wine is the product of many grapes. When they have been trodden, and pressed in the wine-press, the pulp is left as worthless, and the wine is stored.

"Holy Church, too, suffers by being beset in the world as in a wine-press, where, as the wine is separated from the pulp, the wicked are cast away, and the Righteous out to the test.

"Rightly, then, these elements of Bread and Wine designate the Body and Blood of Christ – that is, His Holy Church."

*   *   *

None of these ideas started with Master Simon. Indeed, he quotes Ignatius of Antioch as one of his sources, and all of the others may be traced back to the Greek or Latin Fathers . . . but the extension into finer and more remote "meanings" is entirely typical of Theology starting to go mad: bringing the Desert into the City of God.

The Sermon to the Birds

The Great Golden Legend of Saint Francis of Assisi has been so burnished over the years as to need no further polishing, and his Little Flowers are now preserved in thick layers of pious plastic.

And yet . . . and yet . . . there was once a living man behind all that deceptive gentling, a soul in self-inflicted agony.

*   *   *

There he was at the end of the twelfth century, the young son of a wealthy merchant, "ignorant and unschooled," to quote his own words . . . whose "association with dissolute and pleasure-loving companions led to a wasted early manhood," to quote the words of a later biographer.

And there he was one early February morning at the beginning of the thirteenth century, hearing Mass, when the Priest read from Matthew's Gospel the words of Jesus to the Apostles: *Go, preach, saying, The Kingdom of Heaven is at hand . . . Provide neither gold, nor silver, nor coins in your purse, nor pack for your journey, neither two coats, neither shoes, nor yet staves . . .*

And so, Holy Fool that he was, Francis there and then decided to start his Order of Barefoot Friars: they, too, would "go forth, with neither gold, nor silver, nor pack, nor shoes, nor staff, and with but one coat, and call men to Righteousness."

The Roman Catholic Church was corrupt, rich, rigid with ornate gold and silver embellishments, embroidered with incomprehensible doctrines, its hands bloody with the making and breaking of Kings and Emperors . . . and here was this obvious lunatic wanting to preach the poverty of that other lunatic they thought they'd safely entombed a thousand years ago.

Why he wasn't burned alive as a heretic like Savonarola after him remains a mystery.

*   *   *

Francis was a small, dark-skinned man, with eyes like black olives, the stubble of a beard, dirty, unkempt, haggard . . . and the hagiographies offer him as the "tenderest and sweetest of Christian Saints," give him the affectionate nickname of the "Little Pauper," and even the legends about him are called his "Little Flowers."

125

Beware of diminutives, for they diminish, reduce such awkward people to a more cuddly size, make pets of Saints most churchwardens wouldn't allow into Choral Evensong.

And yes, I *have* seen the down-and-almost-outs, the "Little Brothers" of Saint Francis, being asked to leave Westminster Abbey ten minutes before the Service was due to start.

But there was iron in the soul of the real Francis, thorns on the gnarled stems of his living flowers.

*　　*　　*

Even through the stained-glass *Life*, written "under obedience" by Bonaventura thirty-five years after the "sanctified death" of the "Little Father," we can glimpse the man of all too human flesh and blood struggling not only with the Church but the insane demands of "spiritual warfare against carnal sin."

For, by now, the "sin of the flesh" had become the sin of sins.

And so, with poor innocent Francis torn by the perverted dualism of soul and body, there are all the usual futilities of mortifying (or trying to kill) Brother Flesh.

He ate "but little food, and that of the meanest," even "sprinkling it with ashes" to "destroy the savour and taste" . . . and "hardly ever drinking water," not "though parched with burning thirst."

And he was "always discovering methods of more rigorous abstinence" and "chastising the lusts of the flesh by afflicting it."

The "bare ground for the most part served as a couch unto his wearied body, and he would often sleep sitting, or with a log or stone placed under his head . . ."

He was "wont in the winter season to plunge into a ditch full of his Bride of Snow, that he might both utterly subdue the foe within him, and might preserve his white robe of chastity from the fire of lust."

Whenever this "lover of chastity felt the oncoming of a grievous temptation of the flesh," he "laid aside his habit, and began to scourge himself severely with a cord . . ."

And he said that "one who so much as spoke to a woman could as little avoid contamination therefrom as he could walk upon hot coals and his feet not be burned."

And the name of his Little Sister was Lady Clare.

*　　*　　*

And this is how our Little Brother did preach to the birds.

When Francis had learned the will of Christ, he rose up with great fervour, saying, "Let us then go forth in God's Name."

And with him he took Friar Masseo and Friar Agnolo, holy men both, and setting forth, taking no heed of road nor path, they came to a city called Saburniano.

And Francis began to preach to the people, first commanding the swallows to keep silence until his Sermon were ended. And, the swallows obeying him, he preached with such zeal that all the men and women of that city desired in their devotion to follow after him and forsake the city.

But Francis suffered them not, saying, "Be not in haste to depart . . ."

And so, leaving them much comforted and well disposed to penitence, he departed thence, and came to a place between Cannara and Bevagna.

And he lifted up his eyes, and beheld some trees by the wayside whereon were a multitude of birds, so that he marvelled, and said to his two companions, "Tarry here for me by the way, and I will go and preach to my Little Sisters the Birds."

And he entered into the field, and began to preach to the birds that were on the ground. And anon those that were on the trees flew down to hear him. And all stood still the while Francis made an end of his Sermon. And even then they departed not until he had given them his blessing.

And, according to Friar Masseo, as he thereafter related, Francis went among them, touching them with the hem of his garment, and not one stirred to fly away.

"My Little Sisters the Birds," said Francis, "much are ye beholden to God your Creator, and always and in every place ye ought to praise Him, for that He hath given you a double and a triple vesture.

"He hath given you freedom to go into every place, and also did preserve thee in the Ark of Noah, in order that your kind might not perish from the earth.

"Again, ye are beholden to Him for the element of air which He hath appointed for you.

"Moreover, ye sow not, neither do ye reap, and God feedeth you, and giveth you the rivers and the fountains for your drink.

"He giveth you the mountains and the valleys for your refuge, and the tall trees wherein to build your nests.

"And, forasmuch as ye can neither spin nor sew, God clotheth you and your children.

"Wherefore your Creator loveth you much, since He hath dealt so bounteously with you. And therefore, Little Sisters mine, beware of the sin of ingratitude, but ever strive to praise God."

While Francis was uttering these words, all those birds began to open their beaks in song, and stretch their necks, and spread their wings, and reverently to bow their heads to the ground, showing by their gestures and songs that these words gave them greatest joy.

And Francis was glad, and rejoiced with them . . .

Finally, his Sermon ended, he made the Sign of the Holy Cross over them, and gave them leave to depart.

And all those birds soared up into the air in one flock with wondrous songs . . . and one part flew towards the east, another towards the west, the third towards the south, and the other toward the north.

And each flock sped, singing wondrously . . .

And his words changed the sensibility of Europe, gentled the conscience of Christianity . . . made Vegetarians of the tender-hearted . . .

Even humanised our slaughter-houses.

*   *   *

He was the Greatest Heretic of them all, the Rebel with the Noblest Cause, another Voice crying aloud in the wilderness of the Church.

"Don't you talk of any *Rule* to me," he said to a Congress which included the fearsome Dominic, and many who'd be reporting straight back to the Pope, "neither the *Rule* of Benedict, nor of Augustine, nor of Bernard, nor any Way of Life whatever – except that which God has mercifully granted to me.

"For *He* told me that he wanted me to be a Pauper and a Holy Fool in this world, and would not lead my Brothers in any other Way than this.

"But by your own syllogisms God will confound you . . ."

Yes, the Church should have burned him alive . . . but somehow scraped up the sense to use him as an example of everything it no longer was.

If it had *ever* been.

*   *   *

When he knew he was dying he asked that he be "laid naked on the earth with ashes sprinkled over him," and there he was, finally, "very calm and quiet, staring up at the sky . . ."

And he died "late on a Sunday, after Vespers," while a "great multitude of larks came on the roof of the hut where he was, and, flying about, made a wheel around the Heavens, sweetly singing, likewise praising the Lord."

Yes, *Praised be our Lord for our Sister, Mortal Death, from whom no living man can escape.*

Sleep, my poor dear Brother Francis . . . may you find bliss in the arms of thy Beloved Sister Clare.

Seven Illuminations from Thirteenth Century Manuscripts

Anthony of Padua Preaches before the Pope

The friend of Francis in his coarse brown habit, the Cardinals of the Consistory of Rome in their scarlet robes, His Holiness the Pope in His full Pontificals, with here and there the soft white fringe of ermine, the gleam of gold and silver crosses and rings, the flash of some immortal diamond, the fire of a ruby . . . candle-flames in ascensions of glory, incense . . .

Now in this Consistory "were men of divers nations, to wit, Tuscans and Lombards, French, German, Sclavonians, and English, and divers other tongues throughout the world. Inspired by the Holy Spirit, Anthony did expound the Word of God so effectually, so devoutly, so subtly, so sweetly, so clearly, so wisely, that all understood his words distinctly, even as though he had spoken in the tongue of their native land . . . and all were filled with wonder."

John of Ford Preaches to his Monks

The Abbot of a Cistercian Abbey in Devon stands before his Brethren, who sit, half by half, facing across the Choir of their Church, all in their coarse grey robes, hoods down, waiting for the elected silence to descend upon them, which shall be the silence of their Calling.

Grey their robes, grey the stone of the walls and arches they are still building, grey their breath on the cold air . . . perhaps the star of a candle for their Abbot to preach by, perhaps a few wildflowers in supplication on the dull granite of their Altar . . .

Their Abbot turns a page of their great hand-written Bible . . . perhaps there's a golden gleam of an illuminated capital . . . and then he finds and reads the text of his Sermon:

"*By night on my bed I sought Him Whom my soul loveth, I sought Him, but I found Him not.*

"Jesus, the Bridegroom, has gone, He is not here.

"There is nothing left but loneliness left to the Church, the Bride of Christ, in her bed. All she knows is a constricting narrowness. She is a burden to herself, and she has lost her peace of mind.

"So she hurries out from her lonely room, into the streets and broad ways of the city . . . because she wishes to emulate the

130

generous love of her Bridegroom – for whoever claims to abide in Him must walk as He walked . . . She wants to pour out publicly the streams of her knowledge, distribute her living waters to everybody.

"Seeking her beloved Bridegroom, then, she hurries out to accomplish her purpose in the city, preaching in and out of season, both in the streets and the broad ways . . . speaking wisdom from the Oracles of God to the already instructed, giving the strong meat of the word to the strong, and milk to the babes.

"Her breasts are swelling with milk, and she is not ashamed to suckle the little ones.

"So the beloved Bride of the Lord Jesus, whose only task is to seek Him Whom her soul loves, seeks Him first of all in her bed of hidden and persevering meditation – and she does not find Him.

"Then she seeks Him further in the exercise of Holy Preaching – but, there too, she does not succeed in finding Him.

"Finally, she resorts to the third art of seeking, which is silent and humble listening . . .

"She looks for Him in the room of inner quietness, then she hurries out to take up the anxious responsibility of Preaching, and then she submits to the humility of discipleship, asking about her beloved Bridegroom at the Seat of Teaching . . .

"And now she is wearied, fainting from such great weariness . . . and so He comes at the desire of His Beloved.

"The One she longed for slips into her embrace, to be held all the more tightly, enjoyed the more delightfully, retained the more insistently, seeing how long He was sought, how hardly followed, and how late He was found by His Bride."

Amen, our good Brother John . . . let the Work of God now continue.

And the Brethren rise for the chanting of the next Psalms . . .

A Certain Monk tells of our Holy Brother Benedict in Heaven
Henry, Cardinal Bishop of Albano, before his elevation to High Office had been a Cistercian Monk . . . and so, from fondness of his former Brethren, had a "certain illiterate but plain-spoken Monk in his retinue."

And one Sunday during Lent it happened that Henry, for the amusement of his friends, did ask this Monk to preach unto them . . . and so, under Holy Obedience, he did preach.

Yes, again the coarse grey robe and the scarlet of pomp, the bare feet of the one and the soft white ermine of the other . . . the gold, the silver, the jewels . . . the expectant smile . . .

"When we are all dead and come to the Gates of Paradise," said our Brother, not even able to read a text for his Sermon, "there we shall meet our Holy Brother Benedict.

"Seeing us cowled Monks, he will welcome us in with joy – but when he sees Henry, Cardinal and Bishop, he will marvel at his mitre, and say: *Who art thou?*

"And Henry, Cardinal and Bishop, will say: *I am a Monk of Citeaux.* Then, while Henry pleads hard on his own behalf, Benedict will give sentence thus to the gate-keepers of Paradise: *Lay him on his back, and rip open his belly. If ye find therein unseasoned cabbages, beans, peas, lentils, pulse, and such food, let him be brought in with these Monks. But if ye find him filled with great fish and delicate fare, let him stay outside.*"

And, with these words, our Brother turned to the Cardinal Bishop, and said: "What wilt thou say at *that* hour, poor Henry?"

And the Cardinal Bishop "smiled at these words, and commended the Sermon" of our Brother. Amen.

A Certain Augustinian Friar tells of Preaching

The worn leather sandals, for he is an itinerant, the staff, for the ways are hard, the robes of wool, for the winds are cold . . .

"As Saint Austen saith, *God's Word ought to be worshipped as much as Christ's Body,* for it is more profitable to the soul to hear the Word of God in preaching than to hear any Mass, and rather should a man forbear his Mass than his Sermon.

"By preaching folk be stirred to contrition, to forsake sin and the Fiend, to love God and goodness and be illumined to know their God, to choose virtue from vice, truth from falsehood, and to forsake errors and heresies.

"But by the Mass be they not so.

"If they come to Mass in sin, they go away in sin – and if women come in shrews, as shrews they leave."

A Certain Dominican Monk is Truthful about Preaching

Humbert de Romans, Minister General of the Preaching Order of the Blessed Saint Dominic, sits in the Scriptorium of his Monastery, at work on his book, *The Preparation of Sermons* . . .

The black and white robes, the black of the ink and the white of the page . . . the white of the goose-quill . . . the silence, the inner sadness, the memory of other days around him . . .

Men of exalted position are rarely wont to hear Sermons, he writes, the letters beautiful, the words more black in his heart than any ink. *Note also that poor folk seldom come to church* . . .

132

He replenishes his pen in sorrow . . .
. . . . *seldom to Sermons.*
But cannot go on . . . for did not their Brother Dominic command them to preach unto the Salvation of souls?

Berthold of Regensburg tells of Devils and the Fires to Come
His Brother Franciscan, Roger Bacon, saith that this man before us is "one who, by his single efforts, hath more magnificent profit in preaching than all the other Friars of Saint Francis and Saint Dominic together."
The brown robes, the lean face, those glittering eyes . . .
"Hadst thou but once seen a single Devil in his true form," he saith, his words not yet more than kindling, "I should know for certain that thou wouldst never sin more . . .
"Because if the Satan came out at this moment from this forest hard by, and this city that we see before us were a burning fiery furnace heated through and through, then should ye see such a press of folk as was never yet seen . . . and all of them thronging headlong into that burning fiery furnace of Hell."
There are glances at that forest hard by . . . and *is* that a red glow in the sky over the city?
"These Devils," saith Berthold, "gladly suffer in this Hell, so long as the damned suffer also. They rejoice at every soul they win. They care less for Jews and heretics, because these belong to them already – and even of Christians they win the greater part.
"They haunt Sermons in their hundreds and hundreds, and even in their thousands, though they are neither seen nor heard . . ."
There are glances at neighbours, uneasy shiftings . . . shadows . . .
"And *this* is their cunning," saith Berthold, "for no man who hath once seen the Satan as He is would ever again fall into sin.
"Therefore, splash Him over with tears of remorse and penitence, as we splash a dog with boiling water when he thieves in the kitchen.
"For if thou hast but one mortal sin upon thee at thy death, then must thou to Hell, to be delivered unto this Satan.
"In Hell are all Pagans and heretics . . . and of Bishops, Abbots, and Priors there is no lack . . ."
Yes, there is now permitted the faintest of grim smiles . . .
"And *there*!" Now the thunder-clap of Doom . . . "And *there* do sinners suffer as many deaths as the motes that dance in the sun!"
The considered pause before the opening of those gates of iron . . .
"If thy whole body were of red-hot lead, and the whole

world, from earth to sky, one vast fire, and thou in the midst, *that* is how a man is in Hell: but that he is an hundredfold worse.

"And when, at the Last Day, soul and body are united again, and the two together must fall back into Hell, *then* will the damned feel it as much worse as the plunge from cool dew into a lake of fire."

Another pause . . . longer . . . until the silence is screaming . . .

"And these tortures will endure as many thousand years as there are drops in the sea, or as the number of all the hairs that have grown on man and beast since God first made Adam. And *then*," saith our Brother Berthold of Regensburg, "after all these years, the pains will only be at their beginning . . ."

And *then* doth one of our Sisters start screaming . . .

For it is a true saying, that *unless the Priests preached about Hell, they would surely starve.*

And Doctor Angelicus tells of Great Mysteries

Thomas Aquinas, a Monk of the Preaching Order of the Blessed Saint Dominic, now Abbot of our Brother Benedict's Abbey of Monte Cassino, ascends into his pulpit . . . a "tall and heavy man, thickset . . . large head like a pumpkin, bald . . . skin the colour of new wheat, his nose strong and aquiline, his mouth firm . . . stern . . . one eye larger than the other . . ."

Again the black and white robes, the elected silence . . .

He turns the page, but knows the text by heart, and "throws back his great head, closes his eyes, and grips the handrail of the pulpit so tightly that his knuckles shine white," so that he "gives the appearance of an Admiral on the prow of his ship . . . ordering the attack . . ."

What does he say?

Alas! this Doctor of the Angels hath mastered the Sum of Theology, his words are for the learned, the subtle, whose who can divide an already divided hair into its further divisions . . .

And we look up, hungry for living bread . . . and are given divided hairs arranged in the logical patterns of Theology now *gone* mad.

Theology gone Mad

John Pecham, Archbishop of Canterbury, issued his *Constitutions of Lambeth* towards the end of the thirteenth century. He was a Franciscan Friar, a scholar and poet, a true son of his time, and his instructions on Preaching are typically Medieval.

Every "Pastor had to preach to the people at least four times a year in their own tongue," and "explain the Five Chief Articles of Faith, the Ten Commandments, the Two Great Precepts of Charity in the Gospels, the Seven Corporal Works of Mercy, the Seven Deadly Sins, the Four Cardinal Virtues, and the Seven Sacraments."

And in this formal numerology we have a comparatively simple example of the demented complexity of the religious thought of Thomas Aquinas and all the other Doctors of the Church in their Trinities and in their Divisions: for their ideas came in threes, even sixes and sevens . . . and the more complicated the allegedly "Mystic" relationships between these numbers the happier they were.

It's interesting to remember that Christians began as the Children of God, that Jesus had His Brothers and Sisters, that the Disciples and Apostles addressed their audiences as "Men and Brethren" . . . but by the time of the Exodus back into the Desert it was "Fathers" and "Abbots" – and that *now* it's "Doctors" of the Church.

We have wandered a long way from home, my Brothers.

*   *   *

However, an anything like complete list of such subjects for Sermons as constituted by John Pecham would also have included the Three Eminent Good Works and the Three Evangelical Councils, the Four Sins Crying to Heaven for Vengeance and the Four Last Things to be Ever Remembered, the Four Theological Virtues and the Six Sins Against the Holy Spirit, the Seven Spiritual Works of Mercy and the Seven Contrary Virtues to the Seven Deadly Sins, the Seven Gifts of the Holy Spirit and the Eight Beatitudes, the Nine Ways in Which We May Cause or Share the Guilt of Another's Sin, and the Twelve Fruits of the Holy Spirit.

Even the Sermons of the Apostles, spontaneous utterances from first word to last, were divided into their supposed parts: Formal Greeting to the Hearers, Summary of the Blessings of God on Mankind, Reference to Guilt for Sin, Call to Repentance, Reminder of Judgement to Come, and Final Reference to Christ's Resurrection.

And, with extraordinary ingenuity, the Doctors of the Church were able to fit even the entirely different sort of preaching by Paul into some such pattern . . . and so formulate Rules for the Structure of the Sermon.

By the late thirteenth and early fourteenth century there were several *Manuals* and *Collections* of Sermons and Outlines, even Sets of Notes.

*　　*　　*

Typically, then, a Model Sermon would start with a *thema* or text, usually taken from the Old Testament or the Gospel or Epistle appointed to be read that day during Mass or the Divine Office.

Then would follow the *prothema* or "prelocution," which would cite the Authority or "proof" of the text. This was sometimes an elaborate set of quotations from other parts of the Bible, with secondary support from the Fathers and Doctors of the Church.

Then a Prayer for the success of the Sermon, that it would work for the Salvation or Confirmation of its hearers in the Faith.

Then the text would be repeated, with a "process," or statement of the various main sections into which the Sermon upon it was to be divided.

These sections or "divisions" were of two types: the *infra*, when the Sermon was being preached to fellow clerics, and could thus be "learned" . . . and the *extra*, when preached to the people, and had to be "secular," with "illustrations" from common daily life.

Each division of the "process" was a "principal," and every further division of a principal was a *socius* or "part" . . . with the amplification of these parts often tightly organised and even more complicated.

There could be as many as twenty forms of amplification, involving several of the Classical Modes of Rhetoric: the Historical or Literal, the Allegorical or Personified, the Tropological or Moralised, and the Anagogical or Mystical . . . with a "development" including further citations of Authority, parallels from secular history, and Analogies from the Bible or Lives of the Saints.

Then there would be a Recapitulation, leading into the Application of the whole Sermon to the needs of its hearers.

Finally, there would be another Prayer, perhaps a repetition of the text, and the Blessing and Dismissal.

*　　*　　*

True, not all of the surviving Sermons follow every last requirement of any standard pattern, but there's always some such structure . . . which, of course, it's impossible to demonstrate fully – except at the inordinate length they were preached, usually for an hour or more . . . tens of thousands of almost obsessional words.

Little wonder that the Church had lost or was losing the common people who had once listened to Jesus "so gladly . . ."

The Rule of the Dead

True, it wasn't only the increasing abstract remoteness of Theology that was disabusing the common people about the pretentions of the Church: there was the almost unbelieveable moral corruption of its professional clergy . . . and, more significantly, the impossible restrictions being chained on normal sexual loving by these ecclesiastical celibates.

*   *   *

About the corruption there is little historical doubt.

Pope Sergius the Third "contrived that his bastard son should succeed him as Supreme Pontiff . . ."

Pope John the Twelfth "turned the church of Saint John Lateran into a brothel," and, at his deposition in disgrace, was charged with "sacrilege, simony, perjury, murder, adultery, and incest."

Pope Leo the Eighth died when "struck by paralysis in the act of adultery . . ."

Pope Benedict the Ninth "shocked the sensibility even of a barbarous age" by his "greed and lechery . . ."

Balthasar Cossa, elected Pope to end the Great Schism, freely confessed to "incest, adultery, defilement, and homicide" . . . had "kept his brother's wife as mistress," and "seduced two hundred virgins, matrons, widows, and a few nuns."

Popes, Cardinals, Bishops, all the way down to Monks and Priests, all subjected to the demands of absolute celibacy, and mostly cracking under the inhuman strain. Sodomy, pederasty, and other

139

forms of homosexuality were popular in the Monasteries, flagellation was endemic, and desperate hysterical symptoms were welcomed as "miracles." Secular Priests exploited the Confessional as an easy means of seducing boys and women, with the threat of Hell as the ultimate "persuasion" into bed.

And the common people, who lived in squalid poverty, were lied to, and tricked, and robbed to pay for the gold and silver and jewels and soft white ermine and "great fish and delicate fare" in my Lord Bishop's Palace . . . and rotted in hovels while God was "worshipped" in Abbeys and Cathedrals and Temples made of starving flesh and aching bones . . .

Inasmuch as ye have done it unto the least of these, My Brethren, ye have done it unto Me . . .

*   *   *

There's even less doubt about the pathological restrictions which these perverted "celibates" tried to impose on normal sexual loving . . . with the word "pathological" being rooted in suffering and disease.

"Virginity," said the Church, "was a higher moral state than marriage, and, even within marriage, all sexual acts had to be confined to the minimum required for procreation."

"For a man to love his wife ardently," said Peter Lombard, "was worse than adultery."

The sexual act was "only permitted in one position," which was then described in obsessional detail, with numerous severe penalties for "sinful" variations.

Even *this* sexual act was "illegal on Sundays, Wednesdays, and Fridays," the "Forty Days of Lent and the Forty Days before Christmas," for "three days before partaking in Holy Communion," and "from the conception of a child unto forty days after the birth."

It was also strictly forbidden during "all the days of any Penance imposed by a Priest after Confession as the condition for his Absolution of sins" . . . and these Penances could be from seven days to seven years – sometimes for life.

And, if there weren't prohibitions enough, Thomas Aquinas was always in reserve: "Masturbation," said the Angelic Doctor, "is a greater sin than fornication . . ."

It was even a "sin" for a menstruating woman to enter a church. Yes, woman as the "sewer" . . . the "very Satan" of Jerome . . .
Surely this is Hell . . . but who these Hellish?

*   *   *

Not that any of these Rules of the Dead seemed to do much good.

"We have been absolutely submerged under a flood of fornication, adultery, and incest," said Alcuin, one voice in a chorus, "so that the very semblance of modesty is entirely absent."

And even the behaviour of people in church wasn't at all what the Preachers believed they had an absolute right to expect.

"It irks you to stand decently for a short hour in here," said our Brother Berthold of Regensburg during one of his Sermons. "You laugh and chatter as if you were at a Fair. And ye women, ye never give your tongues a rest from useless talk! One tells the other how glad the maidservant is to sleep, and how loth to work. Another tells of her husband, a third complains that her children are troublesome and sickly!"

Antonio, the Archbishop of Florence, was saying much the same about his Tuscans and clergy: "In the churches they sometimes dance and leap with women. On Holy Days they spend little time in hearing of the whole Mass, but in games, or in taverns, or in brawls at the

141

church doors. They blaspheme God and His Saints, they are filled with lies and perjuries. Of fornication, and of worse sins still, they make no conscience. They use witchcraft and enchantments for themselves and for their beasts. And their Parish Priests care not for the flock committed unto them, do not instruct them through Preaching, or by private admonitions, but walk in the same errors, following their corrupt ways . . ."

A century later it was even worse . . .

"O Priests!" said John Colet, the Dean of Saint Paul's Cathedral, "O Priesthood! O the detestable boldness of wicked men in this our wicked generation! O the abominable impiety of these miserable Priests, of whom this age of ours contains a great multitude, who fear not to rush from the bosom of some foul harlot into the Temple of the Church, to the Altar of Christ, to the Mysteries of God!"

* * *

And the common people were soon to be heard.

* * *

Words of Revolt

John Ball was a poor English Priest of Kent in the fourteenth century, who preached the doctrine of human dignity and equality before God when such Christian ideas were condemned by the Church as heresies. Indeed, almost as usual, the Bishops and Clergy were as good as unanimous in siding with the Kings and Nobility against the common people, and our Brother John was forbidden to preach by Archbishop Langham of Canterbury, excommunicated, and imprisoned several times.

"For this foolish Priest," wrote Froissart in his *Chronicles,* "used often on Sundays after Mass, when the people were coming out of the churches in the villages, to go into yard, and assemble the people about him, and preach."

And what were his words of fire?

"My good people, things cannot go well in England, nor ever shall, till everything be made common, and there are neither villeins nor gentlemen, but we shall all be united together, and the Lords shall be no greater Masters than ourselves.

"What have we deserved that we should be kept thus enslaved?

"We are all descended from one father and mother, Adam and Eve.

"What reasons can they give to show that they are greater Lords than we, save by making us toil and labour, so that they can spend?

"They are clothed in velvet and soft leather furred with ermine, while we wear coarse cloth. They have their wines, spices, and good bread, while we have the drawings of the chaff, and drink water. They have handsome houses and manors, and we the pain and travail, the rain and the wind, in the fields.

"And it is from our labour that they get the means to keep their estates.

"We are called their serfs, their slaves, and if we do not serve them readily we are whipped.

"But we have no person to whom we may complain, or who will hear us, or give us justice . . . We shall have it otherwise, or else we will provide a remedy ourselves.

"And if we be together, all manner of people that are now in bondage will follow us, with the intent to be made free."

*   *   *

143

Little has changed: the rich get richer, the poor get poorer . . . but it's less dangerous to say such Christian words these days.

"For saying which," wrote Froissart, no lover of rebels and heretics, "many of the common people loved him . . . And so they would murmur to each other in the fields and in the roadways, as they came together, affirming the truth that John Ball spoke."

After generations of hunger and repression and brutality, these common people eventually rose in 1381: the Revolt of the Peasants, which was ruthlessly put down by the King and his Lords Temporal, with the willing help of my Lords Spiritual . . . the Church, God help it.

All the ancient weapons of the State were used: lies and false promises, the sword, the club, the rope, the whip . . . and many good men and women, our Brothers and Sisters, were hanged or flogged or branded or imprisoned in the Name of the King, and with the Blessings of my various Lords, the Bishops.

Peace, my Brother John, across the centuries, Love and Peace.

*　　*　　*

But those words smouldered on . . . and, from time to time, when the winds of change were blowing in the right direction, burst into those ancient flames that will never die while Christ lives.

*　　*　　*

"Christ was poor," said John de Wycliffe, "and the Church is rich.

"Christ was meek and low, and the Church full high and proud,

"Christ was suffering and forgave, and the Church will be avenged.

"Christ forsook worldly glory, and the Church seeks it.

"Christ washed the feet of the Disciples, and the Pope will suffer men to kiss his feet while kneeling on their knees.

"Christ came to serve, and the Pope and the Cardinals and the Bishops seek to be served.

"Christ walked on His feet, and His Disciples with Him, to teach and to change the people in cold and in heat, and in wet and in dry, while the Pope and the Cardinals and the Bishops will keep their feet full clean with scarlet and cordwain, and with sandals, with gold, with silver, and silk preciously adorned.

"Christ went in great sweat and labour, while they sit in their proud castles with their proud ways.

"Christ preached and blessed, and they curse and bless full seldom.

"Christ forsook, and they take gifts full great.

"Christ gave, and they fast holden.

"Christ purchased Heaven, and they Lordships on earth to be rich.

"Christ rode on an ass, and they on fat palfreys.

"Christ was pursued, and they pursue.

"Christ was despised, and they despisen.

"Christ gave power, and they take away.

"Christ made free men, and they maken bond.

"Christ brought out prisons, they imprison.

"Christ loosed, and they burden.

"Christ raised to life, and they bringen to death."

*   *   *

The Church never quite managed to get its hooks into our living Brother, but, thirty years after his natural death, they dug up his body and bones, and burnt them . . . throwing the ashes into a brook near Lutterworth.

"This brook conveyed them into the River Avon," wrote Thomas Fuller, "the Avon into the River Severn, the Severn into the narrow seas, they into the Main Ocean – and thus the ashes of Wycliffe were the emblem of his doctrine, which is now dispersed all the world over."

*   *   *

"Ye that be Prelates," said Hugh Latimer, preaching at Saint Paul's Cathedral, not far in time and distance from where he was to be burned alive as a heretic, "Ye that be Prelates, look well to your Office – for right prelating is busy labouring, and not Lording.

"Therefore preach and teach, and let your plough be doing.

"Ye Lords, I say, that live like loiterers, look well to your Office, for the plough is your Office and Charge. If you live idle and loiter, you do not your Duty, you follow not your Vocation. Let your plough therefore be going, and not cease, that the ground may bring forth fruit.

"But they that be Lords will go ill to the plough, for it is no meet Office to them, not seeming for their Estate.

"Because ever since the Prelates were made Lords and Nobles, the plough standeth, there is no spiritual work done, and the people starve.

"For these Prelates hawk, they hunt, they play cards, they dice, they pastime in their Prelacies with gallant gentlemen, with their dancing minions, and with their fresh companions, so that ploughing is set aside – and, by their Lording and loitering, preaching and ploughing is clean gone . . ."

*   *   *

"The pride of great men is now intolerable," said the common people of Norfolk at the beginning of yet another ruthlessly suppressed rebellion against the tyranny of Church and State, "but our condition miserable. These abound in delights and compassed with the fullness of all things, and consumed with vain pleasure, thirst only after gain, and are inflamed with the burning of their desires, but we are almost killed with labour and watching, and do nothing all our life but sweat, mourn, hunger, and thirst . . .

"Nature hath provided for us, as well as for them, hath given us a body and a soul . . . While we have the same form, and the same condition of birth together with them, why should they have a life so unlike to ours, and differ so far from us in calling?

"We desire liberty, and an equal use of all things: this we will have, otherwise these tumults and our lives shall end together."

*   *   *

Patience, but a little while longer, Men and Brethren.

146

Behold! The Hailstorm of the Lord!

And now these words of fire were being spoken not only in England but all over Europe . . . even in Italy, where Rome was now established as the First City of Christendom.

For consider our Brother Savonarola in the Florence of the fifteenth century, who came to believe after ten years as a Dominican Monk that the "Church must be castigated and reformed with the greatest speed" . . . and dared to say so.

He preached on that one theme, with variations: the "Church was ripe for a great scourge," and there were "seven, even eight reasons for this imminent visitation. The wickedness of men, become so terrible that the measure was now full . . . murders, lechery, sodomy, idolatry, astrology, and simony. Then the wickedness of those who should be the Shepherds of the Flock. Then that men ignored the Prophecies of God. Then that the Good had lost strength in every condition of men. Then the decline of Faith in human hearts. Then the extreme corruption of the Church. Then contempt for the Saints of God. And then the decay of Religion."

And he saw himself as the "hailstorm that shall break the heads of those who do not take shelter," and his style was "vigorous, rough," with "graceless gestures" . . . yet he was popular, and the common people heard him as "gladly" as they have heard so many others in their time.

"Behold, I am returned among my children," he'd begin a Sermon, "and so I greet you, again I greet you, and beg you rejoice with me!"

And he attacked everything the cultivated Florentines held most dear: Humanist Philosophy, Poets, Men of Letters, the Arts in general . . . but also the rich and the powerful, and the moral corruption of the Church.

Especially the corruption of the Church . . . because Cardinal Rodrigo Borgia had recently bribed or threatened enough of his fellow Fathers in God to be elected Pope.

*   *   *

He took the name of Alexander the Sixth, and even some Roman Catholic historians admit that he was "unscrupulous and a man of bad life, utterly unworthy of his High Office."

The opinion of his contemporaries was that he was "most wicked, without sincerity, without shame, without truth, without faith, without religion," and "displayed insatiable avarice, immoderate ambition," and "cruelty more than barbarous . . . "

Other historians colour-in a few of those outlines:

One evening the Pope "ordered fifty prostitutes to be sent to his chambers." After the usual sumptuous supper with his son, Cesare, and his daughter, Lucrezia, these prostitutes were ordered to "dance with the servitors and others who were present," at first "clothed," but soon "naked." Then they had to crawl around the floor on their hands and knees, with "many candlesticks so placed as to illuminate their shameless nakedness to best advantage." Finally, "a number of prizes were produced," and it was announced that they would be given to "those men who should have carnal knowledge of the greatest number of the said prostitutes."

*   *   *

"I tell you," said Savonarola, "if Saint Peter came back on earth now, and wished to reform the Church, he could not do so. Nay, he would be put to death. The wickedness of God's Sanctuary cries out aloud from the earth."

And he had the courage (or was foolish enough) to preach the truth to the very people he was "measuring by the plumb-line" of God.

Here's as extract from a Sermon in the presence of Lorenzo de Medici, known as the Magnificent:

"In any city all good and all evil come from the head, and if the head walked in righteousness that city would become the City of God.

"If the head did not so walk, his sin would indeed be great, though it be only the sin of omission.

"But *here*, in Florence, the tyrants of the city were incorrigible and sunk in darkness, and were proud and listened only to flattery. They did not restore what had been taken unjustly, they levied arbitrary taxes, exploited the peasants, oppressed the poor, bribed voters, chose evil officials, and debased the currency . . . all to the great distress of the citizens."

Can you hear *that* in Westminster Cathedral?

And Savonarola well knew his Princes and Lords:

"I ought to begin with Princes and the great, but rarely, if ever, do they go to hear Sermons – and, when they do, they expect to hear things that do not displease them.

"These Princes and great men, as though they did not know they were only men like others, want to be honoured and blessed by all. Yet the true Preacher cannot flatter them. Rather will he attack their vices. Hence, because he does not behave to

148

them like others, they cannot suffer him. He must therefore expect of them tribulation, either openly or by insidious guile."

And he often rose to impassioned eloquence:

"O Italy, all you cities of Italy, *now* is the time for all your sins to be punished. O Italy, for your lust, your avarice, your pride, your ambition, your thieving and extortion, there will come upon you many adversities and many scourges.

"O Florence, O Florence, for your sins, there will come upon you many trials and tribulations.

"On whom can you call?

"O Clergy, who are the principal cause of so many evils, through your evil-doing comes this storm, by your sins have been prepared so many tribulations. Woe, woe, I say unto those that bear the tonsure!

"I have cried out so often, I have wept for you so many times, my Florence . . . I have wished to speak this morning to you, and each and every one openly and sincerely, for I could do no other.

"We turn to Thee, O Lord, Who died for love of us.

"Forgive, forgive, Lord, this Thy people!

"Forgive, Lord, the people of Florence!"

*   *   *

Eventually, after times of apparent success and times of obvious failure, he went too far, got involved in the labyrinthine plottings of the Florentine political parties . . . the Church moved, and the Pope issued a Brief against him. Another quickly followed. Savonarola was now a "scandalous propagator of new dogmatic errors, of heretical propositions, of nonsense" . . . and he was suspended from preaching.

The end was in sight . . . still at a distance, with many convolutions between, but inevitable.

But he went on preaching:

"Come, Leaders of the Church, come Priests, come Friars, come Novices, you go at night to your concubines, and the morning after you go to take the Holy Sacrament . . .

"You sell benefices, and even the Blood of Christ and relics of the Virgin for money . . . you talk only of evil, of fornicating with women, sodomy with boys . . .

"I am ordered by Christ to preach His Truth as long as I draw breath . . .

"Rome may do what she pleases, she will never put out *this* flame . . . the truth will always burst forth . . ."

He organised a "burning of the vanities" in Florence, a "great pyramid of obscene books and pictures, lutes, women's false hair, cosmetics, perfumes, mirrors, dolls, playing-cards, dice, gaming-tables . . ."

"O wretched Church!" he shouted, "listen to me! You harlot! You used to be ashamed of pride and lasciviousness. *Now* you are proud of your sins! Once your Priests had the shame to call their own children their *nephews* – now they are called *sons*, not nephews, *sons* everywhere!"

This was a reference to the Pope's latest bastard . . . and it was yet another faggot of dry wood for the fire being prepared for Savonarola.

*   *   *

And, like so many before him, and so many since, he had this craving to die a martyr . . . for the "death of martyrs is not death, but birth, because it is not death to go to live with Jesus."

"Lord," he prayed, "cause me to be persecuted. I ask Thee this favour – that I may not die in my bed, but that I may shed my blood for Thee, as Thou hast done for me."

His prayer was to be granted.

First, he was excommunicated . . .

> "Lord," he preached, "I who am mere dust and ashes, I beg Thee, Lord, to remain with me. I ask Thee not for gold or silver, not for peace and tranquillity, but only to give me light . . . the natural light of reason and the supernatural light of faith . . .
>
> "O Christ, I turn to Thee. Thou didst die for the truth, and I am content to die for Thy truth. I offer myself to Thee as a sacrifice . . .
>
> "O Rome! You think to frighten me, but I know no fear."

The Pope's anger exploded, letters were sent, orders given: unless Savonarola was handed over, Florence would suffer . . . merchants would be seized in Rome and their goods confiscated . . .

Florence might defy Papal censure, but *this* was trade, money, profit. What can you expect of Big Business?

He was arrested amid "riots and assaults," bound, spat upon, struck, kicked, imprisoned, and "examined diligently" . . . which meant tortured, again and again and again, agony on agony, his arms dislocated, leaving him so maimed that "food had to be put into his mouth for him . . ."

See how those Christians love one another . . .

The Pope sent a "letter of congratulation," accompanied by a "Bull of Plenary Indulgence to all Florentines" . . . all of their sins were now forgiven them, in both this world and the next.

Savonarola was then tried "according to the Law of the

Church" . . . and even during this trial there was further torture . . .

"Now, hear me, O God," he said as he was forced to watch the sadistic preparations, "I confess that I have denied Christ under torture. If I must suffer, I wish to suffer for the Truth. You givest me this penance for having denied Thee. I deserve it. I *have* denied Thee, I *have* denied Thee, I have denied Thee for fear of torture."

When he had been stripped, he kept on repeating: "I *have* denied Thee, Lord, for fear of torture". And as he was slowly drawn up on the rope to have his arms dislocated yet again he said: "Help me, Jesus."

And, eventually . . . eventually . . . half alive, he was burned at the stake as a heretic.

Thus did Roman Catholic murder Roman Catholic in the Name of Christ.

A Rough German Woodcut

So there he stands in the evening of this April day, the year of our One Lord, fifteen-hundred-and-twenty-one, arraigned before the High Council in the city of Worms: Martin Luther, son of a miner, now an Augustinian Friar . . . one foot on the neck of the Middle Ages, the other kicking the Reformation into struggling life.

Medium height, "emaciated from care and study, so that you can almost count his bones through his skin . . ."

He who can do no other. God help him. Amen.

And there sits young Charles the Fifth of the Holy Roman Empire, Archduke of Austria, Duke of Burgundy, Master of the Low Countries, Spain, and Naples.

He who is descended from a long line of Christian Emperors of this noble German Nation, and from the Catholic Kings of Spain, faithful unto death to the Church of Rome . . . flanked by his Lords Temporal and Spiritual, the six Princely Electors of Germany, Dukes, Prelates of that Church, Bishops, Priests, Doctors of Theology and the Law . . . servants of their retinues, soldiers, armed guards . . .

The coarse woollen tunic of the Friar, the hood thrown back, the white girdle, the sandals . . . and the gorgeous embroidered robes and fine soft furs of his Judges in this case of heresy . . . crimson, purple, scarlet, emerald green . . . the gleam of gold, the clank of steel swords . . . and this scattering of books on an oaken table . . .

"Do you wish to defend these books which are recognised as your work?" demands the Official representing the Archbishop of Triers. "Or to retract anything contained in them?"

"Most Serene Lord Emperor," begins our Brother Martin, his voice ringing, clear, penetrating, "Most Illustrious Princes, Most Gracious and Clement Lords . . ."

*   *   *

Except that his words *then* weren't those that shook the world.

In aching truth, it was probably only *one* word that did the shaking . . .

*   *   *

Eleven years before this trial he'd been sent by his Order to Rome as a representative in the settlement of a Monastic dispute – and, in the pious course of visiting all the Shrines and Churches, the Catacombs and Basilicas, venerating the Holy Relics of Martyred Saints, he'd ascended the *Scala Sancta* . . . the Holy Stairs.

These were a flight of twenty-eight marble steps leading to the Papal Chapel in the old Lateran Palace, brought to Rome by the Helen who'd also found the True Cross. These steps were then believed to have been those which had led up to Pilate's Hall in Jerusalem . . . and so the very stones trodden by Christ on His way to Judgement. And this staircase was ascended by the Faithful on their knees as an act of Penitence and Devotion – for if you did that, and said a *Pater Noster* on every step, you would release a soul from Purgatory.

Yes, we have seen the flames of Eternal Hell, heard the screams of the tortured Damned . . . but the doctrine had become so encompassing, so implacable, so merciless, and offered so little hope that anybody at all could ever escape its everlasting punishments, that another and more gentle fate for sinners had emerged from the subtle minds of the various Doctors of the Church: Purgatory.

And off we wander into the Medieval labyrinth . . .

*   *   *

Martinus Lutherus.

What is Purgatory?

Purgatory is that place and state in which souls after death are purged or purified before being allowed into Heaven.

What souls go to Purgatory?

Those souls go to Purgatory that depart this life in Venial sin, or that have not fully paid the debt of Temporal punishment due to those sins of which the guilt has been forgiven.

What is Sin?

Sin is an offence against God, by any thought, word, deed, or omission against the Law of God.

How many kinds of Sin are there?

There are two kinds of sin, Original and Actual.

What is Actual Sin?

Actual sin is every sin which we ourselves commit, there being two kinds, Mortal Sin and Venial Sin.

What is Mortal Sin?

Mortal sin is a serious offence against God, so serious that it kills the soul and deserves Hell, and they who die in Mortal sin will go to Hell for all eternity.

What is Venial Sin?

Venial sin is an offence which does not kill the soul, yet is displeasing to God, and often leads to Mortal sin.

What is Temporal Punishment?

Temporal Punishment is punishment which will have an end, either in this world, or in the world to come.

What is the Temporal Punishment of Purgatory?

The Temporal Punishment of Purgatory is the pain of intense longing for God, and also, as is commonly taught, some pain of the senses, inflicted probably by material fire.

How can you prove that there is a Purgatory?

You can prove that there is a Purgatory from the constant teaching of the Church, and from the Holy Scriptures which declare that "God will render to every man according to his works," that "nothing defiled shall enter Heaven," and that some will be Saved "yet so as by fire."

Can the Souls in Purgatory be helped?

It is of Faith that the souls in Purgatory can be helped by the prayers, the devotions, and the sacrifices of the faithful on earth, most

154

especially by the acceptable Sacrifice on the Altar, and by means of indulgences.

What is an Indulgence?
An Indulgence is the remission before God of the temporal punishment due to those Venial sins of which the guilt has been forgiven, and is either Partial or Plenary.

What is a Partial Indulgence?
A Partial Indulgence is an Indulgence which remits part of the temporal punishment being suffered by a soul in Purgatory, expressed in terms of time – as, for example, thirty days or seven years.

What is a Plenary Indulgence?
A Plenary Indulgence is an Indulgence which remits all of the temporal punishment being suffered by a soul in Purgatory, so that the soul is at once allowed into Heaven amid great rejoicing.

To whom is granted the power to grant Indulgences?
The power to grant Indulgences is granted, by Divine Authority, to the Pope as the Head of the Church. For to him, and to him alone, is committed the dispensation of the whole Treasury of the Church.

How may we obtain an Indulgence?
We may obtain an Indulgence by saying the required prayers, making the required devotions, or performing the required penance . . .

*   *   *

Well, at the top of the *Scala Sancta,* having duly said the "required prayers," made the "required devotions," performed the "required penance," and "kissed each step for good measure," our Brother Martin stood up . . . and years afterwards told his friends that he'd said: "Who knows whether any of it is true or not?"

*   *   *

Though he'd always had such doubts . . . been in terror of the Holy.
With what tongue could *he* possibly address the Creator of the Universe?
Who was *he* to so much as lift up his eyes towards Heaven?
For he was "but dust and ashes and full of sin" in the "presence of the Living, Eternal, and True God" . . . so desperately conscious of

155

the "terrifying gulf" between "Divine Justice" and his own wickedness that he "lost faith" in his own capacity to do anything about his own Salvation.

And he "craved for certainty" that he would "avoid damnation."

Proposition: That man was vitiated by sin, powerless for good, and could contribute nothing to his own Justification before God.

Ergo: To strive for merit was all in vain.

Which doubts and thoughts and scruples, as a good Friar under the Vow of Obedience, he confessed.

"God is not angry with you," he was told. "*You* are angry with God."

And then, in a surprisingly modern piece of psychological understanding, he was ordered by his Superior to study for his Doctor's Degree in Theology, "begin preaching," and "assume the Chair of Bible" at the University of Wittenberg.

Yes, perhaps the Scriptures would be the Balm of Gilead to his soul, perhaps the Holy Spirit would resolve his doubts, answer his questions.

And his "illumination" came up in the Scriptorium of that Monastery at Wittenberg, high in the Tower overlooking the city.

*   *   *

During the studies necessary for the preparation of a Course of Sermons on the Letter of the Apostle Paul to the Christians at Rome, which he preached in the Autumn of 1515, he saw that Paul was writing of the "Justice of God" . . . and our Brother "trembled." For if we received God's "Justice" we would "suffer everlasting torment, inhale sulphurous fumes, and writhe in most fearful incandescent but unconsuming flames."

But in the original Greek of Paul that word "Justice" had a pair of meanings, translated in English as either "justice" or "justification," with similar meanings in German. *Justice* is a "strict enforcement of the Law," as when a Judge pronounces sentence . . . but *Justification* is when the Judge suspends the sentence, or puts the prisoner on parole, or "expresses confidence and personal interest in the prisoner" – so that the prisoner is "reclaimed," and Justice itself is better served than by the "exaction of its uttermost punishment."

"I stood before God as a sinner troubled in conscience," he said, "and I had no confidence that my own merit would assuage Him. Therefore I did not love a Just and Angry God, but rather hated and murmured against Him.

"Night and day I pondered, until I saw the connection between the Justice of God and the statement by Paul that

Justus autem ex fide vivit . . . The just man liveth by faith.

"It was then I grasped that the Justice of God is that righteousness by which, through Grace and sheer Mercy, God Justifies us through Faith.

"Thereupon I felt myself to be reborn, and to have gone through open doors into Paradise . . .

"This passage of Paul became to me a Gate into Heaven."

*   *   *

Proposition: That Salvation could be attained *only* through the recognition of God's power to effect Redemption by the free imputation of His Goodness to those who have Faith in His power so to do.

Ergo: Justification is by Faith Alone.

Quod erat demonstrandum . . .

Of such is the stuff of Theology, with the Reformation built not merely on the cleared foundations of a corrupt Church, but also on that one innocent word *Alone . . .*

And off they go:

"This Satan," said the Pope, "this Son of Iniquity . . . this most evil and pernicious heresy . . ."

The Dominicans called him a "leper with a brain of brass and a nose of iron . . . author of damned and pestiferous errors . . ."

"Are *you* alone wise, Martin?" asked even his friends, "and all the ages wrong? Do you set yourself up against the Fathers and Doctors?"

He soon became "this morbid and troubled Friar" with his "coarse language," whose writings "passed all bounds of decency," being "full of gross obscenities."

By the time of his excommunication he had "abandoned the whole Roman Catholic conception of Christianity," said the Roman Catholic Christians with one accord, "denounced the Pope as the Anti-Christ," and had "introduced the dangerous error that the Scriptures could be read and interpreted by the unqualified" . . . which "inevitably leads to schism and lamentable confusions. Indeed," they said, taking an even longer view in hindsight, "this complete denial of any independent power for good in Fallen Man had terrible implications in that it contained the seeds of all future Protestantism: the Unfree Will, Predestination, the Priesthood of all Believers, the Spiritual Church as opposed to the Actual Church Militant on Earth, and the Attack on the Pope, the Hierarchy, and Sacramentalism."

Nor are they yet done with his body and bones . . . *still,* after these centuries, there are feet kicking away at ashes . . .

"If we wish to find a scapegoat on whose shoulders we may lay the miseries which Germany has brought upon the world," wrote Dean Inge, a Protestant, and no great lover of Roman Catholic Doctrines, "I am more and more convinced that the worst evil genius of that country is not Hitler or Bismark or Frederick the Prussian, but Martin Luther . . . There is very little to be said for this coarse and foul-mouthed man. It is a real misfortune for Humanity that he appeared just at the crisis in the Christian world. Even our own Henry the Eighth was not a worse man, and did far less mischief."

*   *   *

"I cannot and I will not recant anything," said our Brother Martin, "for to go against conscience is neither right nor safe. Here I stand. I cannot do otherwise. God help me. Amen."

Yes, words of fire . . . but the fires they lit hardly went out over Europe for a hundred years.

The Agonies of Glory

After those beginnings of what we know as the Reformation, the Theologians of both armed camps became slightly less interested in abstruse speculations, and concentrated their merciless attentions on attempts to "prove" by the manipulation of Biblical texts that all the "others" were totally wrong, the "spawn of Satan," and deserved nothing better than slaughtering as heretics. Scholarship was sharpened into a weapon, disputation was refined as an instrument of torture . . . and Theology was no longer the "Queen of Sciences," but a whore – with the precisely calculated agonies of death as her gift.

* * *

The sixteenth century in England was what some enthusiasts regard as an Age of Faith or something . . . when Christian butchered Christian in the Holy Name of Christ: Protestants hanged and disembowelled Roman Catholics, Roman Catholics burned Protestants alive, and Protestants variously imprisoned and tortured and murdered other Protestants for daring to disagree about trivial and unverifiable details of doctrine.

Yes, from heresy and schism and those who dare to disagree, *the Good Lord deliver us* . . . but, at the same time as the persecutors prowled the land, searching for whom they could flog and rack and burn or hang or put under the axe, there were also the persecuted only too willing to be persecuted, would-be Martyrs hungering and thirsting after the glories of Martyrdom.

And this so great a cloud of ecstatic witnesses, Protestants and Roman Catholics alike, seemed to welcome the kiss of the whip, and the sharpened steel bit into their joyous flesh as the teeth of an urgent lover . . . even flames were merely the passionate pangs of love fulfilled.

Faith in the substance of things hoped for? the evidence of things not seen? Or festering masochism? the sickness of bigoted minds?
Lord, now lettest Thou Thy Servants depart in peace . . .

* * *

Nothing new in the idea of Martyrdom, being the "voluntary endurance of death for the Christian Faith, or for the preservation of some Christian virtue" – usually understood as the refusal to worship

159

or honour other gods, and the defence of virginity.

Remember our Brother Stephen? or Ignatius of Antioch "lusting after death"? or Polycarp "abiding in the fire unflinchingly"?

Yes, those tens of thousands who likewise refused to deny Christ, and were "butchered to make a Roman holiday" . . . all that "noble army" who voluntarily endured death for the Christian Faith . . . *Praise Them!*

* * *

Little new in the idea of heresy, being the "sin of formal denial or doubt of any revealed truth of the Christian Faith," with the "crime" being the "outward or pertinacious manifestation of the sin."

Because there always *have* been those few stubborn people who either can't or won't see eye-to-eye with the vast majority about Religion or Politics or the correct way to eat a boiled egg . . . it being "allowed by all hands that the primitive way of breaking eggs before we eat them" is "upon the larger end," though many people have "suffered death rather than submit to break their egg at the smaller end."

And there always *will* be those who choose the "wrong" end.

* * *

Neither was there much disagreement between Protestants and Roman Catholics about the principle that heretics should be punished.

"Heresy," wrote the Protestant Lord Coke at the time, "is an infectious leprosy of the soul, and must therefore be cut off, lest it diffuse the contagion."

"Canon Law," wrote the Roman Catholic John Lynch, summing up more recently, "asserted that the Christian State must give the heretic due punishment, and the Church accepted the fact that this might involve burning at the stake."

And most of the heretics who *were* "cut off" had freely consented to the "cutting off" of those who had chosen the other or "wrong" end of the Theological egg – often having been present at the punishment . . . while some had actually taken an active part in the murderous butchery.

Thomas Cranmer, for example: He "personally consigned" the Protestant John Lambert to Roman Catholic flames for the heresy of refusing to believe in Transubstantiation . . . the "miraculous conversion" of the bread and wine at Holy Communion into the "actual Body and Blood of Christ." A few years later he changed his mind, "laid down that belief in this Papist Doctrine was heretical," declared that "those who should persist in such belief should suffer death" . . . and was "instrumental" in the burnings of Roman Catholics as "wilful and unregenerate heretics." And then, finally, he died heroically in Roman Catholic flames as a Protestant heretic himself . . . protesting his faith in "Christ Jesus" to the last.

*   *   *

There was even less new about the ancient "cure" for heresy.

"When you hear any speak ill of the Church," said Saint Louis, of Holy and Blessed Memory, "defend Her not with words, but the sword, which you should thrust into the belly of the heretic as far as it will go."

Or: "Ye shalt be handed over to the Secular Arm, and shalt suffer due penalty, for thus shalt thou be Saved, as saith the Holy Scriptures, *yet so as by fire.*"

Or: "Ye shall be drawn on a hurdle through the open city to the place of execution, and there be hanged and let down alive, and your privy parts cut off, and your entrails taken out and burnt in your sight, then your head to be cut off, and your body divided into four parts, to be disposed of as shall be thought fit . . ."

And may the Lord God Almighty have mercy upon your soul.

No, there was little or nothing new about any of this, neither martyrdom nor heresy . . . least of all the stake, the rope, and the knife.

The new factor was that the grounds for conviction as a heretic became less and less important, more and more unverifiably trivial . . .

"Christ saith that the Bread is His Body," said Justice Browne at one trial. "How say you?"

"Through Christ *call* the bread His Body," said William Hunter, "as He doth also say that He is a Vine or a Door, yet not is His Body turned into bread, no more than He is turned into a Door or Vine. Christ called the bread His Body by a figure of speech."

"Thou art a villain indeed," said Justice Browne. "Wilt thou make Christ a liar?"

And for this difference over a point of Rhetoric was William Hunter burned alive at the stake, "going forward cheerfully," and "embracing the wood of the fire in his arms . . ."

What courage for a "figure of speech" . . . a form of words . . .

*   *   *

Yet they all seemed to share that courage . . .

The Protestant Lawrence Sanders "went with a merry heart towards the fire," and "took the stake in his arms and kissed it" . . . and, "being fastened" and "fire put to him," he "full sweetly slept in the Lord."

The Roman Catholic Richard Reynolds "encouraged his companions" at Tyburn, saying: "We have promise of a Heavenly Supper this night in exchange for our sharp breakfast this morning, to be eaten patiently . . ."

The Protestant Rawlins White, in the presence of his wife and children, "kissed the ground at the stake," and "laid the reeds and the wood about his own person with such a cheerful countenance that all were astonished."

The Roman Catholic Polydore Plasden "kissed the rope," saying: "O sweet Christ, I will never deny thee for a thousand lives."

The Protestant John Hooper "smilingly beheld the stake and the preparations made for him . . ."

The Roman Catholic John Boste was "cut down from the rope while still alive," and, "as his heart was torn from his body," said to the hangman: "God will forgive thee . . . go on, go on . . ."

But does it any longer matter whether they were Protestants or

Roman Catholics? Does entrance into the Kingdom of God depend on which end of the egg you choose?

John Cardmaker "kissed the stake sweetly," and "gave himself to be bound to it most gladly . . ."

Thomas Garnet at Tyburn said: "I am the happiest man alive this day."

John Almond said: "One hour overtaketh another, and though never so long, at last comes death. And yet not death, for *this* death is the Gate of Life unto us, whereby we enter into Everlasting Blessedness."

John Kemble saw the "hangman to hesitate at this dispatch of so old and frail a man," and said to him: "Be not afraid, do thy office. I forgive thee with all my heart. Thou wilt do me a greater kindness than discourtesy."

So they all passed over, and the trumpets sounded for them on the other side . . .

*   *   *

And they all seemed to share an eloquence to shame most Sermons . . . for their words from the stake or the gallows were nearly always terse and simple to the edge of being heart-breaking, more passionate and compelling as preaching than hours from any pulpit.

*   *   *

Rowland Taylor "went to the stake and kissed it . . ."

"Good people," he said when he had been bound, "I have taught thee nothing but God's Holy Word, and those lessons I have taken out of God's Blessed Book, the Holy Bible. And I am now come hither this day to seal it with my blood."

Then a man called Warwick cast a burning faggot of wood at his head, wounding him in the face so that the blood ran down.

"Friend," he said, "I have harm enough, what needed that?"

And then the fire reached his flesh . . .

"Merciful Father of Heaven," he said, "for Jesus Christ's my Saviour's sake receive my soul into Thy hands."

Two Sermons there, both short: one in words, one the deed.

*   *   *

Robert Southwell, at Tyburn, smiled and said: "This my death, my last farewell to this unfortunate life, and yet to me most happy and most fortunate. I pray it may be for the full satisfaction of my sins, for the good of my country, and for the comfort of many others. Which death, although it here seems disgraceful, yet I hope that in time to come it will be to my Eternal Glory."

Remember, Man, he'd written, *that thou art dust!*

*   *   *

"Well," said Nicholas Ridley as he and Hugh Latimer stripped themselves for the stake, "so long as the breath is in my body I will never deny my Lord Christ, and His known Truth. God's Will be done in me . . . O Heavenly Father, I give unto Thee most hearty thanks, for that Thou hast called me to be a professor of Thee, even unto this death. I beseech Thee, Lord God, take mercy on this Realm of England, and deliver the same from all her enemies."

And he and Hugh Latimer were then chained by the smith to the stake, and soldiers brought fire to the wood stacked at their feet.

Thereupon Hugh Latimer spoke thirty-one of the bravest Christian words ever spoken: "Be of good comfort, Master Ridley, and play the man, we shall this day light such a candle, by God's Grace, in England, as I trust shall never be put out."

And the fire took hold, and they embraced the flames, and, eventually . . . eventually . . . with prayers on their searing lips . . . died . . .

"Latimer's famous, if spurious words," wrote Evelyn Waugh, a Roman Catholic, "have not been fulfilled."

Which tells you a lot about Evelyn Waugh.

*　　*　　*

Sermons to break the heart, yes...

But the terrible deaths they suffered were no more terrible than those to which they were calmly prepared to send others.

So were these Martyrs actually insane by our slightly more tolerant standards? or were they merely stubborn? Had they been backed into Theological holes and corners from which their own sinful pride wouldn't let them walk away with dignity? Or were these agonising glories the price they were willing to pay for years of doubt about the inessential details of what they were trying to believe?

Who can search us out and know us? our down-sitting and our up-rising? Who can understand our thoughts?

Such knowledge is still too remote from us, too high in Heaven, too deep in Hell ... and we will never know it.

But what we *can* know is that it was never the teaching of Jesus Christ that resulted in these murders, but the neglect and contradiction of that teaching ... the substitution of the mere traditions of men for Truth.

For Now is no Time to Dissemble

The best formal Sermon ever preached at one of these sixteenth-century Martyrdoms was that by Thomas Cramner, Most Reverend Father in God, late Archbishop of Canterbury.

As we have seen, he first believed this and then believed that, sent others to the rack and to the stake . . . but, finally, was confronted by a Roman Catholic Queen upon the Throne of England: Mary Tudor . . . better known to those who know little other History as *Bloody Mary* . . .

He was charged with "blasphemy, inconstancy, and heresy" in that he "denied the authority of the Roman Catholic Pope in the Realm of England" . . . found guilty, degraded, sentenced, and taken to the stake . . .

And, "being an inconstant man," was there expected to "publicly recant himself" that "all might understand" he "remained a Roman Catholic . . ."

"I will do it," he said, " and that with a good will."

*   *   *

But spake thus unto the people:

"Every man, good people, desireth at the time of death to give some good exhortation, that others may remember the same and be the better thereby. So I beseech God grant me grace that I may say something at this, my departing, whereby God may by glorified and edified.

"For it is, first, a heavy case to see that so many folk be so much doted upon the love of this false world, and so careful for it, that of the love of God or of the World to come they seem to care little . . .

"Therefore, set not your minds overmuch upon this glozing world, but upon God and the world to come . . .

"Love altogether like Brethren and Sisters – for alas, pity it is to see what contention and hatred one Christian man beareth to another, not taking each other as Brother and Sister but rather as strangers and mortal enemies. But I pray you learn and bear well this one lesson, to do good unto all men as much as in you lieth, and to hurt no man, no more than you would hurt your own natural Brother or Sister.

"The next exhortation shall be to them that have great

substance and riches of this world, that they will well consider and weigh three sayings of the Scripture.

"One is of our Saviour Christ Himself, Who saith, *It is hard for a rich man to enter into the Kingdom of Heaven.* A sore saying, yet spoken of Him that knoweth the truth.

"The second is of Saint John, whose saying is this: *He that hath the substance of this world, and seeth his Brother in necessity, and shutteth up his mercy from him, how can he say that he loveth God?*

"The third is of Saint James, who speaketh to the covetous rich man after this manner: *Weep you and howl for the misery that shall come upon you. Your riches do rot, your clothes be moth-eaten, your gold and silver doth canker and rust – and their rust shall bear witness against you and consume you like fire. You gather a hoard or treasure of God's great indignation against the Last Day.*

"Let them that be rich ponder well these three sayings – for if they ever had occasion to show their charity, they have it now at this present, the poor people being so many and victuals so dear.

"And now, forasmuch as I am come to the last end of my life, whereupon hangeth all my life past and all my life to come, either to live with my Master Christ for ever in joy, or else to be in pain for ever with wicked Devils in Hell, and I see before mine eyes presently either Heaven ready to receive me, or else Hell ready to swallow me up.

"I shall therefore declare unto you my very Faith, how I believe without any colour or dissimulation. For now is no time to dissemble, whatsoever I have said or written in time past."

And he then, "to the astonishment of all," recanted his recantation, "written for fear of death" . . . and promised that his "unworthy right hand," which had "written contrary to his heart," should "first be punished in the fire . . ."

So that his "Judges there assembled began to rage, fret, and fume . . ."

But they "could no longer threaten or hurt him," for the "most miserable man in the world can die but once, and he must needs die that day."

And he tried to go on preaching to the people: "As for the Pope, I refuse him as Christ's enemy and Antichrist, with all his false doctrine . . ."

So that his "Judges began to yelp, and bawl . . ."

And Bishop Cole cried, "Stop the heretic's mouth and take him away!"

Then our Brother Cramner was pulled down, and led to the fire, that place where Nicholas Ridley and Hugh Latimer were burnt before him . . .

When the wood was kindled and the "fire began to burn near him, stretching out his arm he put his right hand into the flame, which he held so immovable that all men might see his unworthy hand burned before his body was touched."

And so, "using often the words of Stephen, *Lord Jesus, receive my spirit,* in the greatness of the flame he gave up his life."

*   *   *

"About Cramner," writes the Very Reverend Dunstan Pontifex, of the Order of Saint Benedict, "this much is clear: if he was not an arch-villain, he was no Saint. He was a rather weak, rather timid man, with no very high principles . . ."

Over four hundred years dead, still kicking at ashes . . .

An Epitaph for those ashes?

"The Litany in English was his own handiwork," writes Edward Carpenter, sometime Archdeacon of Westminster, "and his telescoping of the traditional Monastic Offices into Morning and Evening Prayer for the use of lay people has proved itself peculiarly adapted to English temperament and religious feeling."

Yes, Brother Thomas, like you *we have left undone those things which we ought to have done, And we have done those things which we ought not to have done* . . .

But we have taken Temporal Power away from the Church, so that nobody gets burned alive for *following too much the devices and desires of their own hearts* . . .

Not so much a Sermon, More a Symphony in Four Movements

Theology went mad in the speculations and Sermons of the Middle Ages, and those agonies of glory were evidence of its lingering convulsions . . . but even as late as the seventeenth century there were still Preachers who used those formal models of Sermon construction . . . and these give us a last look back before the Protestant Reformation broke up the bath as a way of getting rid of the dirty bath-water.

*　　*　　*

Consider our Reverend Father in God, Lancelot Andrewes, sometime Lord Bishop of Winchester and Dean of the Royal Chapel of King James the First.

For eighteen years, starting in 1606, he preached before the King's Majesty at Whitehall on Christmas Day, always choosing for his theme some part of the Christmas Story: his famous *Sermons on the Nativity.*

Most of these will serve as a demonstration, the first as well as any.

He starts with a main text from the second chapter of the Letter of the Apostle Paul to the Hebrews, the seventeenth verse: *For verily Christ took not on Him the nature of Angels, but He took on Him the seed of Abraham.* This is then repeated in the Latin of the Vulgate, and throughout the Sermon every one of his ninety-five subsidiary texts is quoted in English and Latin, and then minutely examined in both languages . . . with the occasional few words of Greek from the text of the New Testament edited by Erasmus. And there are various supporting quotations from Chrysostom, Augustine of Hippo, and Gregory the Great – again in English and Latin or Greek . . . with a reference to the original Hebrew of the Old Testament. It by now being obvious that his *divisions* were going to be in the *infra* style, as before a learned congregation.

The whole Sermon can be read aloud in a comfortable hour, and consists of fifty paragraphs or divisions, arranged in the clearly recognisable standard structure:

The statement of the *thema* or text in three divisions.

A prelocution, in which the authority for this text is examined in

169

three *degrees* – the last of which is sub-divided into three progressive paragraphs.

Then there's the *process,* or statement of the three main sections into which the rest of the Sermon is to be divided.

Each of these main divisions or *principals* is further sub-divided or *amplified:* the first into four parts, the fourth of which is in three paragraphs; the second into three parts, each variously and tightly sub-divided; and the third into seven parts, again variously sub-divided and inter-related by complicated cross-references.

The Biblical narrative is examined under the four Classical Modes of Rhetoric: as historically literal events, as allegories of our human condition, as lessons for our moral improvement, and as mystical explanations of God's dealings with us.

There is a parallel to this narrative in secular history with a reference to the "dangers that daily compass us about" after the recent Gunpowder Conspiracy . . . and several analogies from the Bible.

There's then a Conclusion, and a final Prayer.

No, it's not so much a Sermon as we hear them today, but more of a Theological Symphony in Four Movements.

* * *

T. S. Eliot regarded Lancelot Andrewes as a "writer of genius," and a better preacher than John Donne. He saw Donne's Sermons as the work of a man who seeks in religion a refuge from the "tumults of a strong emotional temperament which can find no complete satisfaction elsewhere," but in Andrewes a man "so free from confusion or disorder" that his "personality could be readily subdued in the pursuit of principles of right thought and right action."

True, Eliot's views often grew not from balanced criticism but from exasperation or active dislike, from his own frustrated emotions rather than from his intellect. So, in Andrewes he probably saw the man he knew he was himself: "deferential, glad to be of use, politic, cautious, and meticulous, full of high sentence . . . at times, indeed, almost ridiculous . . ."

Yet it's easy to see that Andrewes derives from a "broadly European tradition, expressive of the finest spirit of English culture," with little of the "parochial or provincial" . . . and whose prose has what Eliot called an "ordonance," an "internal agreement of words which encourages precision, relevance, and intensity."

Eliot's well-known poem, *Journey of the Magi,* pays his "homage" to Lancelot Andrewes by beginning with an abbreviated quotation from one of his Sermons on the Nativity, the fourteenth, on the text,

For we have seen His star in the East, and are come to worship Him, preached before James the First, at Whitehall, on Christmas Day, 1622.

We have already seen how Andrewes constructed his Sermons on a standard Medieval pattern, and this is no exception: a text, its divisions, a prelocution, a process, principals, amplifications, inter-relationships and complicated cross-references, dozens of other texts in English and the Latin of the Vulgate, further explications in Greek, allusions to the Fathers of the Eastern Church . . . and so on, a rich complex of meanings and mysteries.

We'll join him towards the end, where Eliot borrows his beginning . . .

*   *   *

"In this coming of the Wise Men we consider, *first*, the distance of the place they came from. It was not hard by, as the Shepherds, but a step to Bethlehem over the fields – *this* was riding many a hundred miles, and cost them many a day's journey.

"*Secondly,* we consider the way that they came, if it be pleasant, or plain and easy – for if it be, it is so much the better.

"Yet this was nothing pleasant, for through deserts, all the way waste and desolate. Nor easy either, for over the rocks and crags of both Arabias, specially Petraea, their journey lay.

"Yet if safe – but it was not, but exceeding dangerous, as lying through the midst of the *black tents of Kedar,* a nation of thieves and cut-throats. To pass over the hills of robbers, infamous then, and infamous to this day. No passing without great troop or convoy.

"Last we consider the time of their coming, the season of the year.

"It was no summer progress. A cold coming they had of it at this time of the year, just the worst time of the year to take a journey, and specially a long journey in. The ways deep, the weather sharp, the days short, the sun farthest off, *in solstitio brumali,* the very dead of winter.

"*Venimus,* we are come, if that be one meaning, *venimus,* we are now come, come at *this* time, that sure is another."

There are fifteen tightly printed pages of such density . . . and even our Brother knows that it's all too much, even for his learned and *infra* congregation: "To enter farther into this would be too long, and indeed they be not in our verse here, and so for some other treatise at some other time." But manages to go on for minutes longer . . .

171

Corporis hæc Animæ sit Syndon Syndon Jesu
Amen.

Martin (I) scup. And are to be sould by R R. and Ben: ffisher

172

not merely "diverse great men," the "most noble, wise, and accomplished of that highly intellectual age," but the "groundlings" in their hundreds, and "you might have seen all grieve, and those here and there unable to restrain their tears."

He was "tall, pale," had a "graceful and impressive delivery," and held his congregations "enthralled, unwearied, unsatiated."

As Logan Pearsall Smith long ago pointed out, "great prose needs a great subject matter, needs great themes . . . Good and Evil, Desire and Disillusion, the briefness of Life and the mystery of Death . . ."

And our Brother John had those and to be sparing.

"The world is a great Volume, and man the Index of that Book. Even in the body of man, you may turn to the whole world . . ."

Any selection from so great a volume must be arbitrary, and I can't even claim to have searched the index . . . because everywhere you may turn to the whole world, and "enclose infinite riches" in a few words.

* * *

He took a high view of his vocation: "The Preacher," he says, is a "watchman placed on a tall tower to sound a trumpet," and his preaching was the "voice of the trumpet . . . the beating of a drum, the tolling of a warning bell . . . a lovely song, sung to an instrument."

I remember our contemporaries . . . yes, *Fled is that music . . .*

He was brisk about enforced clerical celibacy: "Without Christ," he says, "chastity is a castration."

And he was prophetic about some of our Instant Moralists: "Chastity is not chastity in an old man, but a disability to be unchaste."

Again: "It is nothing for a sick man that hath lost his taste to say, *Depart voluptuousness . . .* nothing in an impotent man to say, *Depart wantonness . . .*"

He's chilling about a familiar sort of over-scrupulous Christian who drags around with a very small bag of very small sins to confess to anybody who'll listen: "There is no such cross as to have no crosses."

He talks of sins he had "so laboured to hide from the world" that they "are now hid from his own conscience, and his own memory."

"Take heed how you condemn another man for a heretic," he says, and they could have done with his voice a hundred years earlier, "for God is no respecter of persons."

And he shows scant regard for text-juggling as "proof" of a doctrinal position: "It must be God's whole Book, and not a few misunderstood sentences out of it, that must try thee. Thou must not

"That star is gone, not now to be seen.

"Yet I hope for all that, *venimus adorare,* we be come thither to worship.

"It will be the more acceptable, if *not* seeing it we *still* worship.

"It is enough we read of it in the text – we see it there.

"And indeed, if the same Day-Star be risen in our hearts that was in theirs, and the same beams of it to be seen . . . then we have *our* part in it no less, nay as *much* as they.

"And it will bring us whither it brought them, to Christ.

"Who, at His Second Coming in Glory, shall call forth these Wise Men, and all that have followed the steps of their faith – and *that* upon the reason specified in the text: For I have seen *their* star shining and shewing forth itself by the like beams . . . and as they came to worship Me, so am I come to do them worship.

"A *venite* then, for a *venimus* now.

"Their star I have seen, and give them a place above among the stars.

"They fell down in worship, and I will lift them up, and exalt them.

"And as they offered to Me, so am I come to bestow on them, and to reward them with the endless joy and bliss of My Heavenly Kingdom.

"To which be the power and the glory, For ever and ever. Amen."

* * *

He died at Winchester, on his birthday, in 1626, aged seventy-one years . . . and I expect that Heaven was hard by, but a step over the fields, and that he had a pleasant coming of it.

The Angel from a Cloud

About the Sermons of John Donne I must say much too little rather
than much too much: because, of all the hundreds and hundreds I
have heard or read, *his* and Studdert Kennedy's are those I return to
again and again for pleasure and emotional stimulation. And, though
I love my dear old Woodbine Willie as a man more and more, I will
always prefer the sounding prose of Donne.

There are one-hundred-and-sixty of his Sermons in three great
folio volumes, over three thousand pages of grey print: immensely
long and dense paragraphs, texts hammered and teased into wearying
attenuation, recondite references to almost forgotten controversies
. . . garbage for the Theological archeologist.

Yet, Donne, the Medieval Scholastic born too late, poured the best
and the worst of himself into those Sermons – and it's been his
Literary misfortune that the form is now out of fashion. What writer
these days would even think of writing a Five-Act Historical Drama
in blank verse? Four hundred years ago there were few other options.
Three hundred years ago the Anglican Sermon was at its considerable
peak . . . with John Donne hovering above it, the "Angel from a
cloud . . ."

And his words are of fire and roses, ashes and thorns, disgust and
passion and exultation, despair and serene acceptance . . . and it is for
those words in the wilderness that I revere him.

"I neglect God and His Angels for the noise of a fly, for the rattling
of a coach, for the whining of a door . . . A memory of yesterday's
pleasures, a fear of tomorrow's dangers, a straw under my knee, a
noise in mine ear, a light in mine eye, an any thing, a nothing, a fancy,
a Chimera in my brain, troubles me in my prayer. So certainly is there
nothing, nothing in spiritual things, perfect in this world."

Yes, he had the Poet's "craft and sullen art" to say "what oft was
thought, but ne'er so well express'd."

*   *   *

He'd usually preach for an hour, with his hour-glass always "running
away in the sands and dust of Time" on the ledge of the pulpit . . . and
some of the Sermons, if read as printed, would have lasted for two or
even three "turnings of the glass."

Yet he had "vast congregations" in Old Saint Paul's Cathedral or
at the open-air Paul's Cross, "extreme press and thronging" . . . and

press heavily to thine own damnation every such sentence ... That which must try thee is the whole Book, the tenor and purpose, the scope and the intention of God in His Scriptures."

However, he was at his best in "longer chases ... "

"Because God's Word calls *Preaching foolishness,* you take God at His Word, and you think Preaching a thing under you. Hence it is, that you take so much liberty in censuring and comparing Preacher and Preacher, nay, Sermon and Sermon from the same Preacher – as though we preached for wagers, and as though coin were to be valued from the inscription merely, and the image on the coin, and the person of the image, and not for the worth of the metal."

Mea culpa, Brother John, *mea maxima culpa.*

"Joy is peace for having done that which we ought to have done ...

"To have something to do, to do it, and then to rejoice in having done it, to embrace a calling, to perform the duties of that calling, to joy and rest in the peaceful testimony of having done so – *this* is Christianly done, Christ did it. Angelically done, Angels do it. Godly done, God does it.

"Divers men may walk by the sea side, and the same beams of the sun giving light to them all, one gathereth by the benefit of that light pebbles, or speckled shells, for curious vanity – and another gathers precious pearl, or medicinal amber, by the same light.

"So the common light of reason illuminates us all, but one employs this light upon the searching of impertinent vanities, another, by a better use of the same light, finds out the Mysteries of Religion – and when he hath found them, loves them, not for the sake of the light, but for the natural and true worth of the thing itself.

"If I had the years of Methusala, and his years multiplied by the minutes of his years, which were a fair term – and if I could speak till the Angels trumpets blew, and you had the patience of Martyrs, and could be content to hear me till you were called to meet the Lord Jesus in the clouds, all *that* time would not make up one minute, all those words would not make up one syllable, towards this Eternity ...

"Methusala, with all his hundreds of years, was but a mushroom of a night's growth, to this Day of Eternity – and all the four Monarchies, with all their thousands of years, and all the powerful Kings, and all the beautiful Queens of this world, were but as a bed of flowers, some gathered at six, some at seven, some at eight, all in one morning, in respect of this Day.

"At the Last Day I shall rise from the dead, from the dark station, from the prostration of death, and never miss the sun, which shall be put out – for I shall see the Son of God, the sun of glory, and shine myself, as that sun shines.

"I shall rise from the grave, and never miss this city, which shall be nowhere, for I shall see the City of God, the New Jerusalem.

"I shall look up, and never wonder when it will be day, for the Angel will tell me that *Time shall be no more,* and I shall see, and see cheerfully that Last Day, the Day of Judgement, which shall have no night, never end, and be united to the *Ancient of Days,* to God Himself, who had no morning, never began.

"There I leave you," were the last words of his last Sermon, "to lie down in peace . . . till He vouchsafe you a Resurrection, and an Ascension into that Kingdom which He hath prepared for you with the inestimable price of His incorruptible Blood. Amen."

No use going to Saint Paul's Cathedral for the like of that *these* latter days . . . those times shall be no more.

177

Music at Midnight

Another lovely man was George Herbert, the early seventeenth-century English Poet, who ended his short and uneventful life as an Anglican clergyman in the Wiltshire country Parish of Bemerton . . . where he was a "pattern of virtue to all other wearers of the cloth," and "continued meditating and praying and rejoicing until the day of his death."

He also wrote some of the most beautiful of Religious Lyrics, and preached "most excellent" Sermons . . . but dear old Izaak Walton, whose brief *Life* is still the friendliest source of stories about this loving man, gives us a perfect example of George Herbert's best preaching.

True, it wasn't in a church, not up in a pulpit . . . not even with very many words . . .

*   *   *

"His chiefest recreation was Music," writes Friend Walton, "in which Heavenly Art he was a most excellent Master, and did himself compose many Divine Hymns and Anthems, which he set and sang to his lute or viol: and though he was a lover of retiredness, yet his love to Music was such, that he walked usually twice every week, on certain appointed days, to the Cathedral Church in Salisbury; and at his return would say *That his time spent in Prayer, and Cathedral Music, elevated his soul, and was his Heaven upon earth.*

"But before his return thence to Bemerton, he would usually sing and play his part at an appointed Music Meeting, and, to justify this practice, he would often say, *Religion does not banish mirth, but only moderates and sets rules to it.*

"In one of his walks to Salisbury, he saw a poor man with a poorer horse, that was fallen under his load: they were both in distress, and needed present help. Which Mr Herbert perceiving, put off his Canonical coat, and helped the poor man to unload, and after to load his horse.

"The poor man blessed him for it, and he blessed the poor man, and was so like the Good Samaritan, that he gave him money to refresh both himself and his horse, and told him *That if he loved himself he should be merciful to his beast.*

"Thus he left the poor man.

"And at his coming to his musical friends at Salisbury, they began to wonder that Mr George Herbert, which used to be so trim and clean, came into that company so soiled and discomposed: but he told them the cause.

"One of the company told him *That he had disparaged himself by so dirty an employment.*

"His answer was *That the thought of what he had done would provide Music to him at midnight, and that the omission of it would have upbraided and made discord in his conscience, whensoever he should pass by that place. For if I be found to pray for all that be in distress, I am sure that I am bound, so far as it is in my power, to practise what I pray for. And though I do not wish for the like occasion every day, yet let me tell you, I would not willingly pass one day of my life without comforting a sad soul, or shewing mercy, and I praise God for this occasion. And now let us tune our instruments."*

*   *   *

I wouldn't exchange that for the *Collected Sermons* of any Evangelist you care to name.

The Orthodox true Minister,

The Breaking of Bread from House to House

The most remarkable English Preachers ever to disturb the Church as by Law Established were the Ranters of the later seventeenth century: men and women who believed that they were so mystically "atoned" (or at one) with God that they were incapable of "carnal sin unto destruction."

Between the execution of Charles the First in 1649 and the beginnings of Oliver Cromwell's Protectorate in 1653 there was a surge of passionate religious fervour from what we now call the "grass-roots" of society.

"The old world," said Gerrard Winstanley, "is running up like a parchment in the fire . . ." The Spirit of God seemed to be poured out upon all flesh, sons and daughters uttered prophecy, young men saw visions, and old men dreamed dreams . . . even as the Apostle Peter had foretold at Pentecost, so that the common people "waited daily for Jesus Christ to Return in Glory amid the clouds of Heaven" to "establish not a church but the Kingdom of Righteousness" on the very soil of England.

And, of all the groups and sects and schisms to roam the streets and fields of that troubled world, the Ranters were the most formidable.

*　　*　　*

They were given that name by their massed religious opponents, because their style of preaching was more your Billy Graham American Hot Gospelling than the lukewarm milk-and-water of the usual Anglican pulpit: what it lacked in "learning" it made up for in enthusiasm.

And that's one of the difficulties: we only know what their enemies said and wrote about them – the very bishops and clergymen the Ranters preached against most vehemently. So due allowance must be made for intolerance and misrepresentation – even the invention of unusually tall stories. It wouldn't be the first time that Christians have cooked evidence in the roasting of heretics.

Norman Cohn, in his already classic book, *The Pursuit of the Millennium,* has described and documented them in awesome detail – but one stands out: Abiezer Coppe . . . whose alleged "custom it was to preach stark naked many blasphemies and unheard of Villainies in the Day, and in the Night to drink and lie with a Wench . . . both stark naked . . ."

Yes, chance would have been a fine thing for many of those bishops and clergymen, whose own private lives were not always so sweet-smelling as their own moral exhortations.

He was born in 1619, began his religious life as a "Puritanical," given to "fastings, vigils, and self-mortification." In his own words: "Tears were my drink, dust and ashes my meat, sack-cloth my clothing."

And some of his "Ranting" words are in the great tradition of the genuine Gospel, urgent, about *this* world . . .

"Behold, behold, behold, the eternal God, the Lord of Hosts, Who is that mighty Leveller, is coming, Yea, even at the doors, to Level in good earnest, to Level to some purpose, to Level with a witness, to Level the Hills with the Valleys, and to lay the Mountains low.

"And the Prime Levelling, is laying low the Mountains and Levelling the Hills in Man.

"For this Honour, Nobility, Gentility, Propriety, Super-fluity, hath been the Father of Hellish Horrid Pride, Arrogance, Haughtiness, Loftiness, Murder, Malice, of all manner of wickedness and impiety. Yea, the cause of all the blood that ever hath been shed . . .

"The Lord will plague your Honour, Pompe, Greatness, Superfluity, and confound it into parity, equality, comm-unity . . . and the eternal God, Who is Universal Love, will fill the earth with universal love . . .

"Be wise now, therefore, O ye Rulers, be instructed.

"Kiss Beggars, Prisoners, warm them, feed them, clothe them, money them, relieve them, release them, take them into your houses . . .

"Admit them, they are flesh of your flesh, your own Brethren, your own Sisters, every whit as good . . .

"Loose the bands of wickedness, undo the heavy burdens, let the oppressed go free, and break every yoke. Deal thy bread to the hungry, and bring the poor that are cast out, both of houses and churches, to thy house. Cover the naked, hide not thyself from thine own flesh . . .

"Especially thee, thou Holy, Righteous, Religious Appro-priator . . . you shall weep and howl for the miseries that are suddenly coming upon you, because your riches are corr-upted . . . your gold and silver is cankered, the rust of them is a witness against you . . ."

For these and other words he was arrested, copies of his pamphlets and sermons, "containing many such horrid Blasphemies and damnable and detestable Opinions," were seized, and burnt by the public hangman . . . and he rotted in Newgate Prison for a year-and-a-half.

*   *   *

the Seducer and falfe Prophet.

Other Ranters made equally powerful condemnations of secular power and ecclesiastical privilege – but there are many passages of beautiful spirituality which would be praised under more famous names.

"Men are in Heaven," said Jacob Barthumley, "or Heaven in men, when God appears in the glories and pure manifestations of Himself, in Love and Grace, in Peace and rest and in the Spirit. I find that where God dwells, and is come, and hath taken men, and wrapt them up into the Spirit, there is a New Heaven and a New Earth, and all the Heaven I look ever to enjoy is to have my earthly and dark apprehensions of God to cease, and to live no other life that what Christ lives in me."

For these and other words he was "burned through the tongue" by his Christian Brethren.

*   *   *

And *these* words still stand today.

Joseph Salmon had been imprisoned for preaching "contrary to the Peace and Civil Order of the Commonwealth," and after eighteen months was thus "persuaded" to "recant" of his Ranting . . . but obviously still retained its power.

"I lie quietly secure in the Lord," he said, "while I see the whole world consuming in the fire of envy one against another. I hear much noise about me, but it serves only to deliver me unto the still peace of Divine rest. The formal world is much affrighted, and every form is up in Arms to proclaim open wars against itself . . . Come then, O my soul, enter thou into thy Chamber, shut thy doors about thee, hide thyself in silence for a season till the indignation be blown over."

*   *   *

But let's allow a last more Ranting word to our Brother Coppe.

"Howl, howl, ye Nobles, howl ye Honourable, howl ye Rich Men for the miseries that are coming upon you.

"For our part, we that hear the Apostle preach, will also have all things in common, neither will we call any thing that we have our own.

"Do you as you please, till the plague of God rot and consume . . .

"*We* will not, but will eat our bread together in singleness of heart, *we* will break bread from house to house."

Yes, I can just see him and Francis of Assisi, walking together with their Sister Poverty along the streets of London towards Newgate . . . where the public hangman waits for these heretics, either to burn them or their "words wheresoever they be printed . . ."

*   *   *

Though he could Rant with the best of them when the "Spirit of the Lord was hard upon him," George Fox was never a Ranter: in truth, his "soul was greatly grieved" at their "vapouring and blaspheming . . ."

But he liked the Anglicans even less, referred to churches as "mere

183

steeple-houses," called clergy "professors of religion," found "accounted excellent" preachers to be "empty hollow casks," took to disrupting Services by "standing up in power" or "as in a rapture" to argue the "deep meaning" of texts with the "professor" *and* his congregation . . . and so got one and all "into a fierce contention . . . all on a fire . . ."

"However," he wrote, with that "passionate intensity" of knowing himself to be "utterly in the right truth of the Word" which infuriated so many of his contemporaries, "I maintained the *true* Church, and the True Head thereof . . . till they all gave out and fled away . . . and the Lord's power and glory shined over all."

Yes, I'm afraid that, given the short-fuse and temper of his times, dear old Leather Breeches asked for most of his own troubles: beatings and "rough-handling" by the "rude multitude," imprisonment in "dungeons vile," hunger, cold, the "despite of men . . ."

Yet he said many "true sayings" . . . which remain true today.

"When I heard the bell toll to call people together to the steeple-house, it struck at my life – for it was just like a market-bell, to gather people together that the priest might set forth his ware to sale.

"Oh! the vast sums of money that are gotten by the trade they make of selling the Scriptures, and by their preaching, from the highest bishop to the lowest priest!

"What one trade else in the world is comparable to it? notwithstanding the Scriptures were given forth freely, and Christ commanded His ministers to preach freely, and the Prophets and Apostles denounced Judgement against all covetous hirelings and diviners for money.

"But in this free spirit of the Lord Jesus was I sent forth to declare the word of life and reconciliation freely, that all might come to Christ, Who gives freely, and Who renews up into the Image of God, which man and woman were in before they fell, that they might sit down in Heavenly Places in Christ Jesus."

Amen, and yet again Amen, Brother George!

"He and his Friends," wrote G. M. Trevelyn, "held that Christian qualities matter much more than Christian dogmas. No Church or Sect had ever made that its living rule before."

But what on earth would his Friends of today do if he "stood up as in a rapture" at one of their Meeting Houses?

A Portfolio of English Engravings

Views of the Picturesque

In the seventeenth century the English country churches were usually in a far worse state of repair than even the worst of today: water rotted their foundation, walls crumbled, thatched roofs sagged . . . most were unflagged, their floors strewn with rushes. "Some," writes William Addison, whose *English Country Parson* is a quarry of such salutary information, "had the floor constantly being disturbed for burials, so that it became the custom for juniper and frankincense to be burned . . . to counteract the normal foul smell."

Such were the "damp, mildewed, and unwholesome" places where "Sermons were wont to be preached . . ."

As though *that* wasn't enough to "clip the wings of Rhetorique," it was "not an uncommon thing for a pedlar to arrive at the church door in the middle . . . and call out his wares in a loud voice." When the Preacher "might even bring his Sermon to a hasty conclusion because most of his congregation had deserted him . . ."

The Rector of Credenhill at his Meditations

"An empty book is like an Infant's Soul," saith Thomas Traherne, "in which anything may be written . . . I have a mind to fill this with profitable wonders.

"Things strange yet common, incredible yet known, most high yet plain, infinitely profitable but not esteemed.

"I will not by the noise of bloody wars and the dethroning of kings advance you to glory, but by the gentle ways of peace and love.

"As nothing is more easy than to think, so nothing is more difficult than to think well . . .

"The end for which you were created is that, by prizing all that God hath done, you may enjoy yourself and Him in Blessedness.

"God therefore hath made it infinitely easy to enjoy, by making everything ours, and us able so easily to prize them . . . The Sun serves us . . . The Clouds and Stars minister unto us, the World surrounds us with beauty, the Air refresheth us, the Sea revives the earth and us. The Earth is better than gold because it produceth fruits and flowers.

"You never know yourself till you know more than your body . . .

185

"You never enjoy the world aright, till you see how a grain of sand exhibiteth the wisdom and power of God.

"Your enjoyment of the world is never right, till every morning you awake in Heaven.

"You never enjoy the world aright, till the Sea itself floweth in your veins, till you are clothed with the Heavens, and crowned with the Stars, and perceive yourself to be the sole heir of the whole world . . .

"Yet further, you never enjoy the world aright, till you so love the beauty of enjoying it, that you are covetous and earnest to persuade others to enjoy it."

Had only the Fathers of the Desert known such a man, surely they'd have gathered roses there instead of thorns for the laceration of Christ.

A Sermon on the Mischievous Influence of Words and Names falsely applied

"Bodily Abstinence," saith Robert South, "is often called and accounted *Piety* and *Mortification* . . . most especially when joined with a demure, affected countenance.

"Suppose a Man ambitious, one who poisons the ears of great men by venomous Whispers, and rises by the fall of better men than himself. Yet if he steps forth with a Sunday look and a Lenten face, with a *Blessed* Jesu! and a mournful Dirge for the Vices of the times, Oh! *then* he is a Saint upon Earth, an *Ambrose* or an *Augustine*. I mean not for that earthly trash of book-learning, for, alas! they are above that – or, at least, that's above them. But for Zeal, and for Fasting, for a devout

Elevation of the Eyes, and a holy rage against other Men's Sins.

"And thereby demonstrate to the World what is Christian Abstinence, and what self-mortifying Rigour there is in forbearing a Dinner, that they may have the better Stomach to their Supper."

The Bishop of Down and Conner Preacheth one thing . . .

"Any zeal is proper for Religion," saith Jeremy Taylor, "except the zeal of the sword, and the zeal of anger . . . for if the sword turns Preacher, and dictates propositions by Empire instead of arguments, and engraves them in men's hearts with a dagger, so that it shall be death to believe what I innocently and ignorantly am persuaded of, it must needs be unsafe *to try the spirits, to try all things,* to make inquiry . . .

"This may ruin souls by making hypocrites, or careless and compliant against conscience or without it – but it does not save souls, though peradventure it should force them to a good opinion."

. . . *and doeth another* – because he forced the Irish Catholics in his Diocese to attend Protestant Services in English, when they spoke only the Gaelic, and wanted no part of anything either English or Protestant.

But when did the English ever understand the Irish?

Sinners in the Hand of an Angry God

The most unsympathetic Preacher I have ever come across is Jonathan Edwards, an eighteenth-century American Revivalist, whose unmerciful character chills me, and whose Sermons are my personal warning against the enemies of Christ in the Christian Church.

Facts are plentiful, but comparatively unimportant: born in 1703, the son of a Protestant Minister in a small New England frontier village, educated at newly founded Yale, his powerful preaching started the first waves of what became known as the Great Awakening, married for thirty years, father of twelve children, writer of many books and polemical tracts, died in 1758.

May he rest in Peace . . . though I doubt it.

He had a brilliant intellect, and was one of the truly original minds of his young country . . . but, in religion at least, he had a hard heart.

Yes, his account of the "new transports of religious joy" he "delighted in" shortly before his eighteenth birthday is regarded by some as a classic "springing from the tradition of Augustine and Pascal," and it is undoubtedly a genuine record of a profound experience . . . made all the more extraordinary because the new emotionalism clashed with his intellectual Calvinism.

He described what happened as a "calm, sweet Abstraction of Soul from all Concerns of this World, a Vision of being alone in the Mountains, or some solitary Wilderness, far from all Mankind, sweetly conversing with Christ, and wrapt and swallowed up in God. The Sense I had of Divine Things would often of a sudden kindle up a sweet burning in my Heart, an ardour of my Soul, that I know not how to express."

The "test of religious truth," as he now saw it, was "an *inward* sense of the *heart*," which became "central to all his Revival Preaching," and yet somehow confirmed his Calvinistic belief in the "Sovereignty of God." There was a contradiction between the apparently spontaneous warmth of the heart and the seemingly implacable determinism of the belief.

Yet once see his "truth" in action, understand what *he* meant by that "*inward* sense," and there's no actual contradiction . . . because his heart was as implacable as his doctrine.

Here, then, by way of demonstration, are some mercifully short extracts from his most famous Sermon: *Sinners in the Hands of an Angry God,* preached at the start of the Great Revival in 1741 . . . nearly seven thousand relentless words about the Wrath of God, over an hour from the everlasting pain of fire, a taste of Hell and the unending hopelessness of Doom

*   *   *

His text is a six word phrase from the Song of Moses, "which setteth forth God's mercy and vengeance," in *Deuteronomy,* chapter thirty-two, verse thirty-five: *their foot shall slide in due time.*
    And he begins without formal preamble.
    "In this verse is threatened the vengeance of God on the wicked unbelieving Israelites . . .
    "They were always exposed to *destruction* . . . to sudden *unexpected* destruction . . . and they are liable to fall *of themselves* . . .
    "The reason why they are not fallen already, and do not fall now, is only that God's appointed time is not come . . . for there is nothing that keeps wicked men at any one moment out of Hell, but the mere pleasure, the mere *Sovereign* pleasure of God.
    "He is not only able to cast wicked men into Hell, but He can most easily do it . . . We find it easy to tread on and crush a worm that we see crawling on the earth, it is easy for us to cut a slender thread that any thing hangs by. Thus easy is it for God, when He pleases, to cast His enemies down to Hell . . .
    "We are already under a sentence of *condemnation* to Hell. We not only justly deserve to be cast down thither, but the sentence of the Law of God is gone out against us, and stands against us, so that we are bound over already to Hell . . .
    "We are now the objects of that very same *anger* and wrath of God that is expressed in the torments of Hell . . . God is *very* angry with us, as He is with the many miserable creatures now tormented in Hell, who there feel and bear the fierceness of His wrath. Yea, God is a great deal *more* angry with great numbers that are now on earth. Yea, doubtless, with many that are now in *this* congregation, who it may be are at ease . . .
    "The wrath of God burns against us, our damnation does not slumber, the Pit is prepared, the fire is made ready, the furnace is now hot, ready to receive us, the flames do now rage and glow. The glittering sword is whet, and held over us, and the Pit hath opened its mouth under us.
    "The *Devil* now stands ready to fall upon us, and seize us as

his own, at what moment God shall permit him . . .

"We walk over the Pit of Hell on a rotten covering, and there are innumerable places in this covering so weak that they will not bear our weight, and these places are not seen . . .

"In short, we have no refuge, nothing to take hold of . . . All that preserves us every moment is the mere arbitrary will, and uncovenanted, unobliged forbearance of an incensed God."

He then goes on to develop the "Application" of these thoughts.

"The use of this awful subject may be for the awakening unconverted persons in this congregation . . . for that world of misery, that lake of burning brimstone, is extended abroad under you. There is the dreadful Pit of the glowing flames of the Wrath of God, there is Hell's wide gaping mouth open, and you have nothing to stand upon . . . there is nothing between you and Hell but the air . . .

"Your wickedness makes you as it were heavy as lead, and to tend downwards with great weight and pressure towards Hell. And, if God should let you go, you would immediately sink and swiftly descend and plunge into the bottomless gulf . . . and you would have no more influence to keep you out of Hell, than a spider's web would have to stop a fallen rock.

"There are black clouds of God's Wrath now hanging directly over your heads, full of the dreadful storm, and big with thunder . . .

"The Wrath of God is like great waters that are dammed for the present . . . and the longer the stream is stopped, the more rapid and mighty is its course, when once it is loose.

"If God should only withdraw His hand from the flood-gate, it would immediately fly open, and the fiery floods in the fierceness and Wrath of God would rush forth with inconceivable fury, and would come upon you with omnipotent power . . .

"The bow of God's Wrath is bent, and the arrow made ready on the strings, and Justice bends the arrow at your heart, and it is nothing but the mere pleasure of God that keeps the arrow one moment from being made drunk with your blood . . .

"The God that holds you over the Pit of Hell, much as one holds a spider, or some loathsome insect over the fire, abhors you, and is dreadfully provoked. His Wrath towards you burns like fire, He looks upon you as worthy of nothing else, but to be cast into the fire . . ."

And on and on he goes, relentlessly . . .

"O sinner! Consider the fearful danger you are in!

"It is a great furnace of Wrath, a wide and bottomless Pit,

full of the fire of Wrath, that you are held over in the hand of that God, whose Wrath is provoked and incensed against you . . .

"You hang by a slender thread, with the flames of Divine Wrath flashing about it, and ready every moment to burn it asunder . . .

"It is the fierceness of the fury of God that you are exposed to . . . His *rebuke with flames of fire* . . .

"Thy fury of God! the fierceness of Jehovah! How dreadful that must be!

"What will become of the poor worms that shall suffer it! And whose heart can endure? To what a dreadful, inexpressible, inconceivable depth of misery must the poor creature be sunk who shall be the subject of all this! But He will have no compassion on you, He will not forbear the executions of His Wrath, or in the least lighten His hand . . .

"He will crush you under His feet without mercy, He will crush out your blood, and make it fly . . . He will not only hate you, but He will hold you in the utmost contempt . . .

"And it is *everlasting* Wrath . . . there will be no end to this exquisite horrible misery . . . your punishment will be infinite.

"But this is the dismal case of every soul in this congregation . . .

"We know not who they are, or in what seats they sit . . .

"And it would be a wonder if some that are now present should not be in Hell in a very short time, even before this year is out.

"And it would be no wonder if some persons, that now sit here in the seats of this meeting-house, in health, quiet and secure, should be in Hell before tomorrow morning . . .

"How can you rest one moment in such a condition?

"The Wrath of Almighty God is now undoubtedly hanging over a great part of this congregation.

"Let every one fly from Sodom!

"*Haste and escape for your lives! Look not behind you! Escape to the Mountain, lest you be consumed!*"

And he stopped.

*   *   *

Contemporary accounts of the effects of this Sermon say that, "totally overwhelmed by the immediacy of Doom, strong men clung to the pillars of the Meeting House and cried aloud for mercy."

People, "without one thought to the contrary," expected the

"awful Judgement to be unfolded on that day and in that place."

And one man wrote that he "waited with the deepest and most solemn solicitude to hear the trumpet sound, and the Archangel call, to see the graves open, the dead arise, and the Judge descend in the Glory of His Father, with all the Holy Angels . . ."

Yes, many Preachers have similarly played on the terrors of guilt, battered congregations into fear and panic, wrung "conversions" and "decisions for Christ" out of them by the determined application of intolerable psychological pressures . . . but none has done it so coldly, so hatefully, so wickedly as Jonathan Edwards.

God, in His mercy, give him grace.

*   *   *

Postscript

I'm not in the least concerned with the truth of falsity (or even the mere plausibility) of any particular Creed or Dogma or Theological notion, but when George Whitfield and John Wesley preached during the Great Awakening in the young America and the Revival here in England they also offered the "immediate choice between certain damnation and the acceptance of Salvation" . . . with even more extraordinary results.

It could hardly have been caused by the ham acting of more recent Evangelists . . . all that shouting and arm-waving . . .

Jonathan Edwards "spoke quietly, using no gestures, holding the Sermon book in his left hand . . . and spoke what he had written."

John Wesley, according to Horace Walpole, "spoke his Sermon so fast, and with so little accentuation, that I am sure he has often uttered it, for it was like a lesson being repeated."

True, Walpole noted that "towards the end" Wesley "exalted his voice," and "acted very ugly enthusiasm" . . . but neither Wesley nor Whitfield put in so much as a tithe of what Billy Sunday and Billy Graham poured out in movement and highly-charged emotion.

Yet men and women "broke out into strong cries and tears" . . . "sweated most profusely" . . . "trembled and shuddered" . . . "suffered convulsions" . . ."dropped down as dead," with the "extremities of the body assuming the coldness of a corpse . . . rigidity ensuing . . ."

"Five others sunk down in half-an-hour," wrote Wesley in his *Journal,* "most of whom were in violent agonies, The *pains as of Hell came about them, the snares of death overtook them* . . . One indeed continued an hour in strong pain, and one or two more for three days . . ."

Again, "some were torn with a kind of convulsive motion in every

192

part of their bodies, and that so violently that often four or five persons could not hold one of them."

And other reports tell of people, here and in America, bouncing up and down, jumping, hopping, skipping, "leaping like frogs," crawling around on their hands and knees, "growling, snapping the teeth, and barking and howling like dogs," foaming at the mouth, uttering "piercing shrieks" . . . with many women "arching" or "straddling" their bodies in the standard postures of sexual hysteria.

"It is the Lord's doing!" said the Evangelists, "and wonderful in our sight!"

Two questions: Did men howl like dogs at the end of the Sermon on the Mount? Did women foam at the mouth whenever the Lord finished preaching?

Che Blinded Eagle

The most eloquent Preacher of the early nineteenth century was Edward Irving, son of a Scottish tanner.

Good Scottish education, Edinburgh University, took an extra-curricular Divinity Course, taught for a couple of years to support himself during it, became the Head of an Academy at Kirkcaldy, and was eventually licensed by the Presbytery there to preach.

He was tall, well over six feet, imposing, dark and handsome, but with a slight cast in one eye . . . which Thomas Carlyle, cantankerous as ever, called a "glaring squint."

His style as a Preacher had "ower muckle grandeur" for the liking of his early congregations . . . and, after trying Edinburgh and Glasgow, he was invited to be the Minister of the impoverished Caledonian Church in London. This was little more than a Chapel, in "desperate plight" with a congregation "dwindled to a bare fifty people." They had heard of Edward Irving, and the appeal to him was "something of a last resort." And he preached his first Sermon there to the faithful in July, 1822.

Before the year was out "crowds besieged" the place, and "many fashionable carriages jostled each other in this shabby corner of London." His pulpit became a "National Forum."

Two years later they started to build a new church large enough for the vast new congregations . . . which stands to this day in Regent Square, a great pseudo-Gothic wedding cake.

What held so many people through Sermons of "astonishing length" and "intellectual rigour"?

"It was not genius of eloquence alone," wrote a contemporary, "but something greater – a man all visible in those hours of revelation, striving mightily with every man . . . in an entire personal unity which is possible to very few."

And then came what he genuinely believed to be that ancient Gift of the Spirit: members of his congregation began "Speaking in Tongues" at his meetings . . . and he made the mistake of inviting people to witness this miracle for themselves.

Today it's such a common phenomenon of Evangelical rallies that it hardly ever reaches the News on television – but in those more innocent days the public hadn't yet been case-hardened to the unusual.

Thousands and thousands came, the "tongues burst out at fever-pitch" in what Thomas Carlyle called "bedlam and chaos" . . . and the career of Edward Irving was soon ended in scandal and clerical sour grapes, vituperation, Byzantine controversy, cruelty, personal tragedy, with elements of farce and standard ecclesiastical hypocrisy.

He died at the age of fifty-one, a burnt-out case, his mind a wreck.

And Thomas Carlyle was great-hearted enough to say these moving words about him: "But for Edward Irving I had never know what the communion of man with man means. He was the freest, brotherliest, bravest human soul mine ever came in contact with. I call him on the whole the best man I have ever found in this world, or now hope to find . . . I have heard that the eagle becomes blind in gazing with unveiled eyes upon the sun. Thus he tried to do what no man may do and live – to gaze full into the brightness of the Deity. And so blindness fell upon him."

William Blake had the deepest and simplest vision: "Edward Irving was a Sent Man, but they who are sent sometimes go further than they ought." Yes, William Blake had *been* there . . . *and* come back.

*   *   *

When in full flow, the Sermons of Edward Irving were based on the idea as ancient as any Gift of the Spirit: that preaching which leaves out the dynamic of the Gospel is without power.

And in his day, as in ours, most preaching was too often "more of a matter of philosophy and ethics than a challenge to action," and the Sermon was "more a literary essay than a call to raise men from the dead."

But in him the Gospel was spoken with power enough to be sparing.

> "This is an age of expediency," he said, "both in the Church and out of the Church, and all institutions are modelled upon the principles of expediency, and carried into effect by the rules of prudence . . .
>
> "This expediency has banished the soul of patriotic energy from our Parliament, the spirit of high equity from our legislation, self-denying wisdom from our philosophy . . . And if we look not to it, faith will be strangled . . . Money, Money, Money is the universal cry. Mammon hath gotten the victory, and may say triumphantly *without me ye can do nothing."*

He's equally good on the Church . . . with a prophetic eye seemingly cocked on our own times.

> "If I observe the relaxation on the part of the rulers of the Church, and their indifference to the spiritual charge of their children, their ignorance of the state of families for which they are responsible, and the abuse – I had almost said profanation –

of the Sacrament itself, the indecent haste of its administration . . . ..

"If I observe the outward and visible machinery of the present religious world as it well names itself, their endless and often prayerless committees, their multitudinous and often unhallowed meetings, their lustings and harangues, their numerous travellers upon commission, their flaming and often fallacious Reports, with all the hurry, haste and bustle of the evangelical machinery, can I but be grieved at the fall and the declension of the Church's glory and the common weal?"

What he would say today I can only imagine in "wild surmise," but Christianity has now indeed become little more than an imperfectly understood code of partly political ethics, the Church is even more of a respectable Club for the moderately "successful" middle-class . . . and the "haste and bustle of the evangelical machinery" has now gone into "Power Packed" and pre-packaged American over-drive.

About the Person of Christ he rises majestically on those wings of an eagle:

" I stand here a witness for the Lord Jesus, to tell men what He did for them – and what He did was this. He took flesh and made it Holy, thereby to make you Holy, and He will make everyone Holy who believes in Him. He came into your battle, and trampled under foot Satan, the world, the flesh – yea, all the enemies of living man . . . and was He not Holy? Holy in His Mother's womb, Holy in His Childhood, Holy in all His days. Holy in His Nativity, Holy in His Life and Death, Holy in His Resurrection – and not more Holy in one than in another."

*   *   *

And there is an extract from what I consider to be his best Sermon: his Farewell to the congregation that was kicking him out for heresy.

"My Theology was never in fault around the fires of the poor, my manner never misinterpreted, my good intentions never mistaken . . .

"Here was the popularity worth the having – whose evidences are not in noise, ostentation, and numbers, but in the heart opened and unburdened . . .

"They who will visit the poor shall find the poor worthy to be visited – they who will take an interest, not as Patrons, but as fellow-men, in the condition of the poor, shall not only confer but inherit a blessing. It is the finest office of religion, to visit the widows, and the fatherless, and those who have no helper . . .

"Communion of this kind is likest prayer to Heaven . . .

"There needs no formality of speech, every word being addressed to a present feeling. There needs no parade of benevolence, every gift being offered to a pressing want. There needs no Society, no Committee to make it known . . .

"Would that in this age, when our clergy and our laity are ever and anon assembling in public to take measures for the Moral and Religious Welfare of men, they were found as diligently occupying this more retired, more Scriptural, and more natural religion! Would they were as instant for the poor . . . as they are for the tribes whose dwellings are remote, and whose tongue is strange!"

*　　*　　*

One more moment of his power . . .

"I believe that my Lord did come down and toil and sweat and travail, in exceeding great sorrow, in this mass of temptation with which I and all men are oppressed, did bring His Divine Presence and death-possessed humanity . . . And, in that very state which God had put it after Adam had sinned, did suffer its sorrows and pains, its anguish, its darkness, wasteness, disconsolateness and hiddenness from the Countenance of God . . . and by this faith and patience did win for Himself the Name of the Man of Sorrows and the Author and Finisher of our Faith."

Surely the Second Coming is at Hand

After that first Great Awakening in America there was another one a hundred years later: the "Great Second Advent Awakening" which swept the country immediately before Spiritualism in the middle of the "religiously enthusiastic" nineteenth century.

This was mostly the doing of William Miller, born in 1782, who became a small farmer in New York State, almost on the border of Vermont, when the whole area was still "frontier territory."

From 1816 to 1818, in an attempt to settle his "doubts and uncertainties," he made an intensive private study of the Bible, and found himself "enthralled" by the Books of Daniel and Revelation . . . and "noted that while their Prophecies are generally couched in figurative language," they are "fulfilled literally." By comparing "Scripture with History" he then went on to argue that "if the Prophecies which have been fulfilled in the past provide a key to understanding those yet to be fulfilled, then we should look for a literal Second Advent of Christ."

And his words shook America, if not the world . . .

"Finding all the Signs of the Times and the present condition of the world to compare harmoniously with the Prophetic descriptions of the Last Days, I was compelled to believe that this world had about reached the limits of the period allotted by God for its continuance . . . I was thus brought, in 1818, to the solemn conclusion that, in about twenty-five years from that time, all the affairs of our present state would be wound up . . . about the year 1843 . . .

"I need not speak of the joy that filled my heart in view of the delightful prospect, nor of the ardent longings of my soul for a participation in the Joys of the Redeemed . . . I began to wait, and watch, and pray for my Saviour's Second Coming."

In 1831 William Miller preached on "his" subject for the first time in public, and by 1834 he had become a "full-time Baptist Preacher," with "Prophecy and the Second Coming of Christ" as his only theme.

With growing confidence, and the "confirmation of his calculations" by some of the "most learned Bible scholars of his day," he "set the date as being during the Jewish Year of 21 March 1843 to 21 March 1844."

*   *   *

The setting of such "Prophetic" dates had been a popular activity throughout the early History of the Church, and even as late as the Middle Ages there were regular "Second Coming" Movements . . . but so many disappointments had obviously "dulled the edge" of expectations – and, apart from various European spasms during the times of the Ranters, these "Clarion Calls" were viewed rather warily.

But *this* was the young America . . .

You may arrive at these dates by all manner of ingenious means, but "careful comparison" of the twelve mysterious chapters of the Book of Daniel in the Old Testament and the twenty-two even more mysterious chapters of the Book of Revelation in the New is the most usual . . . and involves complicated considerations of "symbolic days" taken to represent "actual years," various conjectural dates for the reigns and decrees of assorted Assyrian Kings – one of which provides the "start" of the "Prophecy of the Seventy Weeks" or "four hundred and ninety days," *meaning* "four hundred and ninety *years*" . . . which "end" during the year when Christ was Crucified according to Archbishop Usher's Chronology . . .

So there's "matter of high significance" here!

Now also in the Book of Daniel is found the "Prophecy of the two thousand and three hundred days" before the "Sanctuary shall be cleansed." So, on the two further assumptions that this "two thousand and three hundred *years*" started at the same time as the "Seventy Weeks" and that the "cleansing of the Sanctuary" was the same event as the Second Coming, which was to "cleanse the earth by fire," it is then easy enough to "prove" that it would take place 2,300 years after 457 BC . . . that is, late in 1843 or early in 1844, depending on whether it was to be early or late in the Jewish Year – which starts in the Spring.

He preached this "Message" in villages, towns, cities, churches, chapels, halls, and Camp Meetings . . .

And hundreds of thousands of people all over America *believed* . . .

*   *   *

As with Jonathan Edwards, it was never his style of preaching which caused this effect, but the force of the *content*.

"In his public discourses he is self-possessed and ready," wrote the Editor of a New England newspaper, "distinct in his utterance, and very frequently quaint in his expressions. He succeeds in chaining the attention of his audience for an hour and a half to two hours . . .

199

dealing often in terrible denunciations against such as oppose his views . . ."

A reporter wrote that "he is earnest and vehement in his delivery . . ."

Another that "he utters his opinions in a somewhat positive tone, and occasionally appeals to his audience in language of earnest persuasion."

So there was little there of hysteria . . .

But *what* he said caused "strong cryings and tears," men and women "coming forward to kneel in contrition" . . . and the "growing awareness that this present world had only a few brief years remaining . . ."

*　　*　　*

> "Depend wholly on the power of the Spirit," he advised his fellow Preachers in the Movement. "Keep your sword the right side up, the edge to the heart, and your arm well nerved.
>
> "Bring home the blow with an intent to kill.
>
> "Be not afraid of hurting your hearers, wind no silk handkerchiefs around your blade, nor withold any power when you thrust.
>
> "Some are in the habit of hiding a part of the sword, for fear that the enemy will dodge the blow – but this will never do.
>
> "If the enemy roar and make a noise, take courage, double your diligence, for it is a certain sign that your blows are telling home."

Ignatius of Loyola, that other "Soldier for Christ," would have been proud of that sustained military metaphor for what, after all, was only a Sermon . . . words as swords.

*　　*　　*

William Miller's *content* is almost impossible to quote except at the inordinate length he went in for: up to two hours of texts and names and days and years and Biblical Beasts with heads and horns . . . all very much a specialised taste.

But here is a peroration to such a concentrated Sermon, which reveals the man behind the Preacher, and the personal cost he was paying.

> "Time rolls on his resistless course. We are one more year down its rapid stream towards the Ocean of Eternity . . .
>
> "Does your heart begin to quail? Are you ready to give up your Blessed Hope in the Glorious Appearing of Jesus Christ?

200

"Let us hold fast to our Faith without wrath or doubting . . . for I call Heaven and yourselves to witness, my Brethren, that I have never taught anything to make you throw away any part of God's Word.

"I have never pretended to preach anything but the Bible. I have used no sophistry. My preaching has not been with words of man's wisdom.

"I have used no dreams or visions except those in the Word of God.

"I have wronged no man . . .

"Neither have I sought for your honours or gold . . .

"I have preached about four thousand five hundred sermons in twelve years, to at least five hundred thousand people.

"I have broken my constitution and lost my health, and for what?

"That, if possible, I might be the means of saving some . . .

"I hope, my Brethren, you will continue faithful unto the End."

*   *   *

But the "calculated year" came . . . and went.

Intense disappointment . . .

Then another earnest student of "Bible Prophecy" convinced himself and many of the "True Believers" that William Miller had only made a "small error of computation involving a knowledge of Jewish Chronology," and that the "Lord would return on the tenth day of the seventh Jewish month, being the Day of Atonement," which, in 1844, was on the twenty-second of October. The "most learned Bible scholars" again "confirmed" these new calculations . . . hope was renewed, the hundreds of thousands regathered, and even William Miller clutched at this "Prophetic" straw.

The "Great and Terrible Day of the Lord" approached . . . dawned . . .

"Would it be at the noon-hour?"

"Would it be at the hour of evening?"

"Would the Loud Cry go forth at the Midnight Hour?"

And midnight passed . . .

That indeed "terrible" day is known as "The Great Disappointment."

The Second Spring

The most famous Sermon ever preached by a Roman Catholic in this country, at least since the Protestant Reformation, was that read in "silvery tones" by John Henry Newman before Cardinal Wiseman and the Roman Catholic Bishops of England at the First Provincial Synod of Westminster, on the thirteenth of July, 1852.

In 1829 the Catholic Emancipation Act had restored to Roman Catholics most of the Civil Rights which had been denied to them after the execution of Bloody Mary... and the Hierarchy was meeting as a Synod in England for the first time in three hundred years to organise and legislate for the growing number of believers.

And the Oxford Movement had recently reminded the bemused Anglican Church that it had an Historical past more anciently Roman Catholic than Reformed Protestant... with John Henry Newman only the most prominent of those who had "gone over to Papal Rome."

*   *   *

Many people regard him with affection as a man of "dazzling gifts," and he was certainly wide-ranging: Evangelical Anglican clergyman and Roman Catholic Priest, popular Preacher and fashionable lecturer, Fellow and Tutor of Oriel College, Rector of the Roman Catholic University of Ireland, Founder and Director of the Oratory School for Boys, translator, writer of religious books and polemical pamphlets, editor, versifier, controversialist... eventually being made a Cardinal.

According to Geoffrey Tillotson he was "one of the supreme geniuses of nineteenth-century England," and a writer "it is vain to blame and useless to praise."

Martin D'Arcy, a Roman Catholic Jesuit Priest, and so, perhaps, rather free with the gilding, called him a "legendary figure," this "silver-tongued Saint and Englishman clothed in the red of Cardinals"... a "highly sensitive genius whose lips were touched by an Angel with a burning coal."

And what product could possibily match *that* sort of picture on the packet? ... *he was but a man* ...

*   *   *

Newman had studied the art of persuasion.

"The heart is commonly reached," he wrote, "not through the reason, but through the imagination . . . voices melt us, looks subdue us, deeds inflame us." When preaching he used not only his written words, but his voice and facial expressions and gestures to considerable effect, and there are many contemporary accounts of the "thrilling experience of hearing and seeing" him in full flow.

"He has the most entrancing of voices breaking the silence with words and thoughts which were a religious music," wrote Matthew Arnold, "subtle, sweet, meaningful."

"Each separate short paragraph," report others, "was spoken rapidly," but with "fresh clearness of silver intonation." Then, at its close, there was a "pause lasting for nearly half-a-minute," then another paragraph, followed by another pause . . . and his "tone, once you got used to it," sounded like a "fine strain of unearthly music . . ."

*   *   *

The most important fact of his life was his conversion from the Church of England to the Church of Rome, and, like most converts to any Creed, he soon became more of an enthusiast for his new Faith than many of the Cradle Catholics. And, conforming to stereotype, he turned to rend Protestantism: "It is the dreariest of possible religions," he wrote. "The thought of Anglican Service makes me shiver, and the thought of the Thirty-Nine Articles makes me shudder . . . *The net is broken and we are delivered.* I should be a consummate fool (to use a mild term) if I left *the land flowing with milk and honey* for the city of confusion and the house of bondage."

He "converted" at the age of forty-four, was ordained a Priest eighteen months later . . . and was invited to preach this Sermon only five years afterwards. Which, for the monolithic structure of his new Church, was a meteoric rise to fame and prominence. True, he was a "catch", and the standards of Roman Catholic preaching were not high at the time . . . but he did them all proud.

*   *   *

The Sermon was called *The Second Spring,* and was at once a "Celebration of Roman Catholic Emancipation" and a "call to arms" for the "Reconversion of England to the Old Faith."

He took his text from that "enclosed garden" of so many celibate Monks and Priests, *The Song of Solomon* . . . selecting words from three verses in a limping translation of the Latin Vulgate: *Arise, make haste, my love, my dove, my beautiful one, and come. For the Winter is now past, the rain is over and gone. The flowers have appeared in our land.*

And I can't think of anybody except John Ruskin who could have started so beautifully, and kept it up for quite so long . . .

"We have familiar experience of the order, the constancy, the perpetual renovation of the material world which surrounds us.

"Frail and transitory as is every part of it, restless and migratory as are its elements, never-ceasing as are its changes, still it abides.

"It is bound together by a law of permanence, it is set up in unity, and, though it is ever dying, it is ever coming to life again.

"Dissolution does but give birth to fresh modes of organisation, and one death is the parent of a thousand lives.

"Each hour, as it comes, is but a testimony, how fleeting, yet how secure, how certain, is the great whole.

"It is like an image on the waters, which is ever the same, though the waters ever flow.

"Change upon change – yet one change cries out to another, like the alternate Seraphim, in praise and glory of their Maker.

"The sun sinks to rise again, and the day is swallowed up in the gloom of the night, to be born out of it, as fresh as if it had never been quenched.

"Spring passes into Summer, and through Summer and Autumn into Winter, only the more surely, by its own ultimate return, to triumph over that grave, towards which it resolutely hastened from its first hour.

"We mourn over the blossoms of May, because they are to wither – but we know, withal, that May is one day to have its revenge upon November, by the revolution of that solemn circle which never stops, which teaches us in our height of hope, ever to be sober, and in our depth of desolation, never to despair."

He then reminded his hearers, who needed no reminding, that England had once been Catholic, that they had been Emancipated . . . and that it was up to them all to "re-consecrate the soil to God."

"We know not what is before us, ere we win our own – we are engaged in a great, a joyful work. But, in proportion to God's Grace, there is the fury of His enemies.

"They have welcomed us as the lion greets his prey . . .

"To set up the Church again in England is too great an act to be done in a corner. We have reason to expect that such a boon would not be given to us without a cross. It is not God's way

204

that great blessings should descend without the sacrifice first of great sufferings.

"If the Truth is to be spread to any wide extent among this people, how can we dream, how can we hope, that trial and trouble shall not accompany its going forth?

"But can we religiously suppose that the blood of our Martyrs, three centuries ago and since, shall never receive its recompense?

"Those Priests, Secular and Regular, did they suffer for no end?

"The long imprisonment, the fetid dungeon, the weary suspense, the tyrannous trial, the barbarous sentence, the savage execution, the rack, the gibbet, the knife, the cauldron, the numberless tortures of those holy victims, O my God, are they to have no reward?"

That is magnificently put . . . and I stand ashamed at what was done to those heroic men and women at Tyburn and elsewhere.

If only those same Roman Catholics hadn't lit the fires of Smithfield, if only our Brother John had expressed any regret . . .

True, he talks of "*loving* vengeance" on the "guilty" English, and hopes for a "better life" being obtained "for the children of those who persecuted" the Martyrs – but, by this, he meant the "benefits" to be "conferred on them" by that promised "Reconversion" . . . which is not quite the same thought as regret.

And his peroration is even more magnificent.

"You," he said to the Cardinal and Bishops and Priests, "who day by day offer up the Immaculate Lamb of God, you who hold in your hands the Incarnate Word under the visible tokens which He has ordained, you who again and again drain the chalice of the Great Victim – who is to make you fear? what is to startle you? what to seduce you? who is to stop you, whether you are to suffer or to do, whether to lay the foundations of the Church in tears, or to put the crown upon the work in jubilation?"

To be unfashionably honest in these ecumenical days, I reject his Theology, I don't trust his Church . . . but I'd go to the stake for his right to express himself in such golden-mouthed words.

Blood and Fire

We all know the story of the dear old Sally Army . . . and only those with no experience of its street-level compassion, who've never been stirred by the great silver sin-no-more blare of its bands would ever demand the dreary formalism of *Salvation Army*.

Dull would they be of soul who could pass by without a lift of the spirit or a bit of a fond grin when the Sallies are thumping away on the corner, trombones and trumpets and drums and the jaunty lassies rattling their triumphant tambourines, ribbons fluttering, eyes bright, the joy on their faces, clean and singing . . .

Yes! *what* a Friend we Have in Jesus!

* * *

It all began with William Booth, born in 1829 of an illiterate working-man and a handsome Jewess, apprenticed to a pawnbroker at the age of thirteen, lived on the shabby edge of destitution all his early life, converted at fifteen, became a Methodist, moved to London as a pawnbroker's assistant when he was twenty, preached to the "Lost" in his little spare time, married at twenty-six, evangelised his Methodical way through darkest Victorian England with his wife and growing family, started the East London Christian Mission when he was thirty-six . . .

Any of the standard biographies will give you the rest of the standard facts and dates and who and where and sometimes *why* . . .

He was tall in his prime, had big mournful eyes, black hair, a big nose, beautiful hands, a "harsh and uneducated voice," liked his religion as he liked his tea – *hot* . . . suffered persecution, especially from brewers and ponces and several Bishops, founded one of the most successful religious organisations in the recent world, and filled the hearts of thousands with the "unquenchable gaiety of God."

* * *

The beliefs of the Sallies, their "Marching Orders," are four-square and rock-hard on Evangelical Fundamentalism: both Old and New Testaments given by inspiration of the One God in Trinity, Jesus Christ as "truly and properly God and truly and properly man," all men as sinners, "totally depraved" and "justly exposed to the wrath of God," immortality of the soul, resurrection of the body, "Last and

Dreadful Judgement," the "eternal happiness of the righteous" and the "eternal punishment of the wicked."

So if you want *Sermons Designed to be Read as Literature,* expressions of a cultured interest in the Finer Things of Life, or something – well, let's leave General William Booth out of this.

But if you want grand compassion, righteous indignation, mystical love of Jesus Christ demonstrated by practical love of humanity, listen to *this:*

"To attempt to Save the Lost, we must accept no limitations to human brotherhood. As Christ came to call not the Saints but sinners to repentance, so the new message of temporal Salvation, of Salvation from pinching poverty, from rags and misery, must be offered to all.

"To get a man soundly Saved it is not enough to put on him a pair of new breeches, to give him regular work, or even to give him a university education. These things are all outside a man, and if the inside remains unchanged you have wasted your labour.

"But what is the use of preaching the Gospel to men whose whole attention is concentrated upon a mad, desperate struggle to keep themselves alive? You might as well give a tract to a shipwrecked sailor who is battling with the surf which has drowned his comrades and threatens to drown him . . .

"The *first* thing to do is to get him a footing on firm ground, and to give him his room to live."

*   *   *

True, as Vachel Lindsay pointed out, the noise of the Sally Army bands will "play havoc with the Angel Choir" when William Booth enters into Heaven . . . but if *he* isn't there, who ever *can* be?

Who'd even *want* to be?

*   *   *

Postscript

Yes, I *know* that Charles Haddon Spurgeon had a "magnificent voice" and was a "Prince of the Pulpit," that his "Sunday Morning Sermons appeared in Monday's newspapers in the United States," and that I should be in awe of the umpteen volumes of his *Collected Works* . . . but I find him pompous, too proud of his own Spirit-filled "humility" before the Lord.

"Religion is not a thing merely for your intellect," he thunders from the heights of his purpose-built Tabernacle, "it is a thing that demands your faith. As a Messenger of Heaven, I demand that faith. If you do not choose to give it, on your own head be the Doom if you are prepared to risk it. But *I* have done my Duty, I have told you the Truth. That is enough, and there I leave it . . ."

Well, *I* leave it, too, Brother Charles: I'm prepared to risk that you're wrong, that your way is not the only way . . . perhaps not even God's way.

That Lovely Evangelical Nun

We started with the Sermon on the Mount, and have now arrived at the twentieth century of Christian Preaching . . . where the once golden Keys of that ancient Kingdom now seem to have passed into the hands of American Hot Gospelling mass-evangelists and their paler carbon copies.

In *Elmer Gantry*, Sinclair Lewis has written what is now the classic novel about them – but the cool truth has got fiction beaten to its incredulous knees when it comes to Aimee Semple McPherson.

"I'm a Queen in my Kingdom," she said, "and I'm not kidding."

She flourished during the late nineteen-twenties in Los Angeles, and, beyond any question, after Billy Graham she's the most remarkable mass-evangelist of modern times.

*   *   *

Canadian, "child of a one-time Salvation Army lassie and a Methodist farmer," was "dedicated to the Lord before her birth," preached Sermons to "dolls on lined-up chairs" at the age of five, and "converted at seventeen by a roving Preacher, Robert Semple . . ."

"I was hit," she said, "by a shaft of conviction from the mighty bow of Almighty God."

Robert Semple was a Holy Roller Pentecostal, they married within a few weeks of that converting shaft . . . but, tragically, he soon died, "leaving her friendless, penniless, and with a month-old daughter."

She quickly married again, but after the birth of a son she was divorced by her husband on the grounds of "desertion and mental cruelty," her "wildcat habits," and "suicidal threats."

So, to support herself and her children, she set out on what's known in the United States as the "Old Sawdust Trail" . . . preaching an almost totally uninhibited Revivalism from Foursquare Gospel Hall to Baptist Chapel and back again by way of Camp Meeting and hired tent in a field on the outskirts of the next town, the next city . . .

She preached all over America to "audiences of ten to sixteen thousand frantically applauding people," who found her "warmth, womanly charm, and magnetic power of persuasion irresistible."

Little wonder, for she was "bodily beautiful," with a "firm athletic figure . . . sensuously feminine . . . free-striding," and had a "mass of copperish-auburn hair," and a "wide-mouthed smile revealing strong and very white teeth." Her "most striking feature" was a "swift glance from darkly luminous eyes, at once provocative and reassuring . . ."

Her style was dramatic.

"Flooded with limelight," usually tinted "pale-rose," and wearing a "white silk gown with drapings on her arms to resemble wings," she'd "enter from the back" and "sweep down to the platform amid soaring cheers."

Or she'd "zoom down the church aisle straddling a motorcycle, howling about the speed with which we were all going to Hell . . ."

Or, once on the platform, and "bedecked in American football helmet, pantaloons, and shoulder-pads," she "would hurl herself through the air, and grab a tackling-dummy while shrieking threats at the Devil . . ."

After a few years of this preparation she was ready for Los Angeles, arrived at the end of 1918 with "ten dollars and a tambourine" . . . and was shortly able to "build and dedicate Angelus Temple," a huge arena seating "more than five thousand persons." She designed it herself, including such "holy and inspirational attractions" as "eighteen crystal doors" and "eight stained-glass windows with religious scenes" . . . the furnishings alone were "estimated to represent an investment of a million and a half dollars." And her "religious radio station" was one of the first in the world to "utilise this Sanctified way of saying a *word in season* to the unconverted."

Her life was as extravagant as her preaching.

She "bought expensive clothes by the trunk-load," had "over a hundred pairs of shoes," went to the "beauty parlour twice a week," surrounded herself with flowers, and "was known to eat two fair-sized steaks at a sitting . . . followed by pie or strawberry-shortcake."

She married for a third time . . . but was just as soon divorced by her husband on the grounds that she had "made their married life look ridiculous by her behaviour."

One time she disappeared for a month, and afterwards claimed that she had been "kidnapped, chloroformed, gagged, blindfolded, and kept locked up entirely out of touch or communication with the outside world" . . . but it was later established that the whole affair was a criminal conspiracy to cover up the fact that she had been "fornicating under a false name at various secret hideouts in California with the married operator" of her radio station. She was arrested, and tried at a preliminary hearing . . .

And yet, such is the unbounded capacity for self-delusion in these charismatic figures, and the gullibility of those who succumb to their undoubted powers, that when she was released on bail she preached that very evening at her Angelus Temple . . . and was "cheered as no football hero was ever cheered. The enthusiasm was never more frenzied. She radiated confidence, courage, defiance, and stood before her people like a triumphant empress."

*   *   *

It is impossible to do full justice to her preaching, because it relied more on music and "sentimental dramatic scenes" and her own formidable acting abilities than on any mere words . . . you'd need to *see* as well as hear her in flamboyant action.

Sinclair Lewis gives us a glimpse . . .

He was genuinely "fond of her outrageousness," called her "that lovely evangelical nun," and often went to enjoy her performances.

"In white with a scarlet stole and a crimson cross on her somewhat secular breast," he wrote of one occasion, "she gave one hell of a sales talk to God" in aid of funds, "and then tooted a red trumpet!"

She had strung "long clothes-lines down the aisles with clothes-pegs attached," and "howled that the Lord hated the noisy jangle of silver and loved the rustle of paper," then "urged all Christians to hang their contributions on the line."

And here's a reconstruction of another inimitable few minutes . . .

*   *   *

"For three years . . ."
She holds up three fingers, and jabs the air three times.
" . . . there has been a Big Revival . . ."
Her wide-spread arms indicate just how big it has been.
" . . . here in Los Angeles."
She suddenly hugs the whole of the city in her mothering arms.
"Thousands . . ."
She is now already welcoming those thousands.
" . . . have found their way to Jesus."
She turns and gazes up at a huge portrait of Jesus behind her, and then raises her arms in rapture as though at His Second Coming.
There are cries of "Halleluiah!" and "Praise be the Lord!" from the rousing congregation.
She turns and silences them with one slowly lifted hand.
"You . . ."
She points at them with a raking finger, searching one by one.
"You have seen big strong men . . ."
She swells her chest and flexes her biceps.
" . . . stumbling . . ."
She stumbles helplessly across the platform.
" . . . down these very aisles."
She draws herself up proudly, and then leans forward like a mother, encouraging those unseen men to stumble on, to make it to Jesus.

211

"The Devil . . ."
She shouts the word defiantly, wraps her robes around her, and is now the Devil incarnate, her face contorted in hate and rage.
". . . has lost his grip!"
She cowers back, defeated, her fists unclenching.
Cries of "Hallaluiah!"
And so on for another action-packed twenty minutes . . .

* * *

But, eventually, our Sister Aimee lost her own grip, several "sad and abortive" affairs left her more and more sexually unsatisfied, she was involved in "fifty-five law-suits and charges including tax-evasion, bankruptcy, assault, slander, and disputes over legacies" . . . and, at the age of fifty-three, she committed suicide by taking an over-dose of her "regular sleeping-pills . . ."

No, my Little Sister, you were never a Saint . . . but at least you were living flesh-and-blood, and not made of plaster.

* * *

Final Postscript
And then there was Billy Graham's immediate predecessor around the Old Sawdust Trail . . . Billy Sunday.

"Coat off, tie off, his face dripping sweat," he'd "crouch down on all fours, peering over the edge of the platform as into the fiery Pit of Hell, shouting, in raw and rasping voice, his defiance of the Devil and all his hosts."

Even without the use of a microphone he "could make twenty thousand keep their eyes fastened on him from beginning to end," for he "acted out every word he uttered so that those who did not hear it could see it." Like any experienced professional politician or huckster selling shoddy goods on the market he "knew how to draw laughter or applause, how to wait, and when to repeat a line or vary it slightly a second time in order to wring the full response from it."

And the "drama of his performance" was heightened by his "pounding the pulpit, standing on a chair" or "swinging it over his head, sliding across the platform like a fielder saving a home-run, jumping over imaginary gates, pretending to fall, staggering, whirling like a boxer, ducking and weaving, and even doing handsprings."

At the conclusion of his Sermon he "would jump on top of the pulpit and vigorously wave an American flag."

What did he say?

Does it any longer matter?

Woodbine Willie

But we cannot end in those aching depths.

So please, finally, let us consider Geoffrey Anketell Studdert-Kennedy, better known and best loved as "Woodbine Willie" . . . with *Woodbines* being the cheapest and most popular cigarette on sale during the First World War, the only brand the working-class troops could usually afford, and the name they gave to this good man because they came to love him as he had first loved them.

The greatest compliment that "old breed of men" could pay was to give you a rough-edged nickname, the rougher the warmer. "Creeping Jesus" or "Moaning Minnie," *these* were the contemptuous names they gave to the standard-issue Army Chaplain, with good cause – but Woodbine Willie . . . Ah! *he* was on *their* bloody side!

He was naturally pleased at this rough and ready acceptance, but confessed what he saw as his own betrayal of their hard-won trust: "For men to whom I owed God's Peace," he wrote, "I put off with a cigarette."

*   *   *

As with John Donne, I must say much too little rather than much too much: because, though *theirs* are the only Sermons I return to again and again for pleasure and emotional stimulation, it's my dear old Woodbine I love more and more as a man.

And if such love embarrasses you – well, that's *your* problem.

*   *   *

After the first flush of blind patriotism at the beginning of the First World War, the professional incompetence and emotional rigidity of the generals soon caused the horrendous casualties which changed the mood from euphoria to despair, hope to fatalism, simple faith to knowing cynicism.

The Church as by Law Established mewed for German blood, the Bishops preached about the "Righteousness of our Cause" . . . and the men in the trenches spat in the mud, "sick of all the lies that darkened all the earth," clambered over the top, and died with Christ on the bloody wire.

Only a very few Army Chaplains ever gained the respect of these

213

men: and Woodbine Willie was the first . . . and the inspiration of those few others. And the memory survives . . .

*   *   *

He was born and reared in a Leeds industrial slum, and soon discovered that the souls of the common people were blunted and blighted by the rotting hovels they had to live in, the grinding work they had to do . . . they were born free as the Children of Christ, and lived in the chains forged by the Mammon of Commercial Greed.

He became a Minister in the Church of England, went to France as a desperately unorthodox Army Chaplain at the beginning of that War to End War . . . won the Military Cross for Conspicuous Gallantry . . . and, against the long tradition of compulsory church-parades and strutting jingoism, with "Christianity" used as a bone for the dogs of war, he gained the grudging respect, then the wry affection, and finally the love of almost every man he ever met.

"How lovely and honourable it is to die for your country," was the message preached to the troops going up the line to face that iron rain of death and mutilation.

"The old lie," said Wilfred Owen.

Woodbine Willie, though less of a Poet, had his own equally simple words.

> *Waste of Muscle, waste of Brain,*
> *Waste of Patience, waste of Pain,*
> *Waste of Manhood, waste of Health,*
> *Waste of Beauty, waste of Wealth,*
> *Waste of Blood, and waste of Tears,*
> *Waste of Youth's most precious years,*
> *Waste of ways the Saints have trod,*
> *Waste of Glory, waste of God –*
>   *War!*

Exactly the sort of verses that Rudyard would have written had he had the heart and imagination to be a Pacifist.

And, by such easily understood words, what Francis of Assisi did for his contemporaries by reminding them of the simplicity of Jesus Christ as opposed to the pride and corruption of the Church, Woodbine Willie did for the millions who had lost all faith in the English Establishment . . . and were *losing* their faith in more important matters.

*   *   *

Even William Wand, a late Bishop of London, and a conservative among conservatives, remembers him with genuine respect.

"Happy the Preacher who can still make the Old Story come vividly alive to his hearers! I realised this with particular poignancy in France during the First World War. I was standing on the edge of a crowd listening to Studdert-Kennedy preaching in a vast railway shed to the troops on their way to the Front. As we turned away at the conclusion of the Address, I heard a tall Guards sergeant say to his companion, 'My word, that chap's got a heart, hasn't he?' . . . His essential sincerity and his real love of people were strong enough to break through . . ."

Woodbine Willie despised the professional jargon of the Parson, and spoke the language of the trenches to those who died in them, the slang of the streets to those who survived in slums.

So, naturally, he offended the Nice Nellies of both sexes in the Church . . . but he wasn't overly concerned with them. And there were murmurings that he "upset the balance of the Gospel" . . . . but the only balance he ever bothered about was between those arms outstretched on the Cross.

"It was the glory of the Christian Faith," he said, "that there was a Cross in the heart of the Father before there was a Cross on Calvary."

Yes, he was a man of passionate integrity, refreshing humilty, incandescent courage, and spoke with the "unrestrained utterance of a soul in revolt."

"People were turning from a Church which damned souls to build churches," he said, "which sweated working-men to endow charities, and manufactured prostitutes by paying low wages – to build Rescue Homes for fallen women."

And he had an ear for a living phrase: "a shell is just an iron sin."

All I can do to "report him and his cause aright" is cite a very few of my favourite bits and pieces . . .

*   *   *

"The Spirit of War seems to kill and conquer the Spirit of Peace often, but the Spirit of Peace never really dies – it always rises again, and goes on striving to win men to the side of Christ."

"We want a world in which social position is based solely upon social service, and in which there are no idlers, no gorgeous coloured drones."

"God made the Church for the people, and not the people for the Church."

215

"The very first thing that any true friend of Labour has got to make quite clear to the workers is that there is just as little to be got out of Industrial War in the long run as there is out of International War, and that little is considerably less than nothing. If we have learned anything from the past five years of Hell, it is surely that war never gets anything or anywhere . . . It is and it never can be anything but a pure and unmitigated disaster – and my great grouse against that sort of easy talk about 'smashing' the system is that it gives men the impression that they can secure the Millenium by knocking down a policeman. And it is *that* lie which is blinding the eyes of working people to the things that really belong unto their peace."

"You can only work a better system with better people."

"I hope that my words will make young men un-compromising and bitter rebels against the cruelty and folly and waste of war, and plant in their minds a strong, healthy suspicion of the scheming, lying and greed that brings it about – and most of all that it will help to kill in their minds that power of sickly sentimentalism, that idiotic pomp and pageantry of Militarism, which provide the glamour and romance for the mean and dirty shambles that are the battle-fields of the world's great wars."

"Many of the most damnable deeds in history were done by conscientious people. Their conscience was all right, but their creed was all wrong."

"Religion does not relieve us from the duty of thought – it makes it possible for us to begin thinking."

"The political mind is the root cause of war, and the enemy of all progress . . . it is literally starving Europe, and driving it to ruin . . ."

"The only bricks we have are made of clay, so we must use them."

"Those who, under cover of the Freedom of the Press, present for the edification of the proletariat a hotchpotch of all the garbage that can be collected from the Divorce Courts, together with detailed accounts of the private lives of criminals and crooks, we must uncompromisingly declare to be the enemies of God's people."

"Too often what is called Public Opinion is merely Press opinion, and paid for at that."

"If the Church of the twentieth century does not repent, and proclaim open war against war . . . if it is content to remain a department of life, a State institution largely supported by money gained by methods into which is would not be wise to inquire too closely . . . if it makes its aim and object to produce the kind of piety which regards religion as having nothing to do with money, except so far as it is needed for the upkeep of altars and the payment of priests . . . it will discover that neither doctrinal orthodoxy nor ecclesiastical correctness can save it from the doom which God pronounces upon all rotten institutions . . ."

*　　*　　*

He died, worn out, at the age of fifty-six.

Hundreds of thousands of people mourned . . . there were Services and Sermons all over the country.

One packet of *Woodbines* lay on his coffin.

Did I mention at all that he was Irish?

A Few Words Before Going

The custom of the country now expects me to say how very sorry I am if your favourite Preacher or Sermon has been left out.

But you already know your favourite Preacher and can read your favourite Sermon any time you feel a need for words to shake your world.

All I have tried to do is tell you about mine in the hope that you might like to follow some of these lanes and footpaths into unfamiliar acres of the landscape.

With this bonus: If I've irritated you enough to persuade you to have a closer or fresher look at your favourites I'll be delighted!

And I pray that we'll meet after our wanderings at the gates of that One City whose Builder and Maker is God.

In the meantime I'm off down to the Meeting House of The Society of Friends in Goat Lane, Norwich.

Why?

Because, being Friends of dear old George Fox, they don't ever have any Sermons.